On Location 3

Reading and Writing for Success in the Content Areas

Thomas Bye

McGraw-Hill

On Location 3 Student Book, 1st Edition

Published by McGraw-Hill ESL/ELT, a business unit of The McGraw-Hill Companies, Inc., 1221 Avenue of the Americas, New York, NY 10020. Copyright © 2005 by the McGraw-Hill Companies, Inc. All rights reserved. No part of this publication may be reproduced or distributed in any form or by any means, or stored in a database or retrieval system, without the prior written consent of The McGraw-Hill Companies, Inc., including, but not limited to, in any network or other electronic storage or transmission, or broadcast for distance learning.

ISBN: 0-07-288680-3
1 2 3 4 5 6 7 8 9 QPD/QPD 11 10 09 08 07 06 05

ISBN: 0-07-111909-4 (International Student Book)
1 2 3 4 5 6 7 8 9 QPD/QPD 11 10 09 08 07 06 05

Editorial director: Tina B. Carver
Executive editor: Erik Gundersen
Senior developmental editor: Mari Vargo
Developmental editors: Fredrik Liljeblad, Stephen Handorf
Production manager: Juanita Thompson
Cover designer: Wee Design Group
Interior designer: Wee Design Group
Artists: Burgundy Beam, Randy Chewning, Greg Harris, Albert Lorenz, Judy Love, Anni Matsick, Yoshi Miyake, George Ulrich
Photo Researchers: David Averbach, Tobi Zausner, David Macfarlane
Skills Indexer: Susannah MacKay

INTERNATIONAL EDITION ISBN 0-07-111909-4
Copyright © 2005. Exclusive rights by The McGraw-Hill Companies, Inc., for manufacture and export. This book cannot be re-exported from the country to which it is sold by McGraw-Hill. The International Edition is not available in North America.

www.esl-elt.mcgraw-hill.com

Acknowledgments

The authors and publisher would like to thank the following individuals who reviewed the *On Location* program at various stages of development and whose comments, reviews, and assistance were instrumental in helping us shape the project.

Carolyn Bohlman
Main East High School
Chicago, IL

Claire Bonskowski
Fairfax Public Schools
Fairfax, VA

Karen Caddoo
Sheridan Public Schools
Sheridan, CO

Florence Decker
El Paso MS/HS
Franklin, TX

Trudy Freer-Alvarez
Houston Independent School District
Houston, TX

Maryann Lyons
Francisco Middle School
San Francisco, CA

Susan Nordberg
Miami, FL

Jeanette Roy
Miami-Dade County Public Schools
Miami, FL

Steve Sloan
James Monroe High School
North Hills, CA

Leslie Eloise Somers
Miami-Dade County Public Schools
Miami, FL

Marie Stuart
San Gabriel Unified School District
San Gabriel, CA

Susan J. Watson
Horace Mann Middle School
San Francisco, CA

About the Author

Thomas Bye is an educator and consultant in second language learning and teaching. He was a high school teacher and has served as coordinator of bilingual education as well as director of curriculum and strategic planning for a large school district. He has written other programs for English Learners. He is an adjunct faculty member at St. Mary's College. He holds a Ph.D. in linguistics from UCLA.

Dedication

On Location is dedicated to my family, David Bohne and Chipper.

Scope and Sequence

	Unit	Readings	Genres/ Writing Tasks	Reading Strategies	Word Work/ Spelling
1	**I'll Never Forget …** page 2	Teens' own memorable stories from *The New York Times Upfront*	Autobiographical narratives	Questioning the author	Word families: turning verbs or adjectives into nouns by adding suffixes Spelling words that end in *-ence* and *-ance*
2	**Loud and Ugly** page 24	Selections about the loudest and ugliest animals on earth	Field guides	Using a KWL chart Confirming predictions	Word families: turning nouns and verbs into adjectives by adding suffixes Spelling words with the sound /sh/
3	**Surviving Homework** page 46	Advice about homework and study skills	Essays of advice	Flagging ideas Commenting	Word families: related nouns, verbs, and adjectives Spelling words with the sound /ee/
4	**Ancient Worlds** page 68	Magazine articles on mysteries of the ancient world	Short research reports	Using a KWL chart Quick writing	Word families: turning nouns and adjectives into verbs by adding a suffix Spelling words with the sound /f/
5	**Who's Smarter… Cats or Dogs?** page 90	An article from *National Geographic Kids* comparing cats and dogs	Comparison and contrast essays	Comparing and contrasting	Antonyms Pronouncing the hard and soft *g*

Grammar	Organization	Style	Writing Conventions	Content Area Connections	Links to Literature
Past perfect tense	Organizing a personal narrative	Showing, not telling	Commas with compound sentences	Civics	Poem "Oranges," by Gary Soto
Adverbs	Organizing a field guide	Using figurative language	Quotation marks with figurative language	Science Geography	"How" story that explains how the owl got its feathers
Countable and uncountable nouns	Organizing suggestions and supporting reasons	Using direct quotes	Quotation marks for direct quotes	Study Skills	Aesop's fable: "The Fox and the Crow"
Passive sentences	Organizing a research report	Sentence combining	Word processing conventions	History	Poem "Flowers and Songs," in Nahuatl, Spanish, and English
Plural noun forms	Organizing elements of a comparison and contrast essay	Using similes	Contractions	Science	Excerpt from *Fifth Chinese Daughter* by Jade Snow Wong

Scope and Sequence

Unit	Readings	Genres/ Writing Tasks	Reading Strategies	Word Work/ Spelling
6 How to Make Really Neat Stuff page 112	Instructions for making scientific tools and assembling a skateboard	How-to instructions	Using text features Rereading	Prefixes that refer to number or amount Doubling the final consonant before -ed
7 What Were the 1960s Like, Grandpa? page 134	Oral histories	Oral histories	Questioning the author	Word roots Spelling words with the letters ie and ei
8 Pro or Con? page 156	Articles that argue an issue from The New York Times Upfront	Persuasive essays	Reading like a writer Questioning the author	Word families: related nouns, verbs, and adjectives Spelling words with the suffixes -ant and -ent
9 I Can't Put it Down! page 178	Reviews of fiction and non-fiction books written by teens	Response to literature: book reviews	Overviewing Sorting out main ideas from details	Word families: related nouns, verbs, and adjectives Spelling words with the suffixes -able and -ible
10 The Perfect Storm page 200	Magazine articles about hurricanes and tsunamis	Feature articles: explaining processes	Flagging new information and questions Summarizing	Greek and Latin prefixes Spelling words with the letters s and c

Grammar	Organization	Style	Writing Conventions	Content Area Connections	Links to Literature
Articles: *the* and *a/an*	Organizing and formatting how-to instructions	Audience: use of formal or casual tone	Commas with transition words	Science Math: diagrams	Poems "How to Be a Shark" and "How to Say I'm Sorry"
Repeated actions in the past/past ability: *would, used to*, and *could*	Organizing interviews and narrative oral histories	Avoiding sentence fragments and run-ons	Apostrophes to show possession	American history: the 20th Century	Tall tale: Davy Crockett
Conditionals: factual and contrary-to-fact	Organizing a thesis statement, arguments, and support in a persuasive essay	Writing powerful conclusions	Commas with adverbs	Civics	"One-Minute Speech to the U.S. House of Representatives" by Congressman Richard Durbin
Present perfect tense	Organizing a response to literature	Varying types of sentences	Formatting book titles	Literature	Poem "Books Fall Open," by David McCord
Clause connectors	Organizing cause and effect writing	Writing powerful introductions	Commas with adverbial clauses	Earth science	Myth: "The Puna Chief Who Boasted"

To the Student

Welcome to *On Location!* This book is written just for you. *On Location* will help you learn English while you explore the world.

You will read and write about our world—about the loudest and ugliest animals on earth and about mysteries of the ancient world!

You will read and write about interesting people—other students just like you, NASA astronauts, and a woman who played professional baseball.

Should students be allowed to use cell phones in school? Should classrooms have security cameras? You will find out what other students think and express your own ideas in writing.

You will read, discuss, and analyze poems, stories, and myths related to the topics you have studied in each unit.

You will learn new words and skills that will help you in your other classes, such as math, science, social studies, and geography.

Best of all, you will get to work with others—talking, thinking, and making things as you learn English together.

This is going to be a great year. Enjoy the learning process!

Tom Bye

To the Teacher

Welcome to *On Location*—a three-level reading and writing program that provides an enrichment approach to language and literacy development. Specially designed for middle and high school students at beginning to intermediate levels, *On Location* provides a gradual onramp to academic English, allowing English learners the time they need to develop powerful academic reading, writing, and communications skills.

The *On Location* program offers a research-based approach that honors the findings of the National Reading Panel regarding the direct teaching of reading skills combined with the promotion of instructional practices that develop language and literacy through a focus on comprehension. *On Location* also supports the principles of the Cognitive Academic Language Learning Approach (CALLA), teaching learning strategies that help students succeed across the curriculum.

The program recognizes that learning to read and write is developmental, requiring the acquisition of listening and speaking skills and high levels of student engagement. *On Location* provides students with the direct skills instruction they need to master state and local standards within the context of meaningful communication.

On Location promotes the reading-writing connection through a focus on key academic genres—the kinds of writing students encounter in content-area classes and on high-stakes tests. Students read selections that describe, tell a story, analyze, explain, justify a position, and persuade. And they explore the organizational and stylistic features of each genre as they produce their own writing.

PROVIDING AN ON-RAMP TO ACADEMIC LANGUAGE

Student Books

On Location is organized into three levels. Book 1 enables students to meet beginning-level standards for reading, writing, and oral language. Reading selections are fewer than 100 words in length, building basic fluency and comprehension skills. By the end of Book 1, students are able to read simple paragraphs and write well-formed, connected sentences.

Book 2 enables students to meet early intermediate standards. Reading selections are under 300 words in length, providing access to authentic text materials. By the end of Book 2, students are able to read simple multi-paragraph selections and write related paragraphs.

Book 3 enables students to meet intermediate-level standards. Reading selections are less than 800 words in length, providing an onramp to academic text. By the end of Book 3, students are able to produce simple essays—writing that informs, explains, analyzes, and persuades.

The *On Location* books are organized into ten engaging units, each focusing on a particular nonfiction reading and writing genre. Every reading is authentic—giving students opportunities to read a variety of real-world text selections. Because the reading selections come from sources such as *Junior Scholastic* and *Time for Kids*—as well as the Internet—they are always engaging and help students connect to the world around them.

In each unit, students have the opportunity to produce the type of writing that the unit's reading selection exemplifies. Incorporating a "backwards build-up" model, this is how a unit works—

- Students begin by connecting the topic of the unit's reading selections to their own lives and by developing key vocabulary they will need to read with understanding.
- Students tackle a word analysis skill and explore a grammatical structure they will encounter in each reading.

- As students read the selections that model the genre, they work at building fluency and develop reading strategies that help them become active readers.
- After reading, students explore the organization patterns and stylistic features of the selections.
- Students then produce their own writing as they move through the stages of the writing process that culminates with an oral presentation to classmates.

Along the way, students engage in structured listening and speaking activities that promote thinking and discussion, develop understanding, and build motivation. They explore sound/spelling relationships of words and learn common written conventions.

Each unit opens doors to academic content. Students explore topics in science, social studies, and geography and learn essential academic vocabulary and skills to help them tackle grade-level content across the curriculum. Students also read and respond to a literature selection in each unit that relates to the content of the readings in that unit.

On Location is designed for use in a variety of classroom settings.

SCENARIOS	TIME FRAME	STRATEGIES FOR USE
1: **On Location** serves as the primary instructional program.	15–20 hours/unit	➢ Complete all Student Book and Practice Book activities. ➢ Implement all suggestions in the Teacher's Edition. ➢ Use all components of the *On Location* assessment system.
2: **On Location** supplements an adopted basal program, providing students with intensive reading/writing instruction.	10–15 hours/unit	➢ Complete sections B through H in the Student Book. ➢ Complete selected Practice Book activities. ➢ Use Teacher's Edition suggestions as needed.
3: Selected units from **On Location** supplement an adopted basal program, providing opportunities to read and write non-fiction.	6–10 hours/unit	➢ Complete sections B, C, F, G, and H in the Student Book. ➢ Use Teacher's Edition suggestions as needed.

Practice Books

Each level of *On Location* includes a corresponding **Practice Book**. The Practice Book provides students with the opportunity to master the reading skills, vocabulary, and grammar introduced in the Student Book while allowing them to evaluate their own writing and practice test-taking skills. Activities allow students to further explore unit topics, respond to literature selections, and discover how much they learned by completing the activities and writing tasks in the Student Books.

Audio Program

An **audio program** also accompanies each level of *On Location*. The audio program includes activities that develop social and academic listening skills in addition to recordings of all of the reading selections.

Phonics Book

On Location Phonics, which can be used as an introduction to *On Location* or in parallel fashion with Book 1, provides systematic, explicit instruction that helps students who are new to English hear the sound patterns of their new language and use knowledge of sound-letter relationships to read and write high-frequency words and phrases that they hear and see around them. Incorporating a "fast-track" approach, this optional component enables newcomers to learn both language and content from day one. Teaching notes at the bottom of each student page make *On Location Phonics* a self-contained program.

PROMOTING STAFF DEVELOPMENT

Wrap-Around Teacher's Editions

A wrap-around **Teacher's Edition** provides step by step guidance through every lesson, helping the teacher use best teaching practices to—

- introduce new vocabulary and important concepts through use of context
- use a three-stage process to develop active readers that involves reading aloud ("my turn"), having students share the reading task ("our turn"), and independent reading ("your turn")
- guide students through the stages of the writing process.

Teacher Training and Staff Development Video

The *On Location* program includes a powerful staff development video to support implementation of the program. The video provides strategies for teaching reading and writing from a language arts perspective—focusing on best practices such as pre-teaching vocabulary, use of read aloud/think aloud techniques, interactive reading, modeled writing, interactive writing, use of rubrics, and cooperative learning. The training video provides strategies for reading and writing in the content areas and demonstrates how *On Location* can be used effectively.

ENSURING ADEQUATE YEARLY PROGRESS

Assessment System

The *On Location* **Assessment System** includes a placement test, end-of-unit assessments, and end-of-level tests. Task-specific rubrics (or "ChecBrics") help students plan, revise, and evaluate their work.

Teachers can be sure that with its emphasis on academic reading and writing, *On Location* will help their school meet Adequate Yearly Progress (AYP) targets. The *On Location* assessment system supports district accountability efforts by providing tools that enable teachers to evaluate mastery of English language development/English language arts standards.

Welcome to On Location

On Location is a three-level supplementary series that teaches middle-school and high-school English learners to read and write non-fiction. Its gradual on-ramp approach gives learners the time and support they need to develop powerful academic reading, writing, and communication skills.

Tuning In activities provide **engaging listening passages** which introduce students to the topic of each unit.

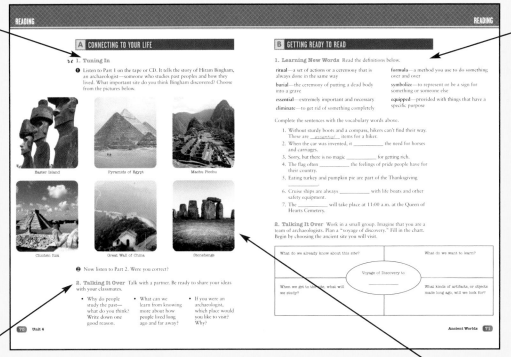

Useful vocabulary is introduced throughout each unit. Students learn new words that will help them understand reading passages, discuss their ideas, and complete their own writing.

Students have multiple **opportunities to discuss ideas** with partners and in groups. **Talking It Over** provides context for the upcoming reading and writing activities. It **makes connections to students' experiences, challenges them to think, and promotes classroom discussion.**

The **predictable organization** of each unit combined with the **variety of genres and topics** provides a **comfortable yet motivating experience** for students.

Vibrant and compelling art and photos bring units to life, illustrating ideas and vocabulary words related to the unit's topic and genre.

Reading passages are accompanied by **relevant and practical reading strategies** that help students **develop a personal set of reading comprehension skills.**

Before You Read activates background knowledge and connects students to the reading topic.

Let's Read contains information about the upcoming reading selection and provides a question or a task that **helps students focus their reading.**

Authentic non-fiction reading selections provide models for student writing while helping students build fluency and develop transferable comprehension skills and strategies for dealing with academic content.

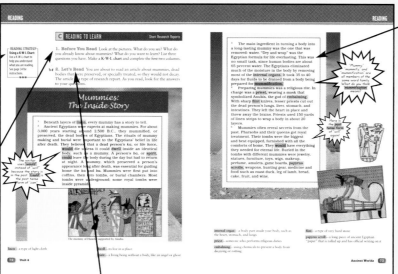

In **Unlocking Meaning**, three activities help students **understand what they are reading and encourage them to reread.** First, students identify the main idea, argument, or proposition. Second, they find details, reasons, or examples. And finally, they think more deeply about the reading.

Before You Move On is a post-reading activity that engages students in analysis and synthesis, retelling, summarizing, or acting on new information.

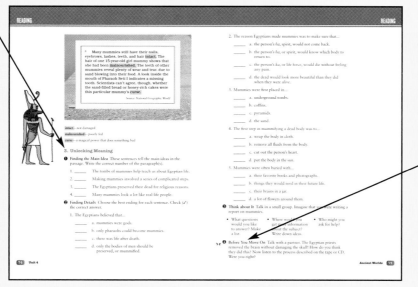

Activities in the *Word Work* section develop word-analysis skills that help students figure out the meaning of vocabulary in the content areas.

Grammar lessons provide instruction and practice around a **grammar point that is relevant to the reading passages and the writing task** in each unit.

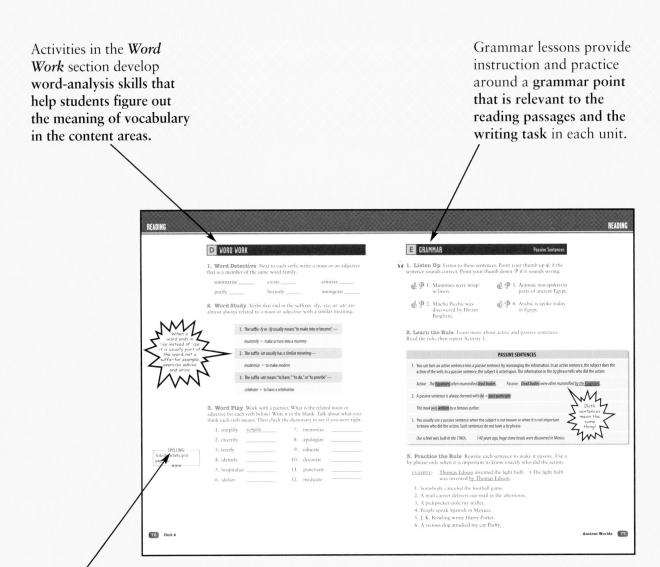

D WORD WORK

1. Word Detective Next to each verb, write a noun or an adjective that is a member of the same word family.

summarize _____   create _____   criticize _____

purify _____   beautify _____   immigrate _____

2. Word Study Verbs that end in the suffixes -ify, -ize, or -ate are almost always related to a noun or adjective with a similar meaning.

> When a word ends in -ise instead of -ize it is usually part of the word, not a suffix—for example, exercise, advise, and arise.

1. The suffix -fy or -ify usually means "to make into or become"—
   mummify = make or turn into a mummy

2. The suffix -ize usually has a similar meaning—
   modernize = to make modern

3. The suffix -ate means "to have," "to do," or "to provide"—
   celebrate = to have a celebration

3. Word Play Work with a partner. What is the related noun or adjective for each verb below? Write it in the blank. Talk about what you think each verb means. Then check the dictionary to see if you were right.

1. simplify   *simple*
2. electrify   _____
3. terrify   _____
4. identify   _____
5. hospitalize   _____
6. idolize   _____
7. memorize   _____
8. apologize   _____
9. educate   _____
10. decorate   _____
11. punctuate   _____
12. medicate   _____

SPELLING:
To do this activity, go to page...

E GRAMMAR   Passive Sentences

1. Listen Up Listen to these sentences. Point your thumb up 👍 if the sentence sounds correct. Point your thumb down 👎 if it sounds wrong.

1. Mummies were wrap in linen.

2. Machu Picchu was discovered by Hiram Bingham.

3. Aramaic was spoken in parts of ancient Egypt.

4. Arabic is spoke today in Egypt.

2. Learn the Rule Learn more about active and passive sentences. Read the rule, then repeat Activity 1.

PASSIVE SENTENCES

1. You can turn an active sentence into a passive sentence by rearranging the information. In an active sentence, the subject does the action of the verb. In a passive sentence, the subject is acted upon. The information in the *by* phrase tells who did the action.

   Active: *The Egyptians often mummified dead bodies.*   Passive: *Dead bodies were often mummified by the Egyptians.*

2. A passive sentence is always formed with *be* + *past participle.*
   This book was written by a famous author.

3. You usually use a passive sentence when the subject is not known or when it is not important to know who did the action. Such sentences do not have a *by* phrase:
   Our school was built in the 1980s.   *140 years ago, huge stone heads were discovered in Mexico.*

> Both sentences mean the same thing!

3. Practice the Rule Rewrite each sentence to make it passive. Use a *by* phrase only when it is important to know exactly who did the action.

EXAMPLE: Thomas Edison invented the light bulb.   • The light bulb was invented by Thomas Edison.

1. Somebody canceled the football game.
2. A mail carrier delivers our mail in the afternoon.
3. A pickpocket stole my wallet.
4. People speak Spanish in Mexico.
5. J. K. Rowling wrote *Harry Potter.*
6. A vicious dog attacked my cat Fluffy.

Spelling activities help students develop knowledge of **spelling patterns** in English.

A preview of relevant vocabulary words prepares students for the reading selection.

A recording of every reading selection is included in the audio program.

New words are glossed below reading selections and are included in the glossary at the back of the book.

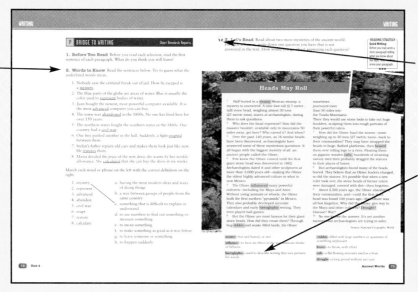

Making Content Connections activities provide opportunities for students to complete tasks that relate to content areas, such as geography, science, and math.

Graphic organizers and other tools promote higher order thinking skills, such as comparing, synthesizing, and inferencing.

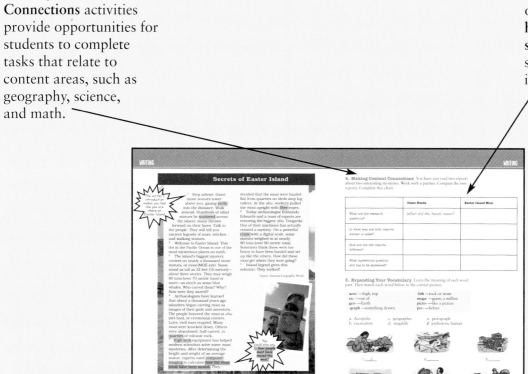

The sequence of activities in the *Writing Clinic* and the *Writer's Workshop* provides students with step-by-step procedures for producing a well-formed piece of academic writing. Students can use these procedures to complete writing assignments in their content area classes.

In **Focus on Organization** and **Focus on Style** activities, students **analyze the selection they have just read.**

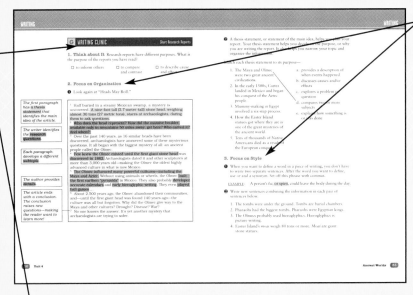

In **Getting It Out** activities, students learn new strategies and work with lists, images, and graphic organizers to plan and develop their own writing.

After students have decided on their topics, they use a graphic organizer, a set of questions, or a specific set of instructions to guide them in their information gathering.

Connect to the Web boxes list helpful and interesting Internet sites where students can learn more about the unit's topic.

Students work gradually toward completing their writing assignments. First, they spend time choosing the topic they'd like to write about.

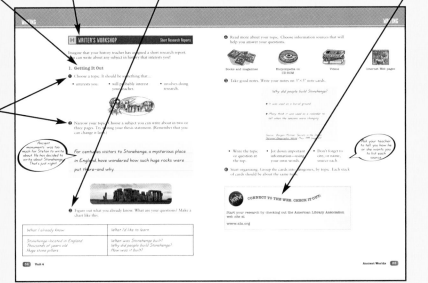

In **Getting It Down,** students turn their brainstorming and planning work into an outline and then a first draft. Models are provided to demonstrate to students exactly what they are expected to do.

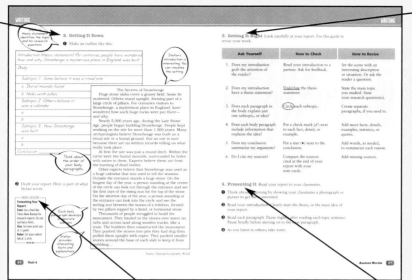

Getting It Right provides students with a combined checklist and rubric ("ChecBric") that helps them evaluate and revise their writing. The ChecBric, which is specific to each writing task, focuses on the skills that students have learned in the unit and provides a basis for evaluating level of performance on the task.

Mini-lessons in the *Writer's Workshop* focus on **writing conventions,** such as capitalization, punctuation, or formatting, that are relevant to the writing assignment.

In **Presenting It** activities, students share their work with their peers. They present their writing to their classmates, then give and receive constructive feedback.

On Assignment activities provide fun exercises related to unit topics. Students learn more about each topic and interact with their classmates while they participate in class art shows, make posters, and conduct interviews.

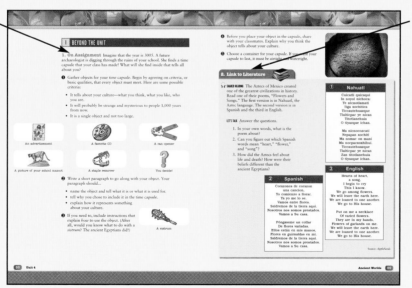

In **Link to Literature** activities, students read poems or fiction selections and participate in guided discussions.

I'll Never Forget...

Read...

■ Teenagers' stories about moments and experiences in their lives that made them change and grow.

Link to Literature

■ "Oranges," a narrative poem by Gary Soto.

Objectives:

Reading:
■ Reading short autobiographical narratives
■ Strategy: Questioning the author
■ Literature: Responding to a narrative poem

Writing:
■ Writing an autobiographical reflection
■ Showing, not telling
■ Keeping a personal journal

Vocabulary:
■ Using vivid adjectives

Listening/Speaking:
■ Listening to a personal narrative
■ Presenting a personal narrative

Grammar:
■ Using the past perfect tense

Spelling:
■ Spelling words that end in *-ance* and *-ence*

This reminds me of...

BEFORE YOU BEGIN

Talk with your classmates.

1. Look at the picture. What is Jessica doing?
2. What could Jessica be thinking about?
3. Do you ever think about people or events from your past? Who and what do you remember?

For help with listening and taking notes, complete Mini-Unit Part A on page 222.

A CONNECTING TO YOUR LIFE

 1. Tuning In Listen to Patty's personal narrative, "Green Salami." Then, write two or three sentences that explain why the incident is so memorable to Patty.

2. Talking It Over Think of your own funny family story. Share your story in a small group.

> I suppose that the high-water mark of my youth in Columbus, Ohio, was the night the bed fell on my father. It makes a better recitation (unless, as some friends of mine have said, one has heard it five or six times) than it does a piece of writing, for it is almost necessary to throw furniture around, shake doors, and bark like a dog, to lend the proper atmosphere and verisimilitude to what is admittedly a somewhat incredible tale. Still, it did take place …
>
> Source: "The Night the Bed Fell" by James Thurber

recitation—something you say that you remember well, like a poem or story

incredible—unbelievable

verisimilitude—the appearance of being true

Read the title of this unit. What do you think the unit is about? Check (✓) the correct answer.

_____ 1. It's about horror stories.

_____ 2. It's about tales of adventure.

_____ 3. It's about personal stories.

_____ 4. It's about how to remember things better.

B GETTING READY TO READ

1. Learning New Words Read the sentences below. Try to guess what the underlined words mean.

Helen Keller

1. Helen Keller was blind and deaf, but she learned to talk, read, and write. She <u>overcame</u> these conditions and went on to college.
2. When Juan broke his arm, it hurt so much he started to scream. The pain was <u>excruciating</u>.
3. Stefan doesn't have a penny to his name! He <u>literally</u> has no money.
4. Tran had a very bad sore throat. After several tests at the hospital, he <u>was diagnosed with</u> strep throat.
5. Maria loved her dog so much. Its sudden death was <u>devastating</u> for her.
6. Carlos loves the *Terminator* movies. He finds action movies <u>engaging</u>.

Match each word or phrase on the left with the correct definition on the right.

1. overcome
2. excruciating
3. literally
4. be diagnosed with
5. devastating
6. engaging

a. to find out from a doctor that you have a particular illness
b. to succeed in dealing with a problem
c. making someone feel extremely sad or shocked
d. extremely interesting
e. extremely painful
f. according to the most basic meaning of a word or expression

2. Talking It Over Work with a partner. Think of the most unforgettable moment or event in your own life. Then, interview your partner, using this chart to take notes. Be ready to share your partner's story with the class.

Who was involved?	What happened?
What was the unforgettable moment? _____	
How did you feel?	Why is the event unforgettable?

C READING TO LEARN

READING STRATEGY
Questioning the Author:
As you read, you can question the author. This will help you understand what the writer thinks and is trying to communicate.

1. Before You Read Think of a problem or issue you have had in your life. What did you do to overcome the problem? Share with a partner.

 2. Let's Read You are going to read about a teen who conquers a problem. As you read, write down one question you would ask him if you could talk to him.

The difficulties that teens experience are often called "growing pains." That's why Henry puts quotation marks around the term.

Facing "Growing Pains" and Overcoming Them

Henry Magram

1   As long as I can remember, I had always been able to outrun my classmates and teammates. But starting when I was in the eighth grade, suddenly I had to outrun knee pain.

2   After scoring great soccer goals, strange and excruciating knee pains began to follow me home. Each time I won my school's Mile Run, new areas of pain and stiffness appeared in my feet and ankles. My knees seemed oddly lumpy. It turned out that at age 13, I was experiencing—literally—what some people call "growing pains."

3   Teens who grow particularly quickly experience this type of pain when their leg bones lengthen faster than their ligaments. While it's not an illness, sports-medicine doctors refer to it as Osgood-Schlatters syndrome. There is no cure except waiting to outgrow it. Many teen athletes like me just limp out of action during the typical growth-spurt years from age 12 to 17 or 18.

4   Before I was diagnosed with Osgood-Schlatters, I had played soccer since I was 3, but suddenly the sport became deadly for me. One afternoon of racing toward the goal in flat-soled soccer shoes—which put added pressure on your ligaments because of the way the shoes flex your feet—can cause severe injury to a taut Achilles tendon. For me, even a vacation at the beach became a danger zone: Walking barefoot in the soft sand was so painful that I returned to Baltimore with torn ligaments.

outrun—to run faster than others

ligament—one of the bands that join your bones together

syndrome—a set of symptoms that show you have a certain medical condition

cure—a treatment or medicine that stops a disease and makes you healthy again

growth spurt—a sudden increase in the growth of your body

flat-soled—used to describe shoes with flat bottoms

pressure—the force or weight that is put on something

flex—to bend part of your body so your muscles become tight

taut—stretched tightly

Achilles tendon—the band of tissue attaching the heel bone to the calf muscle in the leg

5   I had to give up soccer, which was devastating for me in the beginning. Soccer is such an engaging sport, all my friends played it, and it had been so much a part of my life. I didn't think I'd be able to find anything to take its place.

6   Still, I was determined to find a sport in which I could participate. One of my sports heroes is cyclist Lance Armstrong, who overcame cancer to defend his title in the Tour de France. I wanted to follow his example and prevail, despite my Osgood-Schlatters.

7   By the winter of ninth grade, I had discovered several exciting sports that do not exacerbate knee pain: cycling, speed skating, table tennis, discus, and—best of all—crew.

8   Now, after almost four years of playing these new sports, I feel really challenged by them, especially throwing a discus, which involves balance, focus, strength, and an understanding of the physics of spin.

9   I'm now 17 and 6'2". Will I have another painful growth spurt before college? Maybe, but it is rewarding to know that I've already been able to overcome those growing pains and find success in new arenas.

Source: *New York Times Upfront*

speed skating

table tennis

discus

crew

Tour de France—the popular bicycle race held in July, mostly in France

prevail—to win or triumph

exacerbate—to make a bad situation worse

balance—when your weight is evenly spread so that you are steady and don't fall

focus—when you are paying close attention

physics—the study of natural forces

3. Unlocking Meaning

❶ **Finding the Main Idea** Check (✔) the correct answer. "Facing 'Growing Pains'" is the story of a boy who learns...

_____ a. how to play sports, even though he is injured.

_____ b. that he can overcome a problem and go on to be successful.

_____ c. how to grow taller.

_____ d. that he doesn't have to play sports to be popular.

❷ **Finding Details** Choose the best ending for each sentence. Check (✔) the correct answer.

1. Henry is a boy who...

_____ a. raced in the Tour de France.

_____ b. is good at team sports, especially soccer.

_____ c. is chosen captain of the soccer team.

_____ d. hopes to become a PE teacher after he graduates from college.

2. Henry suffers from a condition that causes him to...

_____ a. have severe headaches.

_____ b. suffer pain in his legs, knees, and ankles.

_____ c. black out when he is playing sports.

_____ d. grow very slowly.

3. Osgood-Schlatters is caused by...

_____ a. a torn Achilles tendon.

_____ b. leg bones that grow faster than the ligaments attached to them.

_____ c. playing soccer.

_____ d. a mysterious illness that doctors don't understand.

4. A a result of Osgood-Schlatters, Henry had to give up playing...

_____ a. his favorite sport, soccer.

_____ b. dangerous sports like speed skating.

_____ c. individual sports.

_____ d. table tennis.

5. Henry finds throwing the discus challenging because it involves...

_____ a. skill in making all of your body parts work in just the right way.

_____ b. running very fast.

_____ c. playing hard against another team and winning.

_____ d. throwing a very heavy object.

❸ **Think about It** Work in a small group. Many successful people have had to overcome problems in their lives. What qualities do people who overcome problems often have? List three important qualities. Be ready to share.

a.

Babe Ruth spent his childhood in an orphanage and, as a baseball player, struck out 1,330 times—then went on to the Hall of Fame.

b.

Elvis Presley was thrown out of the Grand Ole Opry after one performance and was told: "You ain't goin' nowhere, son!"

c.

Oprah Winfrey was fired from her television reporter's job and was told: "You're not fit to be on TV!"

❹ **Before You Move On** Think of someone in your own life who has overcome a problem. Write the person a postcard, telling them why you admire him or her.

D WORD WORK

1. Word Detective Sometimes you can guess what a word means by looking for a smaller word or part of a word inside the longer one. Find the smaller words inside the nouns and write them down.

1. **tenderness** smaller word: _____*tender*_____	3. **electricity** smaller word: _____
2. **repentance** smaller word: _____	4. **imitation** smaller word: _____

2. Word Study You can turn many verbs or adjectives into nouns by adding a suffix. Circle the suffixes in the words below. Guess the meanings of the words with and without the suffixes. Then check your dictionary to see if you were correct.

-ness *(state of)*	-ance, -ence *(state of, quality of, act of)*
toughness	assistance
-ity *(condition or quality of)*	**-tion** *(act of, state of)*
capability	communication

SPELLING:
To do this activity, go to page 235.

3. Word Play Work with a partner. Make a noun out of each word by adding the correct suffix from the box. Write a sentence for each noun. Use your dictionary for help.

-ness	-ance	-ence	-ity	-tion

1. rely _____*reliance*_____   7. reckless _____

2. real _____   8. avoid _____

3. acquaint _____   9. act _____

4. attend _____   10. cooperate _____

5. loud _____   11. public _____

6. graduate _____   12. ill _____

E GRAMMAR   Past Perfect Tense

1. Listen Up Listen to the sentences. If the first choice is correct, hold up ☝ one finger. If the second choice is correct, hold up ✌ two fingers.

☝ ✌ 1. a. When the alarm rang, Juan already got up.

b. When the alarm rang, Juan had already gotten up.

☝ ✌ 2. a. Maria screamed and shouted. She had won the lottery!

b. Maria screamed and shouted. She has won the lottery.

☝ ✌ 3. a. I got mad at my dog. He had chewed the furniture!

b. I got mad at my dog. He has chewed the furniture!

☝ ✌ 4. a. I called to talk to my father, but he had already left work.

b. I called to talk to my father, but he already left work.

2. Learn the Rule Learn how to form the past perfect tense. Then do Activity 1 again.

THE PAST PERFECT TENSE
1. To form the past perfect tense, use *had* + the past participle of the verb. The past participle of a regular verb is the base form + *-d* or *-ed* (*lived, waited*). Many verbs have irregular past participles. See page 234, for a list of irregular verbs.   I *had met* Susan once before.
2. Use the past perfect tense to describe a past action or event that was completed before another activity or time in the past. Use the simple past tense to describe the second event: *Juan was late to Maria's party. By the time he finally got there, nearly everyone had left!*   First past event: *Everyone left Maria's party.*   Second past event: *Juan finally got to the party.*

3. Practice the Rule Complete the sentences with the verbs in parentheses. For each sentence, use one simple past form and one past perfect form.

1. By the time we (arrive) _____ at the airport, our plane (take off) _____ .
2. Graciela (not have) _____ any money for the movies yesterday because she (leave) _____ her purse at home.
3. By the time the boring movie (end) _____ , everyone (fall) _____ asleep.
4. Rick (get) _____ a bad grade even though he (study) _____ hard.

F BRIDGE TO WRITING   Autobiographical Reflections

1. Before You Read Have you ever had an opinion about someone that you changed when you got to know him or her? Share an example with a partner.

2. Words to Know Read the sentences below. Try to guess what the underlined words mean. Then read the numbered sentences. Choose the sentence from the box that goes with each numbered sentence and write it on the line.

> They show a lot of <u>dignity</u>.
> It can give you a new <u>perspective</u>.
> This gives them a <u>sense of identity</u>.
> They <u>regret</u> calling each other names.
> They make <u>judgments</u> about others.
> They have <u>traditional values</u>.

1. I respect people who remain calm in difficult situations.
   They show a lot of dignity.
2. Maria and her sister are sorry they had a fight.
   _____
3. People usually have an opinion about other people.
   _____
4. Kids often dress and act in a certain way.
   _____
5. Many people believe in the importance of education and hard work.
   _____
6. Traveling to other countries can change how you see the world.
   _____

READING STRATEGY
Questioning the Author:
As you read, you can question the writer. This will help you understand what the writer is trying to tell us.

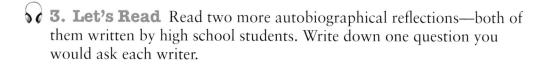 **3. Let's Read** Read two more autobiographical reflections—both of them written by high school students. Write down one question you would ask each writer.

What Racial Profiling Feels Like
By Jemelleh Nurse

Jemelleh's introduction signals a problem. Find the words that tell us something bad is going to happen.

1   Over the summer, I was invited to a pool party at a friend's house in the Atlanta suburbs. My friend lives in a predominantly white neighborhood, but that had never been an issue. I yelled to my mother, "I'm leaving now, I'll call you when I get there." She jokingly yelled back, "OK, stay out of trouble."

2   As I got to my friend's house, three of my other friends pulled up: two boys and a girl, all black. The boys wore hats with the brims facing backward, swim trunks, and white T-shirts. The girl and I had on swimsuits, skirts, and flip-flops. We got out of our cars and started up the driveway. When we heard footsteps coming up behind us, we turned around to see a white police officer.

3   We politely asked him if we needed to move our cars because we thought that was the reason he was following us. When he did not reply, we asked again. He said, "No." We continued up the driveway and the officer, now rushing toward us, ordered us to get on the ground, face down. We turned around to make sure he was talking to us and he yelled again, "Get on the ground, face down!" We did as we were told.

4   The officer asked what we were doing and who lived in the house. We answered all of his questions. Luckily, our friend happened to walk out of her house, with her parents. We thought it was OK to get off the ground, but as soon as we moved, the officer pulled out his gun. I did not know whether to be scared or upset. I was a little of both. The idea of lying face down on the wet ground with a gun pointed at me for walking up a driveway was preposterous! The officer finally let us go, but it was too late. By then, he had already stripped me of my dignity.

5   We went into the house to get cleaned up while my friend's dad talked to the officer. The officer told him that the police were looking for a guy who had stolen a car. I guess because we are black, we automatically became suspects. The officer left without any expression of regret. I was left to ponder his actions and the issue of racial profiling.

6   I have never had trouble with police officers, but I now realize they are people and they carry their own judgments. I can't fault them for being human, but I can fault them for using their positions of power in an abusive way.

7   People fear what they don't understand. Many people, through education, are gaining a better understanding of those of other races. But until society decides that the color of your skin doesn't determine your values or upbringing, then racial profiling will continue.

Source: *New York Times Upfront*

racial profiling—a racist practice by which police stop people of some groups just because of their race

predominantly—mostly

preposterous—completely unreasonable or silly

strip someone of—to take away something from someone

expression of regret—a type of apology

fault—to blame someone

abusive—hurtful to another person

upbringing—the way someone was raised

Visiting Vietnam and Finding a New Identity
by Son Tran

1   I have always thought of myself as an American since I cannot read or write in Vietnamese. I came to America when I was 5, and for a long time it was the only home I knew. But in 1996, my parents and I went back to Vietnam for the first time since we settled in America. The trip changed my whole perspective on who I really am.

2   Before the trip, my parents showed me pictures of Vietnam, and long-forgotten memories came back. I recalled walking with my sister down a dirt road to my grandmother's house. I also remembered a hurricane that made our house, which was made of tree branches, fall. We had to run around the village to find someone who would take us in.

> *Parentheses around a word can say to the reader, "in case you were wondering . . ."*

3   My family left Vietnam in 1988 because of the hardships imposed by the Communist government. (For instance, they changed the currency, so the little savings my parents had lost its value.) My parents had told me that Vietnam was a war-devastated country and a hard place to live. I was about to find out for myself.

4   When we got off the airplane in Ho Chi Minh City (formerly Saigon), the air smelled very strange, but very familiar. I was surprised to find skyscrapers, lavish hotels, and thousands of Vietnamese. Still, I longed to see Tam My, the village where I was born.

5   It took us more than 20 hours traveling by van to reach Tam My. Along the way, my mind was opened to a world that was new to my eyes, but familiar to my heart: the ever-expanding rice fields, tall mountains, and rows of leaning coconut trees. I realized I was finally back home.

6   When we arrived in Tam My, we stayed at my sister's house. (She had remained in Vietnam to care for our grandmother.) My parents were glad to be back where they had spent most of their lives. They were amazed at how the town had grown and happy that it was again peaceful. Because of their bad memories of Communist rule, my parents had begun to resent Vietnam. I was glad to see them recapture their love for their country.

7   On the day that we were to return to America, I looked back at the land and the people of Vietnam. I realized the things I had traded for a better life in America. The trip back to Vietnam allowed me to discover an identity I did not know that I had. I can proudly declare that I am both American and Vietnamese. If asked which is my true home, I would have to say both.

Source: *New York Times Upront*

hardship—something that makes your life difficult

imposed—forced on you

currency—money

devastated—very badly damaged

lavish—luxurious, often expensive

expanding—growing larger

resent—to feel angry about something someone has done to you, often unfairly

recapture—to experience or feel something again

4. Making Content Connections Choose the story that interested you most and involved you most personally. Analyze the incident or experience, then respond. Make a chart.

	Selection: _____	My Own Thoughts and Reactions
1. What was the incident?		
2. What was the most interesting part of the narrative?		
3. Why was the incident so memorable to the writer? What did she or he learn?		

5. Expanding Your Vocabulary

❶ Adjectives can paint vivid pictures in your reader's mind. Adjectives that *sizzle* help you avoid always using words like "good," "weird," "really neat," "sad," and "bad."

Find the word that *does not* go with the word in capital letters. Cross it out. Use your dictionary for help.

HAPPY	jubilant	despairing	tickled pink	elated
ANGRY	gleeful	incensed	infuriated	outraged
UPSET	distressed	agitated	disturbed	untroubled
SURPRISED	astonished	astounded	suspicious	speechless
SCARED	panicked	petrified	terror-stricken	confident

❷ Write five sentences. Use one word from each row above in your sentences.

G | WRITING CLINIC | Autobiographical Reflections

1. Think about It An autobiographical reflection tells—

☐ something that happened to the writer

☐ something that happened to someone famous

Jemelleh tells who, what, and where.

2. Focus on Organization

❶ Read Jemelleh's reflection one more time.

Jemelleh's lead sets the scene for her story. She provides background information that lets us know something upsetting is probably going to happen!

She relates, or tells, the events in time order.

She describes the incident, providing us with details and dialog, or people's actual words.

She describes her own feelings.

She tells how everything turned out.

Over the summer, I was invited to a pool party at a friend's house in the Atlanta suburbs. My friend lives in a predominantly white neighborhood, but that had never been an issue. I yelled to my mother, "I'm leaving now, I'll call you when I get there." She jokingly yelled back, "OK, stay out of trouble."

As I got to my friend's house, three of my other friends pulled up: two boys and a girl, all black. The boys wore hats with the brims facing backward, swim trunks, and white T-shirts. The girl and I had on swimsuits, skirts, and flip-flops. We got out of our cars and started up the driveway. When we heard footsteps coming up behind us, we turned around to see a white police officer.

We politely asked him if we needed to move our cars because we thought that was the reason he was following us. When he did not reply, we asked again. He said, "No." We continued up the driveway and the officer, now rushing toward us, ordered us to get on the ground, face down. We turned around to make sure he was talking to us and he yelled again, "Get on the ground, face down!" We did as we were told.

The officer asked what we were doing and who lived in the house. We answered all of his questions. Luckily, our friend happened to walk out of her house, with her parents. We thought it was OK to get off the ground, but as soon as we moved, the officer pulled out his gun. I did not know whether to be scared or upset. I was a little of both. The idea of lying face down on the wet ground with a gun pointed at me for walking up a driveway was preposterous! The officer finally let us go, but it was too late. By then, he had already stripped me of my dignity.

We went into the house to get cleaned up while my friend's dad talked to the officer. The officer told him that the police were looking for a guy who had stolen a car. I guess because we are black, we automatically became suspects. The officer left without any expression of regret. I was left to ponder his actions and the issue of racial profiling.

I have never had trouble with police officers, but I now realize they are people and they carry their own judgments. I can't fault them for being human, but I can fault them for using their positions of power in an abusive way.

People fear what they don't understand. Many people, through education, are gaining a better understanding of those of other races. But until society decides that the color of your skin doesn't determine your values or upbringing, then racial profiling will continue.

She shares her thoughts.

Jemelleh's conclusion tells us how she felt about the incident and explains what she learned.

❷ Talk with a partner. Write down three examples of *details* in Jemelleh's description of the incident that make her reflection interesting or memorable to read.

3. Focus on Style Good writing "shows, not tells." It paints vivid pictures in the reader's mind and involves others in the story.

❶ Compare these examples. Which do you prefer?

Telling:

The police officer treated us unfairly.

Showing:

We continued up the driveway and the officer, now rushing toward us, ordered us to get on the ground, face down. We turned around to make sure he was talking to us and he yelled again, "Get on the ground, face down!" We did as we were told.

❷ Work with a partner. Choose one of the sentences below as your basis. Then write a short paragraph that shows, not tells. Be ready to share your paragraph.

1. Juan was angry.
2. The pizza tasted good.
3. My math class is boring.
4. Stefan is a handsome boy.

WRITING

H WRITER'S WORKSHOP · Autobiographical Reflections

At the end of the *Voices* column in *The New York Times Upfront* you read these words...

> *Send us your 500-word story, along with your name, address, and phone number. If we publish it, we'll pay you $100.*

You decide to write your own reflection!

1. Getting It Out

❶ Make a timeline that shows important events in your life. Put positive events above the timeline. Put negative events below. Here is Dan's personal timeline—

POSITIVE

Elected fourth grade president

Begin to shave   Meet Tiffany   Make the football team   Get my Chevy Beretta!

Age:	8	9	10	11	12	13	14	15	16

Dog Napoleon dies

Our house burns down

Tiffany dumps me

NEGATIVE

❷ Choose an event, incident, or experience to write about.

❸ What do you remember about the event? Make a memory web. Here is part of what Dan drew.

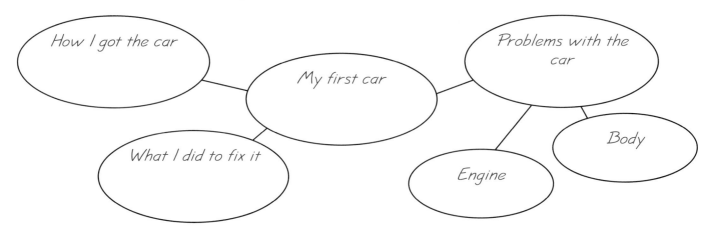

18   Unit 1

❹ Now think about the details. Fold a sheet of paper into three columns. Organize your thoughts and memories...

- Put the events in time order
- Next to each event, write down details you remember
- Jot down how you felt and what you were thinking

Here is a chart Dan started.

What happened	Details	My thoughts and feelings
Cousin Tom called to tell me he has a car for me.	Chevrolet Beretta GTZ... had just gotten my driver's license.	Felt really, really happy-ecstatic!
I decided to take the car.	In really bad shape!	Wanted the car so much I didn't see its problems.
I discovered many problems.	Broken windshield, rusty fenders, etc.	I was eager to learn how to fix things.
The engine stopped running!!! I decided to fix it myself.	I learned about all of the parts.	

❺ Why is the incident important to you? Write one or two complete sentences that explain.

- why you remember the incident
- what you learned about yourself or other people
- how the incident perhaps changed you

I am very proud that I learned to fix my own car. It took a lot of work. To me, my car shines brighter than any new car ever could.

If you can't think of why the incident has meaning to you, consider writing about something else!

❻ Relate the incident to a partner.

Getting my first car was the most exciting day of my life!

2. Getting It Down

❶ Turn your chart into an outline.

---

1. My lead (what I will say to hook the reader): *Getting your first car is . . .*

2. Description of the incident:

    a. What happened first: *Tom told me he had a car I might like . . .*

    b. What happened next: *The car had a lot of problems.*

    c. What happened after that:

3. My conclusion:

    a. Why I still remember the incident:

    b. What I learned about myself:

— MINI-LESSON —

Using Commas:
Put a comma before *and* or *but* in a compound sentence when the second sentence has a subject:

I didn't take the Beretta with me to college, but it's still my one and only car.

❷ Draft your reflection. Here is what Dan wrote—

Dan's first sentence grabs the reader's attention. It's a good lead for his story.

My Dream Chevy

Getting a car is a high point of any 16-year-old's life. Two years ago, my cousin Tom, who is a mechanic, told me he had a car I might like: a 1991 Chevrolet Beretta GTZ. I had just gotten my license, and I was ecstatic! The car was a wreck, but I loved it. Then reality set in.

There were many problems: a broken windshield, rusty fenders, ugly wheels. I made a list of repairs the car needed.

The engine was the first major problem. About a month after I got the car, the head gasket, an engine part that seals in fluids, burst, making it undrivable. The parts were less than $100, so the real cost was the labor. I spent three hours every day after school staring at the shop manual and taking out one part at a time. In two months I had the engine running.

Next, I was ready to shape up the exterior. With the help of my dad, we removed the windshield and began to repair the body. We applied a new coat of bright-red paint. The car sparkled.

The whole project took over a year. My car may not be the most glamorous piece of mechanical excellence, but my pride and persistence have made it shine brighter than any new model off the assembly line.

Dan tells what happened in time order. He gives us lots of details.

Dan could do a little more showing and a little less telling!

Dan's conclusion tells us how he felt about the experience. You can feel his pride!

Source: *New York Times Upfront*

3. Getting It Right Take a careful look at what you have written.
Use this guide to revise your story.

Questions to ask...	How to check...	How to revise if you need to...
1. Does my lead "hook" the reader?	Read your lead to a partner. Ask: "Does my lead make you feel curious?"	Try to make your reader feel like they were there.
2. Do I describe a single important event or incident?	(Circle) the words that describe the event.	Streamline your writing by removing information that does not relate to the event.
3. Does each paragraph help tell my story? Are the paragraphs in time order?	Reread each paragraph. Ask yourself: "How does this paragraph add to the one before it?"	If a paragraph is not related to the paragraphs before and after, think about moving it or leaving it out.
4. For the important parts, do I "show, not tell"?	Highlight vivid examples.	Change two or three "telling" sentences to "showing" sentences.
5. Does my ending reveal how I felt about the incident or experience?	Underline the words that tell how you felt or what you learned.	Expand your conclusion, explaining why you still remember the incident or how you have changed.

4. Presenting It Rather than reading your autobiographical reflection aloud, share your story, in your own words, with your classmates.

❶ Use note cards, based on your written reflection. Make a note card for each event, or thing that happened. Jot down details you want to remember to tell.

❷ Plan how you will introduce and end your story. Don't forget to explain why the incident or experience was important to you.

❸ Rehearse your presentation. Practice your delivery techniques, or skills.

- Use gestures to help make your story come alive.
- Raise or lower the pitch of your voice to show different emotions.
- Slow down or speed up to show that something is important.

❹ Deliver your presentation.

❺ After listening to others, offer a compliment.

1. On Assignment Learn to keep a journal. A journal is a place where you can write your personal thoughts, ideas, feelings, and reflections.

❶ **Think about It**

- When will you write in your journal? Set aside 10 minutes each day.

- What will you use? Choose a notebook—spiral-bound or loose-leaf— or buy a journal with a colorful cover and blank pages.

- What will you include in your journal? Only you will read it.

❷ **Get It Out**

- Think of an incident or experience you had today.

- Reflect on the past. What do you remember and why?

- Reflect on what you have learned each day or what you have read.

❸ **Get It Down**

- Freewrite: write whatever comes to mind for five or ten minutes.

- Make a personal timeline. Add to it every once in a while.

- Make a "future timeline." What will you be doing?

- Describe the world around you. Include your reactions to it.

- Draw a cartoon.

❹ **Get It Right**

- Review what you have written. Make additions, changes, or deletions.

- Revisit past journal entries. Add comments and questions.

- Reflect in writing on how you are growing and changing.

❺ **Use It**

- Use your journal to help you with writing assignments.

- Record information and ideas you don't want to forget.

- Share what you have written with a friend, if you wish.

The next time your teacher asks you to write an autobiographical narrative, your journal will help you get ideas!

SHARED READING A narrative poem tells a story. The speaker is a 12-year-old boy.

LET'S TALK Answer the questions.

1. In what ways is the poem "Oranges" like a story you might read?

2. When the girl chooses a chocolate, this poses a problem for the boy. What is the problem? How does the boy handle it?

3. Find examples of words the poet uses to "show, not tell." What is your favorite image, or picture?

4. Why do you think the speaker remembers this incident?

Oranges
Gary Soto

The first time I walked
with a girl, I was twelve,
Cold, and weighted down
With two oranges in my jacket.
December. Frost cracking
Beneath my steps, my breath
Before me, then gone,
As I walked toward
Her house, the one whose
Porchlight burned yellow
Night and day, in any weather.
A dog barked at me, until
She came out pulling
At her gloves, face bright
With rouge. I smiled,
Touched her shoulder, and led
Her down the street, across
A used car lot and a line
Of newly planted trees,
Until we were breathing
Before a drug store. We

Entered, the tiny bell
Bringing a saleslady
Down a narrow aisle of goods.
I turned to the candies
Tiered like bleachers,
And asked what she wanted—
Light in her eyes, a smile
Starting at the corners
Of her mouth. I fingered
A nickel in my pocket,
And when she lifted a chocolate
That cost a dime,
I didn't say anything.
I took the nickel from
My pocket, then an orange,
And set them quietly on
The counter. When I looked up,
The lady's eyes met mine,
And held them, knowing
Very well what it was all about.
Outside, a few cars hissing past,
Fog hanging like old
Coats between the trees.
I took my girl's hand
In mine for two blocks,
Then released it to let
Her unwrap the chocolate.
I peeled my orange
That was so bright against
The gray of December
That, from some distance,
Someone might have thought
I was making fire in my hands.

Source: *New and Selected Poems* by Gary Soto

ABOUT THE AUTHOR

Gary Soto is a poet and an author of several books for adults and children. He grew up in the San Joaquin Valley of California, and his first book of poetry, *The Elements of San Joaquin*, describes the lives of migrant workers. His books have earned many honors and awards. Mr. Soto lives with his family in Berkeley, CA.

Unit 2 Loud and Ugly

Read...

- Amazing facts about the loudest and the ugliest animals on Earth.

Link to Literature

- A "how" story from Puerto Rico that explains how the owl got its feathers.

Objectives:

Reading:
- Understanding informative expository text
- Strategies: Checking predictions, using a K-W-L chart
- Literature: Responding to a "how" story

Writing:
- Producing writing that informs and explains
- Contributing a page to a class field guide
- Using figurative language to make writing more vivid
- Conducting research on a topic

Listening/Speaking:
- Presenting a report
- Answering questions about information in a chart
- Describing animals and how they live
- Listening to a report

Vocabulary:
- Forming adjectives with the suffixes *-ish*, *-al*, *-ful*, and *-less*
- Learning words for animal sounds
- Learning terms for groups of animals

Grammar:
- Using adverbs of manner

Spelling:
- Spelling the /sh/ sound as in *sheet* and *nation*

Brady Barr goes batty

BEFORE YOU BEGIN

Listen to the tape or CD to hear biologist Brady Barr tell a story about one of the animals that scares him most. Then, talk with your classmates.

1. How does Brady Barr feel about bats? What are his reasons?

2. Imagine that you were with Brady Barr in the cave in Myanmar. Write a short entry in your diary that tells what it felt like.

3. Are there any animals you've seen that you're afraid of? Tell your own story.

A CONNECTING TO YOUR LIFE

🎧 **1. Tuning In**

❶ Listen to the numbered descriptions of the different animals. Write the numbers on the lines next to the animal's names.

_____ American alligator

_____ Nubian vulture

_____ Octopus

_____ Spotted hyena

___/___ Babirusa

_____ Indian peacock

2. Talking It Over Talk with a partner. These six animals can be grouped into two categories. Based on what you now know about these animals, decide what the two categories are. Then put each animal in the correct group.

_____ **Animals**	_____ **Animals**

Think of one more animal you know of that is loud. Describe it. Think of an animal that is really ugly. Tell why.

B GETTING READY TO READ

1. Learning New Words Read the sentences below. Try to guess what the underlined words mean.

1. Stefan is always biting his nails. This is a bad <u>habit</u> of his.
2. Maria walks five miles every morning. It's part of her daily <u>ritual</u>.
3. Lions attack and kill zebras. Zebras are lions' favorite <u>prey</u>.
4. When an enemy comes near, a mother wolf begins to howl. She tries to <u>defend</u> her babies from the attacker.
5. The male alligator tries to scare away other male alligators. He tries to <u>intimidate</u> them by roaring and beating his tail.
6. The hyena opened its mouth and <u>displayed</u> its sharp teeth.

Match each word or phrase on the left with the correct definition on the right.

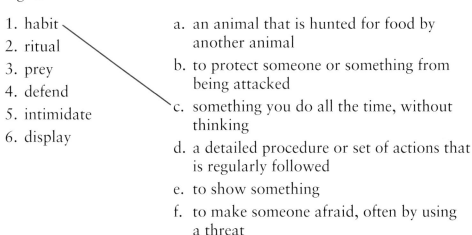

1. habit
2. ritual
3. prey
4. defend
5. intimidate
6. display

a. an animal that is hunted for food by another animal
b. to protect someone or something from being attacked
c. something you do all the time, without thinking
d. a detailed procedure or set of actions that is regularly followed
e. to show something
f. to make someone afraid, often by using a threat

2. Talking It Over Work in a small group. Look at the animals pictured on page 26. Choose the peacock, the hyena, or the alligator. Make a chart like this, and fill in parts 1 and 2. (You will fill in parts 3 and 4 later, after you have read each selection.)

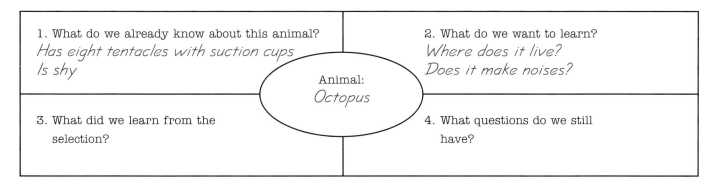

1. What do we already know about this animal?
   Has eight tentacles with suction cups
   Is shy

2. What do we want to learn?
   Where does it live?
   Does it make noises?

Animal:
Octopus

3. What did we learn from the selection?

4. What questions do we still have?

C READING TO LEARN   Field Guides

1. Before You Read Guess three possible reasons that animals might make loud noises.

2. Let's Read As you read, check your guesses. Were you correct?

The Indian Peafowl

1   When it bugles in its high-pitched voice, the male Indian peafowl spreads its tail feathers to form a giant fan—fit for a fashion show! Living in the wild, this cousin of the guinea fowl and pheasant is constantly on the lookout. Danger is never far in the tropical forests where it lives. Leopards and tigers eat peafowl for dinner! At the slightest sound, the peafowl trumpets an alarm that echoes for almost a mile.

2   The Indian peafowl generally flies only when it is in danger. If frightened, it will noisily flap its wings and rise into the treetops.

3   Peafowl are creatures of habit. They sleep roosted in the same tree and trumpet at the same time every day, as if part of a ritual.

4   During courtship, the male peafowl (called peacock) shrieks, "lee-YOW, lee-YOW, lee-YOW." Then, with great showmanship, he spreads his magnificent blue-green tail feathers into a fan and performs a mating dance.

5   The female, or peahen (whose feathers are grayish and who has no fan), easily falls under the charm of the male—and who can blame her? Besides being good-looking, he's a talented singer and dancer!

Source: *The Loudest: Amazing Facts about Loud Animals* by Mymi Doinet

> A bugle and a trumpet are both musical instruments. Guess the meaning of each verb.

> Find examples in the passage to show that the peacock is a "talented singer and dancer."

Address: India and Sri Lanka
Size: Male: About 7 feet (2 meters) long (including tail)
**   Female: About 3 feet (90 centimeters) long**
Weight: From 4.5 to 11 pounds (2 to 5 kilograms)
Favorite food: Buds, seeds, grains, and insects

tropical—existing in the hottest, wettest parts of the world

echo—to make a sound you can hear again and again

courtship—when two people or animals are trying to gain each other's affection

mating—related to animals having sex to produce babies

The Spotted Hyena

1   With a huge burst of laughter, the hyena invites its gang to feast on fresh meat. The hyena is no loner. It lives in a noisy clan of 10 to over 50 animals, which is led by the strongest female in the group. Each evening, the spotted hyenas take off for the hunt, making sounds like very high, piercing laughs. In the savanna, this laughing can be heard almost 2 miles (3.7 kilometers) away. Once they spot their prey, the hungry hyenas run as fast as 30 miles per hour.

2   Then suddenly, they begin to laugh louder and louder to show their glee. There'll be plenty of dinner tonight: their prey—a gnu—is too sick to defend itself.

3   When they laugh, hyenas reveal their powerful jaws. Their premolars can break horn and bone like nutcrackers. Because they are noisy eaters, hyenas attract the attention of other wild animals. Then it may be their turn to be hunted and feasted upon. But not always. By screaming furiously, hyenas can intimidate a lion, sometimes even stealing its meal!

4   When dawn breaks, the hyenas go back to their den. There they sleep and rest their vocal cords until night falls.

Source: *The Loudest: Amazing Facts about Loud Animals* by Mymi Doinet

> The prefix pre- means "before." Molars are back teeth. What are premolars?

> Use hyphens in an adjective phrase with numbers that comes before a noun.

Address: The southern Sahara in Africa

Size: About 5 feet (1.5 meters) long, plus a 10-inch-long (25-centimeter-long) tail

Weight: 88 to 175 pounds (40 to 80 kilograms) (Females are up to 14 percent heavier than males.)

Favorite food: Zebra, antelope, and carrion

feast—to eat a lot of something with enjoyment

loner—someone who often prefers to be alone

piercing—sounding very sharp and unpleasant

savanna—the flat grasslands in tropical regions

den—a cave where an animal lives

vocal cords—the thin bands of muscle in the throat that produce sound

carrion—the flesh of dead animals

The American Alligator

1   The American alligator is the noisiest of all reptiles. Its cries are as loud as the engine of a small plane. Usually, a crocodile wails, or in other words, lets out weak, mournful sounds. But the American alligator roars like a lion!

2   The cries of the American alligator echo through the swamps: the males are trying to intimidate one another. A wild show is about to begin. They stick their short, wide snouts out of the water, displaying their sharp teeth. Bellowing loudly, they whip up their tails and violently beat the water with their jaws. Then, while blowing bubbles with their nostrils, they dive to where the females wait.

3   From May to July, each female American alligator can lay some 40 eggs in nests of grass and mud. The nests measure about 7 feet (2 meters) wide. While they are still in their eggs, the babies let out high-pitched grunts. They are telling their mothers that they will soon be hatching from their shells. Once the babies hatch, the females use their jaws like a cradle. They carefully take each of their babies into their mouths, then carry them to the water, nestled gently between their teeth. Once in the water, the baby reptiles take their first swim.

4   In winter, the American alligator families disappear into the muddy swamp bottom and are silent at last.

Source: *The Loudest: Amazing Facts about Loud Animals* by Mymi Doinet

This is an example of figurative language, or words that form a picture in your mind. Find other examples of figurative language in this passage.

Address: Southeastern United States
Size: From 8 to 16 feet (2.5 to 5 meters) long
Favorite food: Fish, frogs, snakes, and small mammals

mournful—very sad

snout—the long nose of certain animals

bellow—to make a very loud, low noise

high-pitched grunt—a short sound like a pig makes

hatch—to come out of an egg

nestled—located comfortably in a place

swamp—land that is always very wet and covered with water

3. Unlocking Meaning

❶ Identifying the Main Idea Check (✓) the correct answer. You have just read about three animals that make loud noises…

_____ 1. to frighten people.

_____ 2. for specific purposes, or reasons.

_____ 3. to attract a mate.

_____ 4. to show that they are sad.

❷ Finding Details Read the sentences below. Write *T* if the sentence is true and *F* if the sentence is false.

___F___ 1. The Indian peafowl screams only when leopards and tigers are near.

_____ 2. The peacock has much prettier plumage, or feathers, than the peahen.

_____ 3. The peafowl is a herbivore, eating only plants.

_____ 4. The hyena's laughter mostly has to do with courtship and mating.

_____ 5. The leader of a cackle, or group, of hyenas is the strongest female.

_____ 6. Hyenas are nocturnal animals. They hunt their prey at night.

_____ 7. Both the alligator and crocodile are known for their loud roaring.

_____ 8. The male alligator roars mostly to scare off other male alligators.

_____ 9. Baby alligators hatch from their eggs in water.

❸ Think about It Return to your group again. What did you learn from the readings? Finish your chart from page 27. Fill in parts 3 and 4.

❹ Before You Move On Where could you find information to answer the questions you still have about this animal? Make a list.

D WORD WORK

1. Word Detective Sometimes you can guess what a word means by looking for a smaller word or part of a word inside the longer one. Find the smaller words inside the underlined adjectives below and write them in the blanks.

1. <u>foolish</u> man

   smaller word: _____*fool*_____

2. <u>beautiful</u> day

   smaller word: _____

3. <u>homeless</u> person

   smaller word: _____

4. <u>tropical</u> island

   smaller word: _____

2. Word Study You can turn many nouns and verbs into adjectives by adding a suffix. Circle the suffixes in the words below. Guess the meanings of the words with suffixes and without them, then check your dictionary to see if you were correct.

-ish *(like, sort of, or tending toward)*	-ful *(full of, like)*
girlish	playful
greenish	careful
-less *(without, lacking)*	**-al** *(of, related to, or like)*
helpless	personal
humorless	national

—— SPELLING: ——
To do this activity, go to page 235.
■ ■ ■

3. Word Play Work with a partner. Make an adjective out of each word by adding the correct suffix from the box. Write a sentence for each adjective. You can use your dictionary.

-ish	-ful	-less	-al

1. culture _____*cultural*_____
2. power _____
3. waste _____
4. child _____
5. speech _____
6. sensation _____

7. sugar _____
8. region _____
9. plenty _____
10. harm _____
11. brown _____
12. wonder _____

E GRAMMAR

1. Listen Up Listen to these sentences. Point your thumb up 👍 if the sentence sounds correct. Point your thumb down 👎 if it sounds wrong.

👍👎 1. The car stopped sudden.

👍👎 3. The lion roared loudly.

👍👎 2. Lori sang beautifully the song.

👍👎 4. The tiger ate quick.

2. Learn the Rule Learn more about adverbs. Then do Activity 1 again.

ADVERBS
1. Adverbs modify or give more information about verbs by telling *how* something is done. *That huge dog scared me! It came up behind me* **suddenly!**
2. Many adverbs (but not all) are formed by adding the suffix *–ly* to adjectives. Adjective: *A peacock takes* **quick,** *little steps.*   Adverb: *A peacock walks* **quickly.**
3. Adverbs should not be placed between the verb and the object. They almost always come at the end of the sentence or right after the subject. Right: *The lion killed its prey* **quickly.**   Wrong: ~~*The lion killed* **quickly** *its prey.*~~ *The lion* **quickly** *killed its prey.*
4. If a prepositional phrase follows the verb, the adverb can be placed before or after. *The elephant bellowed* **loudly** *at the approaching lion.*   *The elephant bellowed at the approaching lion* **loudly.**

3. Practice the Rule Write an adverb for each adjective below. Then write five sentences. Use one adverb in each sentence.

1. quiet _____*quietly*_____
2. easy _____
3. noisy _____
4. careful _____
5. different _____

6. loud _____
7. rapid _____
8. slow _____
9. sad _____
10. quick _____

READING STRATEGY
Using a K-W-L Chart:
Use a K-W-L chart to help you identify what you know, what you want to know, and what you have learned.

F BRIDGE TO WRITING

Field Guides

1. Before You Read Look at the pictures and titles of the readings on pages 35 and 36. Then look at the K-W-L chart below. Fill in the first two columns.

K: What do I KNOW?	W: What do I WANT to learn?	L: What did I LEARN?

2. Words to Know

Read the definitions. Then complete each sentence with a vocabulary word.

scavenger—an animal that eats food that other animals don't want

environment—the land, water, and air in which people, animals, and plants live

species—a group of animals that can breed with each other

opponent—a person or animal that tries to defeat another in a contest of some sort

carnivore—a meat-eating animal

endangered—used to describe a type of animal that may soon die out, or not exist anymore.

inhabitant—one of the people or animals that lives in a particular place

1. Very few people live in Iceland. This tiny island has only about 300,000 ___*inhabitants*___.

2. Vultures eat almost anything, including dead animals. They are _____.

3. Lions, hyenas, and tigers all eat meat, not plants. They are _____.

4. There are few bald eagles left. This majestic bird is _____.

5. Automobiles are making the air unsafe to breathe. Smog is destroying the _____.

6. Dogs and cats cannot mate. That's because they are different _____.

7. Juan and Carlos often play tennis against each other. They are _____.

3. Let's Read Read about three "ugly" animals. As you read, complete the last column in your chart.

The Nubian Vulture

1   This scavenger—with its naked head and neck—is the most useful garbage collector. This cousin of the eagle soars above the savanna like a glider, spreading its wings, which measure over 3 feet long each. The plains are littered with dead or dying animals. Some are old, sick, or injured; some were killed during fights; and others are the leftovers from a carnivore's feast. When the Nubian vulture's sharp eye spots one of these unfortunate creatures, it dives straight for it.

2   The vulture's featherless neck and head are well adapted to carrion consuming. When the giant bird withdraws its neck and head from a carcass, they are covered with blood. Fortunately, because there are no feathers on its head for the blood to stick to, it dries quickly and flakes off the vulture's head in the hot sun.

3   The Nubian vulture's powerful beak can break the bones of its prey into a thousand pieces. The vulture swallows muscle, skin, and meat. Only lions and hyenas are able to interrupt its feast. The vulture can eat over 2 pounds of meat at each meal. It is a useful scavenger. By ridding the environment of rotting flesh, it keeps colonies of germ-carrying flies in check.

Address: Africa and the Arabian Peninsula
Size: A little over 3 feet (about 1 meter) long
Weight: About 13 pounds (6 kilograms)
Favorite food: Elephant and antelope carcasses

unfortunate—unlucky

carcass—the body of a dead animal

rid—to remove something bad

in check—under control

The Babirusa

1   The babirusa has 2 giant canines that protrude through its upper jaw—and can even puncture its own skull. The male babirusa has 4 tusks: 2 that are sharply curved and 2 that are less curved. The most amazing of these tusks are the 2 that grow through the top of the male's muzzle. The older male babirusa gets, the longer these grow. In curving backward, these gigantic teeth can reach the babirusa's forehead. Sometimes they even grow back into the animal's head!

2   The female babirusa has canines that are much smaller.

3   In the wild, babirusas can easily crack hard nuts with their rigid teeth. They feed mainly on leaves, shoots, and fruits. They do not root in the ground like other species of pigs, but do on occasion use their teeth to dig insects out of rotting trees.

4   To defend itself, the babirusa brandishes its tusks as if they were swords. The curved upper canines are not well suited for injuring opponents, but are quite useful in warding off attack!

5   An excellent swimmer, the babirusa uses its 200-pound (97-kilogram) body like a buoy and can float from island to island to feast on fruit.

6   The babirusa is a shy animal and runs from the presence of humans—and who can blame it? The creature has been widely hunted for its meat. Today, the species is endangered.

Source: *The Ugliest: Amazing Facts about Ugly Animals* by Mymi Doinet

Address: Indonesia
Size: About 3.5 feet (1 meter) long
Weight: Up to 220 pounds (100 kilograms)
Favorite food: Leaves, shoots, and fallen fruit

canine—a long, sharp tooth

protrude—to stick out

tusk— a very long tooth of an animal, like an elephant's

muzzle—the nose and mouth of an animal

shoot—the new part of a plant

brandish—to wave something around in a dangerous way, like a weapon

ward off—to fight off

buoy—an object that floats in the water as a marker

presence—the state of being in a particular place

4. Making Content Connections Work with a partner. Choose a loud animal and an ugly animal. Compare the two and complete the chart.

	Loud animal: _____	Ugly animal: _____
Its main "claim to fame"		
Something we both already knew about the animal.		
Something interesting we both learned.		
Something we would like to learn more about.		

5. Expanding Your Vocabulary Match the name of the animal to the sound it makes.

___f___ 1. roar

_____ 2. bark

_____ 3. hoot

_____ 4. trumpet

_____ 5. howl

_____ 6. croak

_____ 7. grunt

_____ 8. bray

a.

b.

c.

d.

e.

f.

g.

h.

G WRITING CLINIC

Field Guides

1. Think about It Where would you find informational articles and reports?

- ☐ in an encyclopedia
- ☐ in a comic book
- ☐ on the Internet
- ☐ in a magazine
- ☐ in a world atlas
- ☐ in a novel

2. Focus on Organization

❶ Field guides inform and explain. This type of writing describes the characteristics of something. Read, once again, about the Indian peafowl.

The introduction identifies the subject and elaborates, or says more, using specific details.

Each body paragraph develops a different idea.

This paragraph describes. It uses words that relate to the senses—sound and sight.

The conclusion summarizes what we have learned about peacocks. This conclusion amuses the reader!

The Indian Peafowl

When it bugles in its high-pitched voice, the male Indian peafowl spreads its tail feathers to form a giant fan—fit for a fashion show! Living in the wild, this cousin of the guinea fowl and pheasant is constantly on the lookout. Danger is never far in the tropical forests where it lives. Leopards and tigers eat peafowl for dinner! At the slightest sound, the peafowl trumpets an alarm that echoes for almost a mile.

The Indian peafowl generally flies only when it is in danger. If frightened, it will noisily flap its wings and rise into the treetops.

Peafowl are creatures of habit. They sleep roosted in the same tree and trumpet at the same time every day, as if part of a ritual.

During courtship, the male peafowl (called peacock) shrieks, "lee-YOW, lee-YOW, lee-YOW." Then, with great showmanship, he spreads his magnificent blue-green tail features into a fan and performs a mating dance.

The female, or peahen (whose feathers are grayish and who has no fan), easily falls under the charm of the male—and who can blame her? Besides being good-looking, he's a talented singer and dancer!

❷ Your **introduction** identifies the subject and tells what you are going to say about it. Your **conclusion** summarizes what you told the reader or provides an ending the reader will remember.

Work with a partner. Read each passage. Decide whether each is probably an introduction or a conclusion—or either. Be ready to say *why* you think this.

1. A large grizzly bear is one of the strongest animals in the world.
2. It's no wonder the piranha is so feared!
3. When a lion roars, it makes so much noise the ground vibrates under its paws.
4. The mandrill, the most colorful of all mammals, is also a dangerous fighter.
5. An octopus is a sea animal that seems to be all head and arms.
6. So, we see that the coyote really does more good than harm.
7. And then, with a full stomach, the lion roars with contentment before falling asleep in the shade of the acacia trees.

3. Focus on Style Writing that describes often uses **figurative language,** or words and phrases that paint pictures in your mind. Match the phrases on the left with the phrases on the right.

1. The vulture soars above the savannah…
2. Mole rats use their teeth to make tunnels…
3. The skin of a frogfish is neither beautiful nor smooth. It's as rough as…
4. Pipa pipa toads are fat and have flat bodies that look…
5. When it senses danger, the porcupine fish becomes entirely round and its spikes stand up. It looks…
6. When baby lions roar, they sound…

a. …as if they've been run over by a truck.
b. …like a glider.
c. …like a big ball of yarn with needles sticking out all over.
d. …as long as several football fields.
e. …like big house cats with colds.
f. …a block of stone.

H **WRITER'S WORKSHOP** Field Guides

Imagine that your class is writing a field guide about the loudest and the ugliest animals on Earth. Make a page for the book.

1. Getting It Out

❶ Choose an animal to write about. Look at the pictures below for ideas or choose another creature that is either loud or ugly.

Loud Animals

Donkey

Lion

African elephant

Howler monkey

Ugly Animals

Proboscis monkey

Frogfish

Bald uakari

Naked mole rat

❷ What do you already know about the animal—if anything? What do you need to find out? Make a chart like the one below.

The Gray Wolf	
What I already know	*What I need to find out*
Lives in packs *Howls at night*	*Why do wolves howl?* *How do they survive?* *What is their social behavior?*

❸ Find out more about your animal. Try searching the Internet.

- Go directly to a Web page. Type its address in your browser's address box—for example: www.nationalgeographic.com. A site's entry page is called its home page.

- Create shortcuts to your favorite Web pages—called either "bookmarks" or "favorites." This will make it easier to return to the pages you like.

- Do a search using a search engine such as www.google.com. Type important words related to your subject in the box—for example, *babirusa facts*.

❹ Take notes. Make a note-taking sheet based on your questions. Group your facts together. Here are Stefan's notes:

Animal: *Gray Wolf* Basic information: *lives in North America, Europe, and Asia* *2-3 feet high and 4-6 feet long*	What its sounds mean: *uses different sounds to communicate* *moans = to show it is unhappy* *barks = to pick a fight* *howls = to keep the pack together, to warn of danger, to begin the hunt, to return to the den*
Social behavior: *lives in packs (families)* *strongest male is the leader*	How it survives: *it hunts at night* *predators–it kills deer, elk, and sheep* *when in danger, it uses a special howl* *keen sense of hearing–up to 4 miles*

❺ Draw a picture of the animal or download a photograph. Make a map that shows where it lives.

2. Getting It Down

❶ Turn your notes into an outline. Use this model:

Animal: *The Gray Wolf*

Introduction: *The gray wolf is one of nature's best communicators.*

Body:

Topic 1: *Gray wolves like the company of other wolves.*

　　Fact: *They live in packs, or families, of 10 to 12 members.*

　　Fact: *Howling keeps the pack together.*

Topic 2: *They use different sounds to communicate.*

　　Fact: *An evening howl...it's time for the hunt.*

　　Fact: *A morning howl...the hunt is over.*

　　Fact: *There is a special howl to warn of danger.*

Topic 3:

　　Fact:

　　Fact:

Conclusion: *When you are in the woods*

Stefan's introduction identifies the subject and tells us what he is going to write about.

❷ Now turn your outline into a page for the field guide. Add a picture and map. Here is what Stefan wrote:

Each paragraph develops a different topic. Each topic relates to the main focus—the howling of wolves.

— MINI-LESSON —

Using Quotation Marks with Figurative Language:
Use quotation marks around words that are used in a special way to create an image:
The wolf leader is the one with the loudest "voice."

Stefan uses adjectives and figurative language.

　　There is no need for cell phones in the gray wolf family! Gray wolves communicate with their relatives by growling, barking, and howling.

　　Gray wolves love the company of other wolves. They live in packs, just like a family. There are usually 10 to 12 members. The strongest male is the leader. He is the one with the loudest "voice." Howling helps keep the pack together—like a family "sing along."

　　Gray wolves use different sounds to communicate. When they are unhappy, they moan and groan. When they want to pick a fight, they bark. When night falls, they use a special howl to call each other together for the hunt. When dawn breaks, a different howl tells the pack that it's time to return to their den. And, another howl says to the pack, "Danger ahead!" With their keen sense of hearing, the gray wolf can hear a howl for help almost 4 miles away.

　　The gray wolf is a predator. The wolf lets out a special howl of delight when he spots his prey—often a moose, deer, or caribou. Although wolves sometimes attack domestic animals like cattle and sheep, they are not dangerous to humans.

　　When you are in the wilderness, you may hear the eerie howling of wolves. Don't be afraid! The wolves are just singing a chorus whose tune only they understand!

Stefan's conclusion summarizes his report.

3. Getting It Right Now take a careful look at what you have written. Use this guide to revise your page.

Ask yourself	How to check	How to revise
1. Does my introduction identify the animal and focus on what I want to say about the animal?	Ask a partner to read your introduction, then say back what your report is about.	Add a title to your page.
2. Does each body paragraph relate to the subject? Does each develop a different topic?	Compare what you have written with your outline.	Remove information that doesn't relate to the topic or reorganize your paragraphs.
3. Do I use adjectives and figurative language?	<u>Underline</u> each adjective and example of figurative language.	Add more adjectives or use a simile ("like a day without sunshine …")
4. Do I include a picture of the animal and a map that shows where it lives?	Put a star (★) next to the picture and a check mark (✓) next to the map.	Add a picture and/or map.
5. Does my conclusion summarize or "tie up" what I have told the reader?	Reread your introduction, then your conclusion. Do the two "fit" together?	Paraphrase, or restate, your conclusion in different words. Or, leave your reader with an interesting fact, thought, or question.

4. Presenting It Share your page with your classmates.

❶ Begin by showing the picture of your animal and naming it.

❷ Read your report aloud. Read slowly and speak clearly.

❸ Ask if anyone has any questions.

❹ As you listen to each of your classmates' reports, take notes. Write down a question of your own about something in the reports, then ask it.

1. On Assignment

❶ We use special words to describe groups of specific types of animals.

A **pride** of lions

A **herd** of cattle

A **flock** of geese

❷ Work with a partner. Use your research skills to match the correct group term below with each animal. Note: Sometimes more than one term is used with certain animals.

army	band	brood	cloud
colony	convocation	flutter	herd
hive	knot	leap	pack
quiver	school	swarm	

What do you call a group of...?

a.

ants

b.

bats

c.

bees

d.

butterflies

e.

chickens

f.

cobras

g.

coyotes

h.

dogs

i.

eagles

j.

elephants

k.

fish

l.

frogs

❸ Which team found the most answers? How did they find out?

SHARED READING Many cultures have "how" stories. A "how" story is a story that explains how things—often animals—got the way they are. Read how the owl got his feathers.

LET'S TALK Answer the questions.

1. Why is this story called a "how" story?

2. Retell the story, using your own words.

3. Do you know a "how" story about another animal? Tell your classmates.

ABOUT THE AUTHOR

Martha Hamilton and **Rich Weiss** are a husband-wife team. They have been telling stories together for 25 years. They live in Ithaca, New York.

How Owl Got His Feathers
A Story from Puerto Rico

1 Long ago, the animals gave large parties and balls. Everyone was invited. They wore their finest outfits and had a great time dancing and feasting.

2 One day, the birds decided to have a grand ball. They wanted every bird to be there. They sent Hawk to knock on all the birds' doors to invite them.

3 When Hawk got to Owl's house and gave him the invitation, Owl was worried. You see, back then Owl did not have feathers. Owl said, "All the other birds will be there in their finest feather suits. They'll make fun of me. I can't possibly go."

4 Hawk told the other birds what Owl had said. They decided each one of them would lend Owl a feather so that he could have a fine suit of feathers and come to the ball. Hawk collected the feathers of different colors and gave them to Owl. He warned Owl that each feather had to be returned to its owner after the party.

5 Owl arranged the feathers very carefully. Everyone at the ball agreed that Owl looked quite handsome in his new suit. He was so pleased. But during the ball he couldn't help thinking about how he would look when it was over. He hated the thought of having to return the feathers. So when no one was looking, he stole away from the ball and hid in the forest.

6 When the party was over, the other birds looked for Owl so they could get their feathers back. But he was nowhere to be seen.

7 To this day, Owl still wears the same fine suit, and the other birds are still looking for him. That is why Owl is never seen by day. He comes out only at night when other birds are sleeping.

Source: *How and Why Stories: World Tales Kids Can Read and Tell* by Martha Hamilton and Rich Weiss

ball—a dance

steal away—sneak away

Surviving Homework

Read...

- Tips for teenagers on how to survive homework.

Link to Literature

- One of Aesop's fables, "The Fox and the Crow," which is about giving advice.

Objectives:

Reading:
- Understanding an essay of advice
- Strategies: Flagging ideas as you read, commenting
- Literature: Responding to a fable

Writing:
- Writing an essay of advice
- Understanding your audience
- Using direct and indirect quotes

Vocabulary:
- Recognizing word families: Related nouns, verbs, and adjectives
- Understanding slang

Listening/Speaking:
- Listening and responding to a poem
- Changing the words you use, depending on audience
- Listening for ideas and taking notes
- Making a short oral presentation

Grammar:
- Understanding countable and uncountable nouns

Spelling:
- Spelling the /ē/ sound as in *see* and *tea*

BEFORE YOU BEGIN

Talk with your classmates.

1. Look at the picture of Jackie. What is happening? Write a caption for the picture.
2. Do students have too much homework? What do you think?
3. If you could give Jackie advice, what would you say to her?

A CONNECTING TO YOUR LIFE

1. Tuning In

a. Listen to Stefan and Lori talk about homework. What is Stefan's problem?

☐ He doesn't like doing homework. ☐ He doesn't have enough time to do his homework ☐ He keeps losing his homework

b. Talk with a partner. What advice would you give Stefan?

2. Talking It Over

What do kids think about homework? How do you feel about it? Complete the survey below. Circle your answers.

Ten Complaints Kids Have about Homework

	Often true	Sometimes true	Not true
1. "Homework is so boring! I'd rather do the laundry or clean my room."	1	2	3
2. "I have too much homework. It stresses me out."	1	2	3
3. "I don't have time for homework. I have too many other things to do."	1	2	3
4. "I have trouble concentrating."	1	2	3
5. "I put big assignments off until the last minute."	1	2	3
6. "I bring home the wrong work."	1	2	3
7. "I'm confused about what I'm supposed to do."	1	2	3
8. "I wait until the last minute to study for tests."	1	2	3
9. "I can't get organized."	1	2	3
10. "I can't study at home. It's too noisy."	1	2	3

Tally, or count, your surveys, then discuss in a small group.

• What is the #1 homework complaint in your group?

• Why is this complaint #1?

Read the title of this unit. What do you think the unit is about? Check (✓) the correct answer.

_____ 1. It's about ideas for avoiding homework.

_____ 2. It's about a survival class.

_____ 3. It's about ideas for dealing with homework.

_____ 4. It's about ideas for getting straight A's.

B GETTING READY TO READ

1. Learning New Words Read the sentences below. Try to guess what the underlined words mean.

1. Tran has a hard time making himself do his homework. He just isn't <u>motivated</u>.
2. Kate has set two major <u>goals</u> for the future: to go to college and to become a doctor.
3. Stefan has six classes and plays sports after school. He has a very busy <u>schedule</u>.
4. Chimeng dislikes filling out worksheets. He hates boring <u>assignments</u>.
5. We give Chipper treats for doing tricks. Our dog loves <u>rewards</u>!
6. Juan's little brother already knows the alphabet. He is making <u>progress</u> learning to read.
7. I can't do my homework when the TV is on. I just can't <u>concentrate</u>.

Kate's goals are to go to college and become a doctor.

Complete each sentence with a vocabulary word from above.

1. People who have ____*goals*____ know what they want to achieve or get done.
2. When you can't _____, you are unable to pay attention.
3. If you're moving ahead, then you're making _____.
4. Someone who is _____ has a reason for doing something.
5. When the teacher gives you a(n) _____, it's work you have to do.
6. When you make a(n) _____, you list activities and events you plan to do.
7. A(n) _____ is something pleasant you get for doing something.

2. Talking It Over Work in a small group. List the five homework assignments you like the least in order. Compare your list with other groups' lists.

C READING TO LEARN

1. Before You Read

a. This article appeared in *TIME for Kids*. Does it describe a typical day for you?

Too Much Homework!

[1] It's a typical day for Molly Benedict. The 8th-grader gets home from Presidio Middle School in San Francisco, California. She does not break for cookies; she does not phone a friend. She even walks right past the TV. Molly heads straight for the computer in the basement and starts writing a page-long book report on Harry *Potter and the Sorcerer's Stone* by J.K. Rowling.

[2] After half an hour of work and some helpful suggestions from her mother for improving the report, Molly has a quick snack and starts chipping away at more than 100 math problems. She moves on to social studies— labeling all the countries and bodies of water on a map of the Middle East. Then it's time for science. She studies the way blood circulates through the human body for an upcoming test. All that's left is practicing the piano, a little fine-tuning on that book report, dinner and— finally!—sleep.

[3] Does Molly's schedule sound familiar? "I don't have a lot of time to do just whatever," says Molly. "My friends and I think it's a lot of work."

Source: "Too Much Homework!: American kids spend more time than ever on homework. Will their hard work pay off?" *TIME for Kids*, January 29, 1999. Used with permission from TIME for Kids Magazine

break for—take time for

improve—to make better

chip away at—to reduce something slowly

circulate—to flow

upcoming—happening soon

fine-tuning—the process of making something perfect

b. Why do kids have so much homework? Talk with a partner. List three reasons.

2. Let's Read Homework expert Cathy Spalding offers tips, or helpful advice, to teens on the Internet at <u>homeworktips.about.com</u>. Read some of her tips for surviving homework.

┌─ **READING STRATEGY** ─
Flagging Ideas:
As you read, place sticky notes next to interesting or important ideas so you can find them again easily.

Back   Forward   Stop   Refresh   Home   AutoFill   Print   Mail

Get Motivated

I always do my math homework first. Then the rest doesn't seem so awful!

¹ What do you do when you just can't get yourself to do homework? You know it has to be done, but it is the last thing you want to spend your time doing. How are you going to get yourself motivated? Here are eight tips to improve your motivation to study.

² Set goals for yourself. They don't have to be big ones, in fact, the smaller the better. Start by setting goals you know you can <mark>attain</mark> easily. For instance, a goal such as getting straight A's on your next report card would be nice, but it is a major goal. An easier one would be taking a page of notes for your report on <mark>Inuksuks</mark>.

³ Set a schedule for studying and write it down. Why write it down? Something about the written word makes it harder to ignore. Once you've written that you'll do it, it's harder to not do it.

⁴ Do the homework you dislike the most first. Also, if there is homework you find most difficult, do it first while your mind is still <mark>fresh</mark>. However, if you have a number of small assignments and one major assignment to work on, doing the small ones first will make it seem like you are making progress quicker.

⁵ Ask for help from your parents. If you don't ask, they will <mark>assume</mark> you either don't need help or don't want help.

⁶ Use rewards to mark your progress. You could "allow" yourself to go to a movie on Friday night if you get your history project completed by then, or you could take a snack break once you get the first thirty algebra questions completed.

⁷ Find a way to turn your homework assignments into something that interests you. If you have a choice of topics, choose something you've always wanted to learn about. If you have to do geometry homework, think about how you could use it when you want to become an <mark>interior designer</mark>. If you are researching Russia and your interest is in wildlife, find out what species you would find there (would you believe about 65% of the world's brown bears?).

⁸ Some of these tips could work for you. Try them out. It's time to get motivated.

Source: about.com

Local machine zone

<mark>attain</mark>—to achieve or reach

<mark>Inuksuks</mark>—human-like stone figures found in Nova Scotia

<mark>fresh</mark>—not tired and able to think clearly

<mark>assume</mark>—to believe something is true without knowing

<mark>interior designer</mark>—a person who gives ideas about color, style, furniture, and art in a home or building

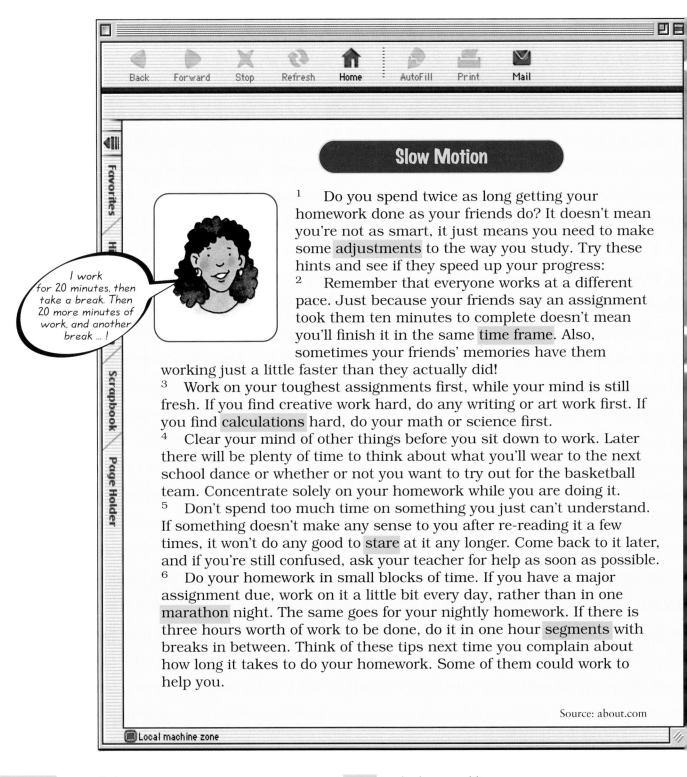

Slow Motion

1   Do you spend twice as long getting your homework done as your friends do? It doesn't mean you're not as smart, it just means you need to make some adjustments to the way you study. Try these hints and see if they speed up your progress:

2   Remember that everyone works at a different pace. Just because your friends say an assignment took them ten minutes to complete doesn't mean you'll finish it in the same time frame. Also, sometimes your friends' memories have them working just a little faster than they actually did!

3   Work on your toughest assignments first, while your mind is still fresh. If you find creative work hard, do any writing or art work first. If you find calculations hard, do your math or science first.

4   Clear your mind of other things before you sit down to work. Later there will be plenty of time to think about what you'll wear to the next school dance or whether or not you want to try out for the basketball team. Concentrate solely on your homework while you are doing it.

5   Don't spend too much time on something you just can't understand. If something doesn't make any sense to you after re-reading it a few times, it won't do any good to stare at it any longer. Come back to it later, and if you're still confused, ask your teacher for help as soon as possible.

6   Do your homework in small blocks of time. If you have a major assignment due, work on it a little bit every day, rather than in one marathon night. The same goes for your nightly homework. If there is three hours worth of work to be done, do it in one hour segments with breaks in between. Think of these tips next time you complain about how long it takes to do your homework. Some of them could work to help you.

Source: about.com

I work for 20 minutes, then take a break. Then 20 more minutes of work, and another break … !

adjustment—a small change

time frame—a period of time

calculation—a step in doing math

stare—to look at steadily

marathon—used to describe an event that lasts a long time

segment—a section or piece

3. Unlocking Meaning

❶ Finding the Main Idea The suggestions for "surviving" homework are all meant to help students …

☐ fit homework into busy schedules   ☐ be more successful students   ☐ convince their teachers not to give so much homework

❷ Finding Details Read the suggestions below. Write *GM* if it comes from "Get Motivated" or *SM* if it comes from "Slow Motion."

GM 1. It's a good idea to set goals for yourself that you can achieve.

_____ 2. Give yourself a reward when you finish all or part of an assignment.

_____ 3. Try to think of ideas for making your homework more fun and less boring.

_____ 4. Do the hardest tasks first—when you have the most energy.

_____ 5. Put other interests aside when you begin your homework.

_____ 6. Make a study schedule for yourself.

_____ 7. If you don't understand something after reading it a few times, come back to it later.

❸ Think about It What are your own homework tips? Work in a small group. Talk about the pros and cons of *one* idea. Make a chart.

More Bright Ideas for Homework	Pros (why this might be a good idea)	Cons (why this might be a bad idea)
Listen to music	It can help you relax.	It can make it harder to concentrate.

❹ Before You Move On Talk with a partner. What should a teacher do when students don't do their homework? Write three ideas, then share with your classmates.

D WORD WORK

1. Word Detective Words that look alike can sometimes belong to the same family. Read the list of verbs. Write an adjective that is a member of the same family in the blank. Make a guess!

1. motivate   *motivated* _____
2. write   _____
3. bore   _____
4. confuse   _____
5. interest   _____
6. harm   _____

2. Word Study Members of a word family look similar, but they have different but related meanings and different jobs in a sentence. Make up another sentence for each word.

VERB	ADJECTIVE	NOUN
study	studious	student
Juan *studies* hard.	Juan is *studious*.	Juan is a good *student*.

SPELLING:
To do this activity, go to page 236.

3. Word Play Work with a partner. Complete the word family chart. Use your dictionary for help. Choose three families and write a sentence for each word.

Verb	Adjective	Noun
act	*active*	activity
taste		taste
	amazing	amazement
bore	boring	
	assigned	assignment
write	written	

E GRAMMAR   Countable and Uncountable Nouns

 1. Listen Up Listen to these sentences. Point your thumb up ☝ if the sentence sounds correct. Point your thumb down ☟ if it sounds wrong.

☝ ☟ 1. I have three homeworks tonight.

☝ ☟ 2. I have a lot of textbooks.

☝ ☟ 3. Tom has a lot of stuff in his room!

☝ ☟ 4. I learn new vocabularies every day.

2. Learn the Rule Study the rules, then do Activity 1 again.

You can use "a/an" with countable nouns that are singular but not plural.

COUNTABLE AND UNCOUNTABLE NOUNS

1. Nouns are either countable or uncountable.

   Some countable nouns: book, assignment, problem, worksheet, notecard.
   Some uncountable nouns: homework, schoolwork, handwriting, vocabulary, money, music, stuff.

2. Countable nouns can be made plural by adding –s or –es.

   Singular: *I left a book in my locker.*
   Plural: *I left both books in my locker.*

3. Uncountable nouns have only one form and cannot be counted.

   Right: I have a lot of homework tonight.   Wrong: I have a lot of homeworks tonight.
   Right: I don't have much money.   Wrong: I don't have many moneys.

---

3. Practice the Rule Circle the correct noun forms.

EXAMPLE: Do we have any (⟨homework⟩/homeworks) tonight?

1. We have 30 math (problem/problems) to do for homework.
2. Ms. Johnson has trouble reading some of her students' (handwriting/handwritings).
3. Could you lend me some (money/moneys)?
4. I have too many (book/books) in my backpack! It's heavy!
5. I keep a binder for each of my (class/classes).
6. I have two homework (assignment/assignments) tonight!
7. There's a test on the new (vocabulary/vocabularies) tomorrow.

F BRIDGE TO WRITING

1. Before You Read Think of reasons that it's hard to do homework... *at home*. Write them down, then share with a partner.

2. Words to Know Read the definitions below for each word.

topic—a subject that people talk, read, or write about

project—a carefully planned piece of work

distraction—something that takes your attention away from what you are doing

procrastinate—to delay doing something you ought to do

absorb—to learn or understand

reinforce—to practice what you learn so that you remember or understand it

priorities—things that are most important and need attention before anything else

Complete each sentence with a vocabulary word from above.

1. I can't concentrate on my homework when the TV is on. The noise is a _distraction_ .

2. Juan enjoys reading books about baseball and football. Sports are a _____ he is interested in.

3. Lori had to drop some of her favorite after school activities because she didn't have enough time to do her homework. Her schoolwork is one of her top _____ .

4. Carlos and Stefan are working on a _____ for the science fair. They are making a model of a volcano.

5. Doing workbook activities can help _____ skills you have just learned.

6. When you read something too fast, it's often hard to _____ the information.

7. "I want you to begin your homework right now," Mom said. "Don't _____ anymore!"

3. Let's Read Students often complain that they have trouble concentrating when they try to do their homework. Learn how to concentrate. As you read, write one more idea of your own.

READING STRATEGY
Commenting:
Jotting down your own ideas as you read is one way of reading actively. When you read actively, you remember and understand more.

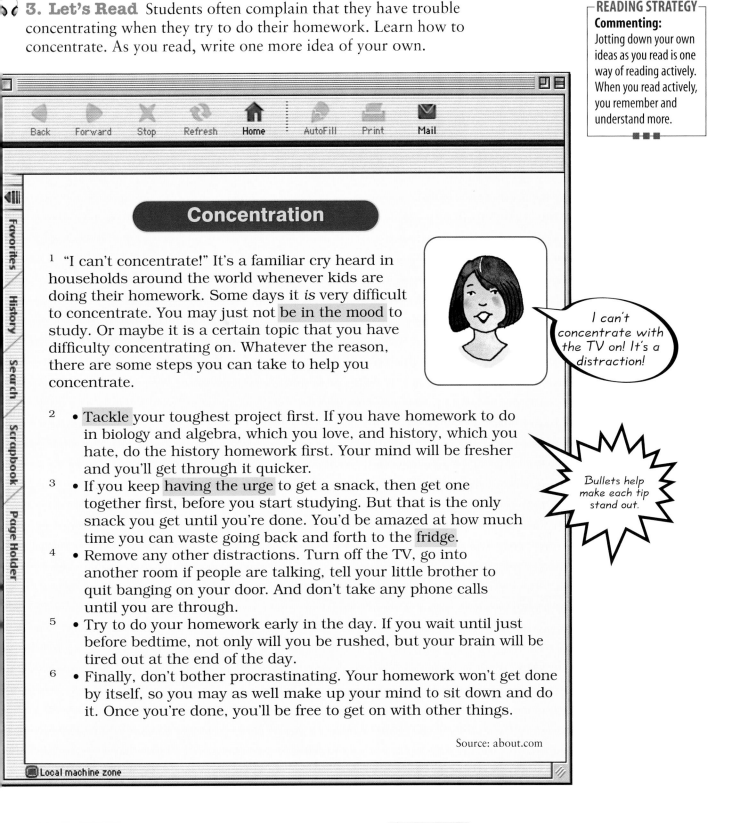

Concentration

1 "I can't concentrate!" It's a familiar cry heard in households around the world whenever kids are doing their homework. Some days it *is* very difficult to concentrate. You may just not be in the mood to study. Or maybe it is a certain topic that you have difficulty concentrating on. Whatever the reason, there are some steps you can take to help you concentrate.

I can't concentrate with the TV on! It's a distraction!

2 • Tackle your toughest project first. If you have homework to do in biology and algebra, which you love, and history, which you hate, do the history homework first. Your mind will be fresher and you'll get through it quicker.

3 • If you keep having the urge to get a snack, then get one together first, before you start studying. But that is the only snack you get until you're done. You'd be amazed at how much time you can waste going back and forth to the fridge.

Bullets help make each tip stand out.

4 • Remove any other distractions. Turn off the TV, go into another room if people are talking, tell your little brother to quit banging on your door. And don't take any phone calls until you are through.

5 • Try to do your homework early in the day. If you wait until just before bedtime, not only will you be rushed, but your brain will be tired out at the end of the day.

6 • Finally, don't bother procrastinating. Your homework won't get done by itself, so you may as well make up your mind to sit down and do it. Once you're done, you'll be free to get on with other things.

Source: about.com

be in the mood—to want to do something or feel you might enjoy something

tackle—to start dealing with a difficult problem

have the urge—to suddenly want to do something

fridge—(*informal*) a refrigerator

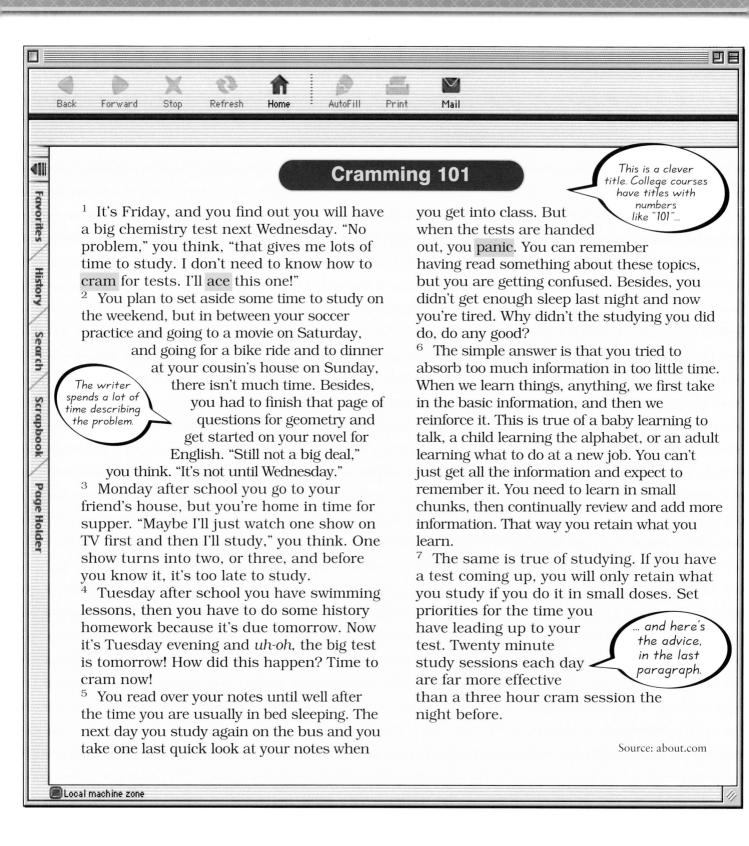

Cramming 101

This is a clever title. College courses have titles with numbers like "101"...

1 It's Friday, and you find out you will have a big chemistry test next Wednesday. "No problem," you think, "that gives me lots of time to study. I don't need to know how to cram for tests. I'll ace this one!"

2 You plan to set aside some time to study on the weekend, but in between your soccer practice and going to a movie on Saturday, and going for a bike ride and to dinner at your cousin's house on Sunday, there isn't much time. Besides, you had to finish that page of questions for geometry and get started on your novel for English. "Still not a big deal," you think. "It's not until Wednesday."

The writer spends a lot of time describing the problem.

3 Monday after school you go to your friend's house, but you're home in time for supper. "Maybe I'll just watch one show on TV first and then I'll study," you think. One show turns into two, or three, and before you know it, it's too late to study.

4 Tuesday after school you have swimming lessons, then you have to do some history homework because it's due tomorrow. Now it's Tuesday evening and *uh-oh*, the big test is tomorrow! How did this happen? Time to cram now!

5 You read over your notes until well after the time you are usually in bed sleeping. The next day you study again on the bus and you take one last quick look at your notes when you get into class. But when the tests are handed out, you panic. You can remember having read something about these topics, but you are getting confused. Besides, you didn't get enough sleep last night and now you're tired. Why didn't the studying you did do, do any good?

6 The simple answer is that you tried to absorb too much information in too little time. When we learn things, anything, we first take in the basic information, and then we reinforce it. This is true of a baby learning to talk, a child learning the alphabet, or an adult learning what to do at a new job. You can't just get all the information and expect to remember it. You need to learn in small chunks, then continually review and add more information. That way you retain what you learn.

7 The same is true of studying. If you have a test coming up, you will only retain what you study if you do it in small doses. Set priorities for the time you have leading up to your test. Twenty minute study sessions each day are far more effective than a three hour cram session the night before.

... and here's the advice, in the last paragraph.

Source: about.com

---

cram—(*informal*) to study a lot of information quickly

ace—(*informal*) to get the best grade possible on a test or assignment

panic—to suddenly feel frightened

3. Making Content Connections

Here are two more complaints kids have about homework. Think about your own experiences. Complete the chart. Then discuss each question in small groups.

	"Homework is boring"	"I'm too busy to fit homework into my schedule!"
1. What is an example from your own life?	*All we ever do is worksheets.*	
2. Why is this a problem for you?	*Worksheets don't make me think.*	
3. What advice would you give to other students?		

4. Expanding Your Vocabulary

Look again at the first paragraph of "Cramming 101." The author uses slang, or informal words or expressions, to make it seem like she is talking to the reader.

<u>With slang:</u>   I don't need to know how to cram for tests. I'll ace this one!

<u>Without slang:</u>   I don't need to know how to learn a lot of information quickly. I'll get a perfect score on this test!

Match the "homework slang" on the left with the meanings on the right.

Warning: Remember who your audience is! Slang can sound inappropriate or rude to adults. When in doubt, avoid using slang.

a. pile on
b. burn out
c. go bonkers
d. brainiac
e. catch some z's
f. ease the pain
g. hit the books
h. bomb out

_____ to do very poorly
___a___ to give a lot of something
_____ to make something easier and more fun
_____ to feel crazy
_____ to become exhausted
_____ an intelligent person
_____ to take a nap
_____ to study hard

G WRITING CLINIC — Essays of Advice

1. Think about It "Advice writing" can have many forms. Talk with a partner. How do each of these columns offer advice to readers? Think of at least one more example of advice writing.

- The "Dear Abby" column
- A consumer report
- How to fix something
- A restaurant review column

2. Focus on Organization

Reread part of the selection. Learn how to give advice in writing.

Identify the **problem** in your introduction. Let your readers know **what you are going to tell them.**

Write a separate paragraph for each suggestion.

Provide **reasons** to support your suggestions.

Provide **examples** to help your reader.

Use your final paragraph to encourage your reader.

What do you do when you just can't get yourself to do homework? How are you going to get yourself motivated? Here are eight tips to improve your motivation to study.

Set goals for yourself. They don't have to be big ones, in fact, the smaller the better. Start by setting goals you know you can attain easily ...

Set a schedule for studying and write it down. Why write it down? Something about the written word makes it harder to ignore. Once you've written that you'll do it, it's harder to not do it.

Use rewards to mark your progress. You could "allow" yourself to go to a movie on Friday night if you get your history project completed by then, or you could take a snack break once you get the first thirty algebra questions completed.

Find a way to turn your homework assignments into something that interests you. If you have a choice of topics, choose something you've always wanted to learn about. If you are researching Russia and your interest is in wildlife, find out what species you would find there ...

Some of these tips could work for you. Try them out. It's time to get motivated.

Can you think of one more example to make homework assignments more interesting?

3. Focus on Style

❶ People's actual words help make your writing lively and interesting. You can imagine the words that might be in your reader's head.

It's Friday, and you find out you will have a big chemistry test next Wednesday. "No problem," you think, "that gives me lots of time to study. I don't need to know how to cram for tests. I'll ace this one!"

Or, you can quote other people's words to make your point.

"When a test is coming up," says Lori, "I study a little bit each day rather than trying to cram everything in my head the night before."

Using someone's actual words helps make advice believable. Compare how a person's words can be used.

- How are they written differently?
- Why would you use direct quotes instead of indirect quotes?
- Why would you choose to use indirect quotes?

The person's exact words	A sentence with a direct quote	A sentence with an indirect quote
I cut down on TV watching.	"I cut down on TV watching," said Juan.	Juan said he cut down on TV watching.

❷ Practice using quotes. Write sentences with direct and indirect quotes for each quote below on a separate piece of paper.

1. Carlos: "I make a homework schedule each week."
2. Lori: "I try not to talk on the phone."
3. Parveen: "I do my homework after school."
4. Juan: "I do my homework during homeroom."
5. Maria: "I catch up on my homework on the weekends."
6. Tran: "I set aside time each day to do homework."
7. Wen-Ying: "I do my homework on the bus."
8. Stefan: "I do my homework before I watch TV."

H WRITER'S WORKSHOP · Essays of Advice

Imagine that your class is writing an advice manual for teenagers called "Homework Tips for Dummies." Write a section for the book that gives advice for a common complaint teens have about homework.

1. Getting It Out

❶ Think about common complaints that teenagers have about homework.

1. "When I read my textbooks, I can't remember what I read!"

2. "I can't seem to get organized!"

3. "I always seem to lose my homework or leave my books at school!"

4. "I often wait until the last minute to study for tests!"

5. "Homework stresses me out!"

6. "It's almost *impossible* to study at home!"

❷ Choose *one complaint*. Brainstorm your own ideas for solving the problem. Make a brainstorm web. Here is what Stefan brainstormed.

Turn up lights so they are bright.

Take a stretch break every so often.

Splash cold water on my face.

I fall asleep when I read.

Talk to a family member about what I've read.

Don't read with the TV on.

❸ Your classmates might also have good ideas. Talk to them and record their ideas in the speech bubbles.

❹ Now add the ideas you like to your brainstorm web.

2. Getting It Down

❶ Turn the ideas and suggestions in your web into an outline. Use this model. Here is Stefan's outline:

Complaint: *When I read a textbook, I nearly always fall asleep.* .

Basic advice for: *staying awake* .

Suggestion #1: *Don't get too comfortable* .

Detail: *Sit at your desk* .

Quote: *"Don't lie down to read." (Juan)* .

Suggestion #2: *Break the assignment into smaller parts* .

Detail: .

Quote: .

Suggestion #3: *No TV or radio!* .

Detail: .

Quote: *"I can't concentrate when the TV is on...." (Lori)* .

MINI-LESSON

Using Punctuation Marks with Quotation Marks:

Punctuation marks go *inside* quotation marks.

Right: "I get up early to do my homework," said Juan.

Wrong: "I get up early to do my homework", said Juan.

■ ■ ■

❷ Now turn your outline into an essay. Here is part of what Stefan wrote:

Do your eyes slam shut the minute you open your textbook? Here are a few basic tips that can help lighten your lids the next time you have a long chapter to read:

If you want to pay attention to what you're reading, don't get too comfortable. Many students sit at a desk when they're reading. "Don't lie on your bed," advises Juan. "You're sure to fall asleep."

Break the assignment into parts.

Get rid of distractions. Turn off the radio and TV. "I can't concentrate when the TV is on," says Lori. "And the radio makes me fall asleep."

. . .

Stefan states the complaint clearly and tells us what he is going to say. The words he uses are clever.

Stefan uses quotes to help him make his points.

I don't understand the second tip. Stefan needs to say a lot more!

3. Getting It Right Take a careful look at what you have written. Use these questions to revise your work.

Questions to Ask...	How to Check...	How to Revise...
1. Do I state the complaint or problem clearly in my introduction. Do I tell the reader what I am going to say?	Underline the sentence that states the complaint or problem.	Add a sentence that states the complaint.
	Put a wavy line under the words that signal what you are going to say.	Add a sentence that begins, "Here are several tips for..."
2. Do I put each suggestion in a separate section or paragraph?	Put a star (★) before each tip.	Reorganize your advice manual so that each tip is separate and clearly stated.
3. Do I include details, examples, and reasons?	Put a check mark (✔) next to each detail or example.	Add details and examples to your paragraph.
4. Do I include quotes for each suggestion?	Circle each quote.	Add quotes that support each suggestion.

4. Presenting It

❶ Get into a group with classmates who have written about the same homework complaint.

❷ Decide who wrote the most interesting introduction. Have that person introduce the problem to the class. Then take turns presenting solutions to the problem.

❸ Ask your classmates if they have any ideas that you didn't think of.

❹ When other students are giving their presentations, take notes. Use this guide. Be ready to try out one idea tonight, then report back to your classmates on how well it worked.

Complaint	Suggestions
	1. _____
	2. _____
	3. _____

1. On Assignment An unknown middle school student wrote this poem about homework.

> *How do you decide which homework assignment is most important?*

Homework in every subject.

Tell me what to do first.

Which is more important?

Each teacher says that his subject is.

How can I be organized when I can't even remember my schedule?

Source: Love Me When I'm Most Unlovable: The Middle School Years

❶ What do you do when you have two or three homework assignments? Talk with a partner.

❷ Many students keep a weekly homework schedule. Make your own schedule.

1. Using a ruler, make a calendar like this. Make a column for each night of the week and a row for each subject.
2. Write down the assignment for each subject.
3. Budget time to do the assignment.
4. Keep a schedule for at least one week.

Subject	Monday	Tuesday	Wednesday	Thursday	Friday	Saturday	Sunday
English							
Math							
Science							
Social Studies							

> *Read pages 87-93. Answer the questions on page 94.*
>
> *4:00-4:45.*

2. Link to Literature

SHARED READING Advice can be offered in many ways. The Greek storyteller Aesop told fables that give advice. Fables tell stories that have animals as characters. Read "The Fox and the Crow."

LET'S TALK Discuss the questions.

1. What does the Fox want that the Crow has?
2. How does the Fox get what he wants?
3. What is the moral (advice) of the fable? Use your own words.

ABOUT THE AUTHOR

Aesop lived in Greece, probably from about 620 to 560 B.C. We don't know much about his life, but his fables are still used today to teach moral lessons to children. Two of his most famous fables are *The Tortoise and the Hare* and *The Boy Who Cried Wolf*.

The Fox and the Crow

A Fox once saw a Crow fly off with a piece of cheese in its beak and settle on a branch of a tree. "That's for me, as I am a Fox," said Master Fox, and he walked up to the foot of the tree.

"Good morning, Mistress Crow," he cried. "How well you are looking today: how glossy your feathers, how bright your eye. I feel sure your voice must surpass that of other birds, just as your figure does; let me hear but one song from you that I may greet you as the Queen of Birds."

The Crow lifted up her head and began to caw her best, but the moment she opened her mouth the piece of cheese fell to the ground, only to be snapped up by Master Fox. "That will do," said he. "That was all I wanted. In exchange for your cheese I will give you a piece of advice for the future— Do not trust flatterers."

Master/Mistress—titles for the male and female heads of the household, used in the past

surpass—to be better than

caw—to make a crowing sound

flatterer—someone who gives a compliment that is not sincere

Ancient Worlds

Read...

- Fascinating reports about Egyptian mummies, the 3,000-year-old Olmec heads of Mexico, and the mysterious stone statues of Easter Island.

Link to Literature

- An Aztec poem, originally written in the Aztec language, Nahuatl.

Objectives:

Reading:
- Reading articles about the ancient world
- Strategies: Using a K-W-L chart, quick writing
- Literature: Interpreting an Aztec poem

Writing:
- Writing a short research report
- Developing a thesis statement
- Taking notes
- Sentence combining

Vocabulary:
- Learning verb suffixes: *-ify*, *-ize*, and *-ate*
- Using knowledge of affixes to unlock word meaning

Listening/Speaking:
- Listening to a description of a famous ancient site
- Comparing and discussing research
- Taking notes of a presentation

Grammar:
- Understanding passive sentences

Spelling:
- Spelling the /f/ sound as in *fun* and *elephant*

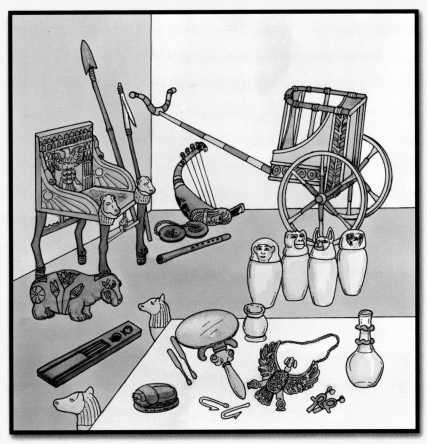

Secrets of a royal mummy's tomb

BEFORE YOU BEGIN

Talk with your classmates.

1. Look at the picture. What do you see?
2. Which objects are no longer used? Which are still used today?
3. What do the artifacts, or objects, tell about ancient Egypt? Help your teacher make a list of facts.

A · CONNECTING TO YOUR LIFE

1. Tuning In

❶ Listen to Part 1 on the tape or CD. It tells the story of Hiram Bingham, an archaeologist—someone who studies past peoples and how they lived. What important site do you think Bingham discovered? Choose from the pictures below.

Easter Island

Pyramids of Egypt

Machu Picchu

Chichén Itzá

Great Wall of China

Stonehenge

❷ Now listen to Part 2. Were you correct?

2. Talking It Over
Talk with a partner. Be ready to share your ideas with your classmates.

- Why do people study the past— what do you think? Write down one good reason.

- What can we learn from knowing more about how people lived long ago and far away?

- If you were an archaeologist, which place would you like to visit? Why?

B GETTING READY TO READ

1. Learning New Words Read the definitions below.

ritual—a set of actions or a ceremony that is always done in the same way

burial—the ceremony of putting a dead body into a grave

essential—extremely important and necessary

eliminate—to get rid of something completely

formula—a method you use to do something over and over

symbolize—to represent or be a sign for something or someone else

equipped—provided with things that have a specific purpose

Complete the sentences with the vocabulary words above.

1. Without sturdy boots and a compass, hikers can't find their way. These are _essential_ items for a hiker.
2. When the car was invented, it _____ the need for horses and carriages.
3. Sorry, but there is no magic _____ for getting rich.
4. The flag often _____ the feelings of pride people have for their country.
5. Eating turkey and pumpkin pie are part of the Thanksgiving _____.
6. Cruise ships are always _____ with life boats and other safety equipment.
7. The _____ will take place at 11:00 a.m. at the Queen of Hearts Cemetery.

2. Talking It Over Work in a small group. Imagine that you are a team of archaeologists. Plan a "voyage of discovery." Fill in the chart. Begin by choosing the ancient site you will visit.

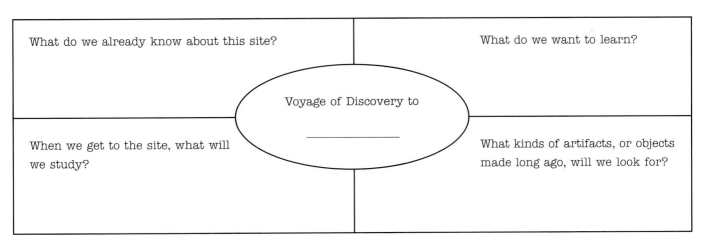

What do we already know about this site?

What do we want to learn?

Voyage of Discovery to

_____

When we get to the site, what will we study?

What kinds of artifacts, or objects made long ago, will we look for?

C READING TO LEARN   Short Research Reports

1. Before You Read Look at the pictures. What do you see? What do you already know about mummies? What do you want to learn? List three questions you have. Make a **K-W-L chart** and complete the first two columns.

2. Let's Read You are about to read an article about mummies, dead bodies that were preserved, or specially treated, so they would not decay. The article is a type of research report. As you read, look for the answers to your questions.

Mummies:
The Inside Story

1   Beneath layers of <u>linen</u>, every mummy has a story to tell.

2   Ancient Egyptians were experts at making mummies. For about 3,000 years starting around 2,500 B.C., they mummified, or preserved, the dead bodies of Egyptians. The rituals of mummy making and burial were important to the Egyptians' belief in life after death. They believed that a dead person's *ka*, or life force, **would** die unless it could **dwell** inside an identical body, such as a mummy. A person's *ba*, or **spirit**, **could** leave the body during the day but had to return at night. A mummy, which preserved a person's appearance long after death, was essential for guiding home the *ka* and *ba*. Mummies were first put into coffins, then into tombs, or burial chambers. Most tombs were underground; some royal tombs were inside pyramids.

> The writer uses "*would*" instead of "*will*" because the story is in the past. "*Could*" is the past tense form of "*can*."

The mummy of Hunefer supported by Anubis

linen—a type of light cloth

dwell—to live in a place

spirit—a living being without a body, like an angel or ghost

3   The main ingredient in turning a body into a long-lasting mummy was the one that was removed: water. "Dry and wrap" was the Egyptian formula for life everlasting. This was no small task, since human bodies are about 65 percent water. The Egyptians eliminated much of the moisture in the body by removing most of the internal organs. It took 35 to 40 days for fluids to be drained from a body being prepared for mummification.

4   Preparing mummies was a religious rite. In charge was a priest, wearing a mask that symbolized Anubis, the god of embalming. With sharp flint knives, lesser priests cut out the dead person's lungs, liver, stomach, and intestines. They left the heart in place and threw away the brains. Priests used 150 yards of linen strips to wrap a body in about 20 layers.

5   Mummies often reveal secrets from the past. Pharaohs and their queens got royal treatment. Their tombs were the biggest and best equipped, furnished with all the comforts of home. They would have everything they needed for eternal life. Buried in the tombs with different mummies were jewelry, statues, furniture, toys, wigs, makeup, perfume, amulets, game boards, papyrus scrolls, weapons, hunting gear, medicine and food such as roast duck, leg of lamb, bread, cake, fruit, and wine.

"Mummy," "mummify," and "mummification" are all members of the same word family. What do you think "mummification" means?

Here is the past tense form of "will" again!

internal organ—a body part inside your body, such as the heart, stomach, and lungs

priest—someone who performs religious duties

embalming—using chemicals to prevent a body from decaying or rotting

flint—a type of very hard stone

papyrus scroll—a long piece of ancient Egyptian "paper" that is rolled up and has official writing on it

> 6   Many mummies still have their nails, eyebrows, lashes, teeth, and hair **intact**. The hair of one 15-year-old girl mummy shows that she had been **malnourished**. The teeth of other mummies reveal plenty of wear and tear, due to sand blowing into their food. A look inside the mouth of Pharaoh Seti I indicates a missing tooth. Scientists can't agree, though, whether the sand-filled bread or honey-rich cakes were this particular mummy's **curse**.
>
> Source: *National Geographic World*

intact—not damaged

malnourished—poorly fed

curse—a magical power that does something bad

3. Unlocking Meaning

❶ **Finding the Main Idea** These sentences tell the main ideas in the passage. Write the correct number of the paragraph(s).

1. _____   The tombs of mummies help teach us about Egyptian life.

2. _____   Making mummies involved a series of complicated steps.

3. _____   The Egyptians preserved their dead for religious reasons.

4. _____   Many mummies look a lot like real-life people.

❷ **Finding Details** Choose the best ending for each sentence. Check (✓) the correct answer.

1. The Egyptians believed that...

_____   a. mummies were gods.

_____   b. only pharaohs could become mummies.

_____   c. there was life after death.

_____   d. only the bodies of men should be preserved, or mummified.

2. The reason Egyptians made mummies was to make sure that...

_____ a. the person's *ba*, spirit, would not come back.

_____ b. the person's *ba*, or spirit, would know which body to return to.

_____ c. the person's *ka*, or life force, would die without feeling any pain.

_____ d. the dead would look more beautiful than they did when they were alive.

3. Mummies were first placed in...

_____ a. underground tombs.

_____ b. coffins.

_____ c. pyramids.

_____ d. the sand.

4. The first step in mummifying a dead body was to...

_____ a. wrap the body in cloth.

_____ b. remove all fluids from the body.

_____ c. cut out the person's heart.

_____ d. put the body in the sun.

5. Mummies were often buried with...

_____ a. their favorite books and photographs.

_____ b. things they would need in their future life.

_____ c. their brains in a jar.

_____ d. a lot of flowers around them.

❸ **Think about It** Talk in a small group. Imagine that you were writing a report on mummies.

- What questions would you like to answer? Make a list.

- Where would you get more information about the subject? Write down ideas.

- Who might you ask for help?

❹ **Before You Move On** Talk with a partner. The Egyptian priests removed the brain without damaging the skull! How do you think they did this? Now listen to the process described on the tape or CD. Were you right?

D WORD WORK

1. Word Detective Next to each verb, write a noun or an adjective that is a member of the same word family.

summarize _____   create _____   criticize _____

purify _____   beautify _____   immigrate _____

2. Word Study Verbs that end in the suffixes *-ify*, *-ize*, or *-ate* are almost always related to a noun or adjective with a similar meaning.

When a word ends in -ise instead of -ize, it is usually part of the word, not a suffix—for example, exercise, advise, and arise.

1. The suffix *-fy* or *-ify* usually means "to make into or become"—

   mummify = make or turn into a *mummy*

2. The suffix *-ize* usually has a similar meaning—

   modernize = to make *modern*

3. The suffix *-ate* means "to have," "to do," or "to provide"—

   celebrate = to have a *celebration*

3. Word Play Work with a partner. What is the related noun or adjective for each verb below? Write it in the blank. Talk about what you think each verb means. Then check the dictionary to see if you were right.

1. simplify   *simple* _____   7. memorize   _____
2. electrify   _____   8. apologize   _____
3. terrify   _____   9. educate   _____
4. identify   _____   10. decorate   _____
5. hospitalize   _____   11. punctuate   _____
6. idolize   _____   12. medicate   _____

—— SPELLING: ——
To do this activity, go to page 236.

E | GRAMMAR   Passive Sentences

1. Listen Up Listen to these sentences. Point your thumb up 👍 if the sentence sounds correct. Point your thumb down 👎 if it sounds wrong.

👍 👎 1. Mummies were wrap in linen.

👍 👎 3. Aramaic was spoken in parts of ancient Egypt.

👍 👎 2. Machu Picchu was discovered by Hiram Bingham.

👍 👎 4. Arabic is spoke today in Egypt.

2. Learn the Rule Learn more about active and passive sentences. Read the rule, then repeat Activity 1.

PASSIVE SENTENCES

1. You can turn an active sentence into a passive sentence by rearranging the information. In an active sentence, the subject does the action of the verb. In a passive sentence, the subject is acted upon. The information in the *by* phrase tells who did the action.

   Active: *The Egyptians often mummified dead bodies.*   Passive: *Dead bodies were often mummified by the Egyptians.*

2. A passive sentence is always formed with *be* + past participle:

   This book was written by a famous author.

Both sentences mean the same thing!

3. You usually use a passive sentence when the subject is not known or when it is not important to know who did the action. Such sentences do not have a *by* phrase:

   Our school was built in the 1980s.   *140 years ago, huge stone heads were discovered in Mexico.*

3. Practice the Rule Rewrite each sentence to make it passive. Use a *by* phrase only when it is important to know exactly who did the action.

EXAMPLE: Thomas Edison invented the light bulb. → The light bulb was invented by Thomas Edison.

1. Somebody canceled the football game.
2. A mail carrier delivers our mail in the afternoon.
3. A pickpocket stole my wallet.
4. People speak Spanish in Mexico.
5. J. K. Rowling wrote *Harry Potter*.
6. A vicious dog attacked my cat Fluffy.

F | BRIDGE TO WRITING — Short Research Reports

1. Before You Read Before you read each selection, read the first sentence of each paragraph. What do you think you will learn?

2. Words to Know Read the sentences below. Try to guess what the underlined words mean.

1. Nobody saw the criminal break out of jail. How he escaped is a <u>mystery</u>.
2. The blue parts of the globe are areas of water. Blue is usually the color used to <u>represent</u> bodies of water.
3. Juan bought the newest, most powerful computer available. It is the most <u>advanced</u> computer you can buy.
4. The town was <u>abandoned</u> in the 1800s. No one has lived here for over 150 years.
5. The northern states fought the southern states in the 1860s. Our country had a <u>civil war</u>.
6. One boy pushed another in the hall. Suddenly, a fight <u>erupted</u> between them.
7. Stefan's father repairs old cars and makes them look just like new. He <u>restores</u> them.
8. Maria divided the price of the new dress she wants by her weekly allowance. She <u>calculated</u> that she can buy the dress in six weeks.

Match each word or phrase on the left with the correct definition on the right.

1. mystery	a. having the most modern ideas and ways of doing things
2. represent	b. a war between groups of people from the same country
3. advanced	c. something that is difficult to explain or understand
4. abandon	d. to use numbers to find out something or measure something
5. civil war	e. to mean something
6. erupt	f. to make something as good as it was before
7. restore	g. to leave someone or something
8. calculate	h. to happen suddenly

3. Let's Read Read about two more mysteries of the ancient world. For each selection, write down one question you have that is not answered in the text. How would you go about answering each question?

READING STRATEGY
Quick Writing:
Before you read, write a short paragraph telling what you know about the topic. After reading, revise your paragraph.

Heads May Roll

1   Half buried in a steamy Mexican swamp, a mystery is uncovered. A nine-foot-tall (2.7-meter-tall) stone head, weighing almost 30 tons (27 metric tons), stares at archaeologists, daring them to ask questions.

2   Who does the head represent? How did the massive boulder, available only in mountains 50 miles away, get here? Who carved it? And when?

3   Over the past 140 years, as 16 similar heads have been discovered, archaeologists have answered some of these mysterious questions. It all began with the biggest mystery of all: an ancient people called the Olmec.

4   Few knew the Olmec existed until the first giant stone head was discovered in 1862. Archaeologists dated it and other sculptures at more than 3,000 years old—making the Olmec the oldest highly advanced culture in what is now Mexico.

5   The Olmec influenced many powerful cultures—including the Maya and Aztec. Without using animals or wheels, the Olmec built the first earthen "pyramids" in Mexico. They also probably developed accurate calendars and early hieroglyphic writing. They even played ball games.

6   But the Olmec are most famous for their giant stone heads. How did they create them? Through bug-ridden and snake-filled lands, the Olmec sometimes journeyed more than 50 miles into the Tuxtla Mountains. There they would use stone tools to take out huge boulders, sculpting them into rough portraits of their powerful rulers.

7   How did the Olmec haul the stones—some weighing up to 30 tons (27 metric tons)—back to their communities? They may have strapped the heads to huge, flatbed platforms, then heaved them over rolling logs to a river. Floating them on gigantic wooden rafts, hundreds of straining, sweaty men then probably dragged the statues to their places of honor.

8   But archaeologists found many of the heads buried. They believe that as Olmec leaders changed, so did the statues. It's possible that when a new ruler took over, the stone heads of former rulers were damaged, covered with dirt—then forgotten.

9   About 2,500 years ago, the Olmec abandoned their communities, and—until the first giant head was found 140 years ago—the culture was all but forgotten. Why did the Olmec give way to the Maya and other cultures? Drought? Disease? War?

10   No one knows the answer. It's yet another mystery that archaeologists are trying to solve.

Source: *National Geographic World*

steamy—hot and humid, or wet

influence—to have an effect on the way someone thinks or behaves

hieroglyphic—used to describe writing that uses pictures for words.

-ridden—filled with large numbers or quantities of something unpleasant

heave—to throw, with effort

raft—a flat floating structure used as a boat

drought—a long period without any rain

Secrets of Easter Island

The writer's introduction makes you feel like you are there on Easter Island.

¹ Step ashore. Giant stone statues tower above you, gazing **eerily** into the distance. Walk around. Hundreds of other statues lie **scattered** across the island, many thrown forward on their faces. Talk to the people. They will tell you ancient legends of wars, witches, and walking statues.

² Welcome to Easter Island. This dot in the Pacific Ocean is one of the most mysterious places on earth.

³ The island's biggest mystery centers on nearly a thousand stone statues, or *moai* (MOE-eye). Some stand as tall as 32 feet (10 meters)— about three stories. They may weigh 80 tons (over 70 metric tons) or more—as much as some blue whales. Who carved them? Why? How were they moved?

⁴ Archaeologists have learned that about a thousand years ago islanders began carving *moai* as images of their gods and ancestors. The people honored the *moai* at *ahu* (AH-hoo), or ceremonial centers. Later, civil wars erupted. Many *moai* were knocked down. Others were abandoned, half-carved, in **quarries** of volcanic rock.

⁵ **High-tech** equipment has helped modern scientists solve some *moai* mysteries. After determining the height and weight of an average statue, experts used **computer imaging** to calculate how the *moai* must have been moved. They decided that the moai were hauled flat from quarries on sleds atop log rollers. At the *ahu*, workers pulled the *moai* upright with **fiber** ropes.

⁶ Today archaeologist Edmundo Edwards and a team of experts are restoring the biggest *ahu*, Tongariki. One of their machines has actually created a mystery. On a powerful **crane** with a digital scale, some statues weighed in at nearly 90 tons (over 80 metric tons). Scientists think these were too heavy to have been hauled and set up like the others. How did these *moai* get where they were going?

⁷ Island legend gives this solution: They walked!

Source: *National Geographic World*

You could also say, "... how people must have moved the *moai*."

---

eerily—in a strange and frightening way

scattered—thrown around in many directions

quarry—a place where rock is dug out of the ground

high-tech—the most technologically modern

computer imaging—creating pictures on a computer

fiber—the woody part of a plant

crane—a large machine used to move heavy things

4. Making Content Connections You have just read two reports about two interesting mysteries. Work with a partner. Compare the two reports. Complete this chart.

	Olmec Heads	Easter Island Moai
What are the research questions?	*What did the heads mean?*	
In what way are both reports similar or alike?		
How are the two reports different?		
What mysterious question still has to be answered?		

5. Expanding Your Vocabulary Learn the meaning of each word part. Then match each word below to the correct picture.

acro- —high, top	-lith —rock or stone
ex- —out of	mega- —giant, a million
geo- —Earth	picto- —like a picture
-graph —something drawn	pre- —before

a. Acropolis   c. geographer   e. pictograph
b. excavation   d. megalith   f. prehistoric human

1. __f__

2. _____

3. _____

4. _____

5. _____

6. _____

G WRITING CLINIC

Short Research Reports

1. Think about It Research reports have different purposes. What is the purpose of the reports you have read?

☐ to inform others ☐ to compare and contrast ☐ to describe cause and effect

2. Focus on Organization

❶ Look again at "Heads May Roll."

The first paragraph has a thesis statement that identifies the main idea of the article.

The writer identifies the research questions.

Each paragraph develops a different subtopic.

The author provides details.

The article ends with a conclusion. The conclusion raises new questions—making the reader want to learn more!

¹ Half buried in a steamy Mexican swamp, a mystery is uncovered. A nine-foot-tall (2.7-meter-tall) stone head, weighing almost 30 tons (27 metric tons), stares at archaeologists, daring them to ask questions.
² Who does the head represent? How did the massive boulder, available only in mountains 50 miles away, get here? Who carved it? And when?
³ Over the past 140 years, as 16 similar heads have been discovered, archaeologists have answered some of these mysterious questions. It all began with the biggest mystery of all: an ancient people called the Olmec.
⁴ Few knew the Olmec existed until the first giant stone head was discovered in 1862. Archaeologists dated it and other sculptures at more than 3,000 years old—making the Olmec the oldest highly advanced culture in what is now Mexico.
⁵ The Olmec influenced many powerful cultures—including the Maya and Aztec. Without using animals or wheels, the Olmec built the first earthen "pyramids" in Mexico. They also probably developed accurate calendars and early hieroglyphic writing. They even played ball games ...
⁶ About 2,500 years ago, the Olmec abandoned their communities, and—until the first giant head was found 140 years ago—the culture was all but forgotten. Why did the Olmec give way to the Maya and other cultures? Drought? Disease? War?
⁷ No one knows the answer. It's yet another mystery that archaeologists are trying to solve.

❷ A thesis statement, or statement of the main idea, helps you plan your report. Your thesis statement helps you decide on the purpose, or why you are writing the report. It also helps you narrow your topic and organize the information.

Match each thesis statement to its purpose—

1. The Maya and Olmec were two great ancient civilizations.
2. In the early 1500s, Cortez landed in Mexico and began his conquest of the Aztec people.
3. Mummy-making in Egypt involved a six-step process.
4. How the Easter Island statues got where they are is one of the great mysteries of the ancient world.
5. Tens of thousands of Native Americans died as a result of the European conquest.

a. provides a description of when events happened
b. discusses causes and/or effects
c. explores a problem or question
d. compares two or more subjects
e. explains how something is or was done

3. Focus on Style

❶ When you want to define a word in a piece of writing, you don't have to write two separate sentences. After the word you want to define, use *or* and a synonym. Set off this phrase with commas.

EXAMPLE: A person's *ba*, or spirit, could leave the body during the day.

❷ Write new sentences combining the information in each pair of sentences below.

1. The tombs were under the ground. Tombs are burial chambers.
2. Pharaohs had the biggest tombs. Pharaohs were Egyptian kings.
3. The Olmecs probably used hieroglyphics. Hieroglyphics is picture writing.
4. Easter Island's *moai* weigh 80 tons or more. *Moai* are giant stone statues.

H WRITER'S WORKSHOP

Short Research Reports

Imagine that your history teacher has assigned a short research report. You can write about any subject in history that interests you!

1. Getting It Out

❶ Choose a topic. It should be something that...

- interests you.
- will probably interest your teacher.
- involves doing research.

❷ Narrow your topic. Choose a subject you can write about in two or three pages. Try writing your thesis statement. (Remember that you can change it later.)

> "Ancient monuments" was too much for Stefan to write about. He has decided to write about Stonehenge. That's just right!

For centuries visitors to Stonehenge, a mysterious place in England, have wondered how such huge rocks were put there—and why.

❸ Figure out what you already know. What are your questions? Make a chart like this.

What I already know	What I'd like to learn
Stonehenge–located in England Thousands of years old Huge stone pillars	When was Stonehenge built? Why did people build Stonehenge? How was it built?

❹ Read more about your topic. Choose information sources that will help you answer your questions.

Books and magazines

Encyclopedia on CD-ROM

Videos

Internet Web pages

❺ Take good notes. Write your notes on 3″×5″ note cards.

> *Why did people build Stonehenge?*
>
> • *It was used as a burial ground*
>
> • *Many think it was used as a calendar to tell when the seasons were changing*
>
> *Source: Burgan, Michael. "Secrets in the Stones." National Geographic World. May, 1999. (page 27)*

- Write the topic or question at the top.
- Jot down important information—using your own words.
- Don't forget to cite, or name, source each.

Ask your teacher to tell you how he or she wants you to list each source.

❻ Start organizing. Group the cards into categories, by topic. Each stack of cards should be about the same topic.

CONNECT TO THE WEB. CHECK IT OUT:

Start your research by checking out the American Library Association web site at

www.ala.org

Stefan's thesis statement identifies the topic and his research questions.

2. Getting It Down

❶ Make an outline like this.

Introduction (thesis statement): For centuries, people have wondered how and why Stonehenge, a mysterious place in England, was built.

Body:

Subtopic 1: Some believe it was a ritual site.

a. Burial mounds found.

b. Holes with ashes.

Subtopic 2: Others believe it was a calendar.

a.

b.

Subtopic 3:: How Stonehenge was built.

a.

b.

Conclusion: _____

Think about the order of your body paragraphs.

Stefan's introduction is interesting. You can visualize the setting.

The Secrets of Stonehenge

Huge stone slabs cover a grassy field. Some lie scattered. Others stand upright, forming part of a large circle of pillars. For centuries visitors to Stonehenge, a mysterious place in England, have wondered how such huge rocks were put there—and why.

Nearly 5,000 years ago, during the Late Stone Age, people began building Stonehenge. People kept working on the site for more than 1,500 years. Many archaeologists believe Stonehenge was built as a ritual site or a burial ground. But no one is sure because there are no written records telling us what really took place.

At first the site was just a round ditch. Within the circle were two burial mounds, surrounded by holes with ashes in them. Experts believe these are from the burning of dead bodies.

Other experts believe that Stonehenge was used as a huge calendar that was used to tell the seasons. Outside the entrance stands a huge stone. On the longest day of the year, a person standing at the center of the circle can look out through the entrance and see the first rays of the rising sun hit the top of the stone. On the shortest day of the year, a person standing at the entrance can look into the circle and see the setting sun between the stones of a trilithon, formed by two pillars topped by a lintel, or horizontal stone.

Thousands of people struggled to build the monument. They hauled in the stones over water on rafts and across land along wooden tracks, like a train. The builders then constructed the monument. They pushed the stones into pits they had dug then pulled them upright with ropes. They packed smaller stones around the base of each slab to keep it from wobbling....

❷ Draft your report. Here is part of what Stefan wrote.

— MINI-LESSON —

Formatting Your Report:

Font: Use a font like Times New Roman for research reports. Do not use fancy fonts.
Size: Set your print size at 12 point.
Ruler: Set your indent tab at ¼ inch.

Each body paragraph develops a separate subtopic.

Stefan provides interesting facts and explanations.

Source: *National Geographic World*

3. Getting It Right Look carefully at your report. Use this guide to revise your work.

Ask Yourself	How to Check	How to Revise
1. Does my introduction grab the attention of the reader?	Read your introduction to a partner. Ask for feedback.	Set the scene with an interesting description or situation. Or ask the reader a question.
2. Does my introduction have a thesis statement?	<u>Underline</u> the thesis statement.	State the main topic you studied. State your research question(s).
3. Does each paragraph in the body explain just one subtopic, or idea?	Circle each subtopic.	Create separate paragraphs, if you need to.
4. Does each body paragraph include information that explains the idea?	Put a check mark (✔) next to each fact, detail, or example.	Add more facts, details, examples, statistics, or quotes.
5. Does my conclusion summarize my arguments?	Put a star (★) next to the conclusion.	Add words, as needed, to summarize each reason.
6. Do I cite my sources?	Compare the sources cited at the end of your report with your note cards.	Add missing sources.

4. Presenting It Read your report to your classmates.

❶ Think about beginning by showing your classmates a photograph or picture to get them interested.

❷ Read your introduction. Clearly state the thesis, or the main idea of your report.

❸ Read each paragraph. Pause slightly after reading each topic sentence. Pause briefly before moving on to the next paragraph.

❹ As you listen to others, take notes.

1. On Assignment Imagine that the year is 3005. A future archaeologist is digging through the ruins of your school. She finds a time capsule that your class has made! What will she find inside that tells all about you?

❶ Gather objects for your time capsule. Begin by agreeing on criteria, or basic qualities, that every object must meet. Here are some possible criteria:

- It tells about your culture—what you think, what you like, who you are.
- It will probably be strange and mysterious to people 1,000 years from now.
- It is a single object and not too large.

An advertisement

A favorite CD

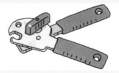

A can opener

A picture of your school mascot

A staple remover

You decide!

❷ Write a short paragraph to go along with your object. Your paragraph should...

- name the object and tell what it is or what it is used for.
- tell why you chose to include it in the time capsule.
- explain how it represents something about your culture.

❸ If you need to, include instructions that explain *how* to use the object. (After all, would you know what to do with a *sistrum*? The ancient Egyptians did!)

A sistrum

❹ Before you place your object in the capsule, share with your classmates. Explain why you think the object tells about your culture.

❺ Choose a container for your capsule. If you want your capsule to last, it must be airtight and watertight.

2. Link to Literature

SHARED READING The Aztecs of Mexico created one of the greatest civilizations in history. Read one of their poems, "Flowers and Songs." The first version is in Nahuatl, the Aztec language. The second version is in Spanish and the third in English.

LET'S TALK Answer the questions.

1. In your own words, what is the poem about?
2. Can you figure out which Spanish words mean "heart," "flower," and "song"?
3. How did the Aztecs feel about life and death? How were their beliefs different than the ancient Egyptians?

① Nahuatl

Cuicatli quicaqui
In noyol nichoca:
Ye nicnotlamati
Tiga xochitica
Ticcautehuazque
Tlalticpac ye nican
Titotlanehuia
O tiyazque ichan.

Ma nicnocozcati
Nepapan xochitl
Ma nomac on mani
Ma nocpacxoxhihui.
Ticcautehuazque
Tlalticpac ye nican
Zan titotlanehuia
O tiyazque ichan.

② Spanish

Corazones de corazon
una cancion,
Yo comienzo a llorar.
Ya yo me lo se.
Vamos entre flores.
Saldremos de la tierra aqui.
Nosotros nos somos prestados.
Vamos a Su casa.

Póngaseme un collar
De flores variadas.
Ellos están en mis manos,
Flores en guirnaldas en mi.
Saldremos de la tierra aqui.
Nosotros nos somos prestados.
Vamos a Su casa.

③ English

Hearts of heart,
a song,
I begin to cry
This I know.
We go among flowers.
We will leave the earth here.
We are loaned to one another.
We go to His house.

Put on me a necklace
Of varied flowers.
They are in my hands,
Flowers of garlands on me.
We will leave the earth here.
We are loaned to one another.
We go to His house.

Source: *AppleSeeds*

Who's Smarter... Cats or Dogs?

Read...

- An article from *National Geographic Kids* that compares dogs and cats—their talents, their brainpower … even their bathroom habits.

Link to Literature

- An excerpt from *Fifth Chinese Daughter* by Jade Snow Wong.

Objectives:

Reading:

- Understanding text that compares and contrasts two subjects
- Strategy: Comparing and contrasting two subjects as you read
- Literature: Responding to a comparison of two people

Writing:

- Organizing and writing an essay that compares and contrasts
- Using contractions
- Using similes to enliven your writing

Vocabulary:

- Recognizing antonyms
- Learning adjectives that can describe both animals and people

Listening/Speaking:

- Understanding an oral comparison of two subjects
- Giving an oral presentation
- Taking notes as you listen to an oral presentation

Grammar:

- Making nouns plural

Spelling:

- Pronouncing the letter *g*

BEFORE YOU BEGIN

Talk with your classmates.

1. Look at the picture. What do you think is happening? Talk with a partner.
2. Which one is smarter—the dog or the cat? Why?
3. Do you have pets? Are they intelligent? How do you know?

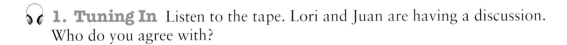

A CONNECTING TO YOUR LIFE

1. Tuning In Listen to the tape. Lori and Juan are having a discussion. Who do you agree with?

2. Talking It Over Take this survey. Circle your answers.

1. Which are smarter—dogs or cats?   dogs   cats
2. Which is more exciting to watch on TV—football or soccer?   football   soccer
3. Which takes more skill—singing or playing the piano?   singing   playing the piano
4. Who acts more grown up—boys or girls?   boys   girls
5. Which is more dangerous— skateboarding or rollerblading?   skateboarding   rollerblading
6. Which tastes better—chocolate or vanilla?   chocolate   vanilla

Find two other students who agreed with you on one of the survey questions. Talk in a small group. List three reasons you all answered the question the way you did. Be specific.

Read the title of this unit. What do you think the unit is about? Check (✓) the correct answer.

_____   1. It's about the care and feeding of pets.

_____   2. It's about how two subjects are the same or different.

_____   3. It's about why dogs are the smartest animals.

_____   4. It's about observing and writing about wild life.

B GETTING READY TO READ

1. Learning New Words Read the sentences below. Try to guess what the underlined words mean.

1. A sports car and an SUV are such different types of vehicles. It would be silly to try to <u>compare</u> them.
2. When I walked in the room, everyone stopped talking. I came to the <u>conclusion</u> that everyone was talking about me.
3. Our class debated whether to ban junk food at school. Lori spoke <u>in favor of</u> the ban. Tran argued against it.
4. A lot of kids think our science teacher is way too strict. Chimeng disagrees. He often speaks up <u>in defense of</u> the teacher.
5. Stefan wants to learn and do well in school. He is a highly <u>motivated</u> student.
6. People say that police arrested the burglar. He is now <u>reportedly</u> in jail.
7. Blue makes me feel calm. That's because I <u>associate</u> it with the sky and the ocean.

Now match each word to the definition.

1. compare	a. protecting someone or something from criticism
2. conclusion	b. supporting one thing over another
3. in favor of	c. very eager to do or achieve something
4. in defense of	d. to describe how two or more things are similar to or different from each other
5. motivated	e. according to what people say
6. associate	f. something you decide after thinking about all the information you have
7. reportedly	g. to make a connection in your mind between one thing and another

2. Talking It Over Talk in a small group. Discuss the special traits of dogs and cats.

> A **trait** is a particular characteristic that someone or something has.

	Dogs	Cats
Positive qualities or **traits**		
Negative qualities or traits		

C READING TO LEARN
Comparison and Contrast Essays

For help with making a Venn diagram, complete Mini-Unit Part B on page 224.

READING STRATEGY

Comparing/ Contrasting:

When two subjects are discussed, identify similarities and differences as you read. This will help you see how much you understand.

■■■

---

1. Before You Read If you lived in a dangerous neighborhood, which would you rather own—a dog or a cat? Talk with a partner.

2. Let's Read Learn more about what makes dogs and cats special. Make a Venn diagram. As you read, list the ways that dogs and cats are the same and different.

Who's Smarter ... Cats or Dogs?

1   Meeeowww!

2   Socks, an outdoor cat belonging to Cindy Robb of Suttons Bay, Michigan, was yowling so loudly that he woke up his owner at 3 A.M. "It sounded like Socks was inside the house," says Robb.

3   She stumbled down the stairs and felt a blast of cold air hit her smack in the face. Robb discovered the kitchen door standing open and a burglar roaring out of the garage in her husband's pickup truck.

4   Very few small-town robberies make the national news, but this one did. Why? People were amused to learn that the family's clever cat sounded the alarm—while their so-called watchdog (who sleeps in the garage!) didn't make a peep.

5   So there you have it, an easy answer to the debate over which are smarter: cats or dogs. But is it really that simple? To help you decide, *National Geographic Kids* compares the two animals. So keep reading and draw your own conclusions.

IN DEFENSE OF DOGS ... DOGS PLAY THE PIANO

6   Forget "sit" and "shake." Chanda-Leah, a 10-year-old toy poodle, settles down at a computerized keyboard and plunks out "Twinkle, Twinkle, Little Star." Flashing red lights under the white keys tell her which notes to hit.

7   "She loves to show off," says owner Sharon Robinson of Hamilton, Ontario, in Canada, who says the secrets to training are practice and patience. That must be true because besides the Vanessa Carlton routine, Chanda performs a record-breaking 468 other tricks! She's the trickiest canine ever listed in Guinness World Records.

"Canine" is a technical term for dog. What do you think "feline," "bovine," and "porcine" mean?

---

yowl—to make a long, sad cry

peep—a small sound

IN FAVOR OF FELINES ... CATS WALK TIGHTROPES

8   Animal trainers of cats that appear in movies and TV commercials train the feline actors to walk on tightropes, wave at crowds, and open doors.

9   "Cats can do a lot, like jump through hoops, retrieve toys, and give high fives," says veterinarian Bonnie Beaver of Texas A & M University. But unlike dogs, they won't work for praise. "Cats are motivated by food," she says, "and it's got to be yummy."

IN DEFENSE OF DOGS ... DOGS "GO" ON CUE

10   To housebreak a pup, take him outside and watch closely. When he starts to urinate, say the same phrase, such as "right there," each time. Within weeks, he'll associate the phrase with the action.

11   Buffy, a keeshond belonging to Wade Newman of Turin, New York, has never had "an accident" in the house. In fact, the smart dog sometimes plans ahead. Once, called in for the night, she came running. "But suddenly she stopped, cocked her head, and took off in the other direction," Newman says. "I was kind of annoyed." But it turned out Buffy was simply getting ready for bed—by "going" first, after which she obediently ran back to Newman. Now, that's thinking ahead!

IN FAVOR OF FELINES ... CATS FLUSH

12   Russ and Sandy Asbury were alone in their Whitewater, Wisconsin, home when they suddenly heard the toilet flush. "My husband's eyes got huge," says Sandy. "Did we have ghosts?"

13   Nope. Their cats just like to play with toilets. Boots, a 2-year-old Maine coon cat, taught himself to push on the handle that flushes. Then his copycat brother, Bandit, followed. "It's kind of eerie," Sandy admits. "Bandit follows me into the bathroom and flushes for me—sometimes even before I'm finished!"

14   Now the cats use the stunt to get attention. They go into a flushing frenzy if supper's late!

15   These cats just play in the bathroom, but some cats can be trained to use the toilet instead of a litter box. For their lucky owners, cleanup is just a flush (instead of a scoop) away. Meanwhile, Fido's just drinking from the toilet.

tightrope—rope or wire above the ground that someone walks on in the circus

retrieve—to bring back something

on cue—at just the right moment

urinate—to get rid of liquid waste from your body

keeshond—a type of dog from the Netherlands

copycat—someone who copies other people's clothes, actions, etc.

frenzy—the state of being very excited or anxious

IN DEFENSE OF DOGS ... DOGS SNIFF OUT PROBLEMS

15 Sometimes dogs can drive you crazy! That reportedly happened to one woman whose sheepdog started to sniff at her back every time she sat down. Exasperated, she asked her husband to take a look. All he saw was a dark mole. Nothing to worry about, thought the woman. Then one day she was sunbathing when her dog tried to nip off the mole with its teeth.

16 That did it. The woman went to the doctor and found out the mole was a deadly form of skin cancer. Her dog probably saved her life.

17 Dogs' noses have about four times as many scent cells as cats' noses and 14 times more than humans'. It makes some breeds terrific at sniffing out mold, termites, illegal drugs, missing persons, and, apparently, even cancer. Now, if only those noses didn't feel so cold!

Based on information in the paragraph, what are scent cells?

IN FAVOR OF FELINES ... CATS LISTEN

18 Even when you think they're sleeping, cats are listening. Their hearing is so acute that they can pinpoint a field mouse's squeak. To find out where the mouse is hiding, they rotate their ears like satellite dishes. One story about a cat shows how it put this ability to good use.

19 A small plane had crash-landed in the ocean, and a cargo vessel steamed over to help. Finding no survivors, the disappointed crew gave up hope. Darkness fell. Suddenly the crew's mascot, a cat, howled and started racing around on the front of the ship. The startled sailors shined searchlights on the water and found a woman survivor. She was 100 yards away—the length of a football field. The cat heard her, alerted the crew, and became a feline hero!

Source: *National Geographic Kids*

---

exasperated—very annoyed

pinpoint—to find the exact location of something

rotate—to turn something around a fixed point

cargo vessel—a ship that carries goods or products

3. Unlocking Meaning

1. **Finding the Main Idea** According to the reading selection, which of the following sentences best states the main idea of the selection?

   _____ 1. Dogs are definitely smarter than cats.

   _____ 2. Cats are most likely smarter than dogs.

   _____ 3. It's hard to say which is smarter—dogs or cats.

2. **Finding Details** Read each statement about dogs or cats. Match the statement to the section in which it is found.

   a. Dogs play the piano   d. Cats flush
   b. Cats walk tightropes   e. Dogs sniff out problems
   c. Dogs "go" on cue   f. Cats listen

   __b__ 1. This animal loves treats a lot more than compliments.

   _____ 2. This pet plans ahead for trips to the bathroom.

   _____ 3. This animal could give a concert.

   _____ 4. This pet has an amazing sense of smell.

   _____ 5. This is an animal with a sharp sense of hearing.

   _____ 6. This pet is very particular when it comes to the bathroom.

3. **Think about It** Do a survey in your class. How many people have pets? What kinds of pets do they have? Your teacher will write the information on the board. Form a group with classmates that have different pets. Discuss these questions. Give examples to support your ideas.

   • Is your pet intelligent?
   • Does your pet understand language?
   • Does your pet have feelings?

4. **Before You Move On** Think of someone you know well—your best friend, a family member, or a teacher. What makes them "smart"? What have you observed, or noticed? Write three or four sentences, and then share.

D WORD WORK

1. Word Detective Match each word in the first column with the word that has the opposite meaning in the second column.

1. boring   a. yucky
2. patient   b. pleased
3. yummy   c. interesting
4. calm   d. noisily
5. disappointed   e. impatient
6. quietly   f. agitated

2. Word Study An antonym is a word that has the opposite meaning of another word.

Candy is <u>sweet</u>.	Lemons are <u>sour</u>.
A Great Dane is a <u>large</u> dog.	A Chihuahua is a <u>small</u> dog.

You can sometimes form antonyms by adding a prefix that means "not," such as *un-*, *il-*, *im-*, or *ir-*. Think of one more example of a word you know that begins with the prefix *un-*.

un + helpful	unhelpful
il + legal	illegal
im + patient	impatient
ir + regular	irregular

SPELLING:
To do this activity, go to page 237.
■ ■ ■

3. Word Play Work with a partner. Write an antonym for each word on a separate piece of paper. You can make antonyms for five of the words by adding a prefix. Use your dictionary for help. Then write a sentence for each antonym on your paper.

lucky	huge	responsible	tall
bad	rough	heavy	wide
popular	polite	love	legible

E GRAMMAR   Plural Noun Forms

1. Listen Up Listen to these sentences. Point your thumb up 👍 if the sentence sounds correct. Point your thumb down 👎 if it sounds wrong.

👍👎 1. I bought two loafs of bread.

👍👎 2. Cats are amazing animals.

👍👎 3. Dogs have four foots.

👍👎 4. Mr. Lee has three childrens.

👍👎 5. Cats' tooths are sharp as knifes.

👍👎 6. I know two womans.

2. Learn the Rule Read the rules, then try Activity 1 again.

PLURAL NOUN FORMS

1. For most nouns, add –*s* to make a plural. When the noun ends in -*ch*, -*sh*, -*s*, -*x*, or -*z*, add –*es*.
   *I love both dog**s** and cat**s**.*   *Cats can move their ears like satellite dish**es**.*

2. When a noun ends in vowel + -*y*, add -*s*. If a noun ends in a consonant + -*y*, drop the -*y* and add -*ies*.
   *Cats are not as smart as monkey**s**.*   *Cats have many different abilit**ies**.*

3. Some nouns have irregular plural forms.
man—men	child—children	mouse—mice	foot—feet
woman—women	ox—oxen	person—people	tooth—teeth

4. Some nouns have the same singular and plural forms.
species—species	deer—deer	fish—fish	fruit—fruit

5. Some nouns that end in –*f* or –*fe* take the plural form –*ves*.
half—halves	knife—knives	thief—thieves	shelf—shelves
calf—calves	life—lives	leaf—leaves	

3. Practice the Rule Rewrite each sentence. Use the plural forms of the nouns in parentheses.

1. The (child) are crying.
2. The (fork) and (knife) are on the table.
3. Cats love to eat (fish).
4. I'm missing my two front (tooth).
5. (Cat) love to eat (mouse).
6. We have three (church) in town.
7. Those (lady) are very friendly.
8. Those (man) are friendly, too.

F | BRIDGE TO WRITING

1. Before You Read Look at the pictures in the reading. What more do you think this reading might tell you about dogs and cats?

2. Words to Know Read the definitions.

predict—to guess what will happen before it happens

unconscious—unable to see, feel, or think, often because you are very sick or have had an accident

accompany—to go somewhere with someone

body language—body positions and movements that show what you are thinking or feeling

talent—a natural ability to do something well

species—a group of animals of the same kind that can breed together

Complete each sentence with a vocabulary word from above.

1. Usually, dogs aren't allowed on the bus. But Margo is blind, so her dog can _____ her.

2. Ana Luisa can play the piano, the trumpet, and the saxophone. She has a lot of musical _____.

3. It might rain next week or it might not. It's always difficult to _____ the weather.

4. After the car accident, Rob was _____. He didn't wake up for three days.

5. Chipper is a dog and Midas is a cat. They are members of different _____.

6. Stefan always backs away when girls get too close to him. His _____ tells others that he is shy.

3. Let's Read As you read, add to your list of ways in which dogs and cats are alike and different.

┌─READING STRATEGY─┐
Comparing/ Contrasting:
When two subjects are discussed, identify similarities and differences as you read. This will help you see how much you understand.

Who's Smarter ... Cats or Dogs? (continued)

IN DEFENSE OF DOGS ... DOGS PREDICT SEIZURES

1 Lindsay, a golden retriever, had been lying quietly at Carol Folwell's side as they traveled in an airplane. Suddenly the dog began bumping against Folwell's legs. "There's something wrong with your dog," said a woman in the neighboring seat.

2 "No, I think there's something wrong with me," Folwell answered. An airline attendant quickly gave her a pillow and helped her lie down in the aisle at the rear of the plane. Minutes later, Folwell's arms flailed, her body stiffened, and she fell unconscious.

3 Folwell has epilepsy, a brain disorder. She used to fall during seizures, banging her head or breaking her arm. But now she has Lindsay, who is allowed to accompany her anywhere, to warn her. "Lindsay is a blessing" says Folwell. "I haven't gotten hurt since I've had her."

4 How can the dog tell when a seizure is coming? She may notice some chemical or electrical change or a tiny shift in Folwell's body language. Nobody knows for sure. But one thing is certain: Dogs that can predict seizures have a very valuable talent.

IN FAVOR OF FELINES ... CATS PREDICT EARTHQUAKES

5 Early one evening in 1976 people in northeastern Italy were all asking the same question: What was wrong with their cats? Many pets were running around, scratching on doors, and yowling to go out. Once out, they didn't come back (except for mother cats, who returned to get their kittens). Then, later that day, a major earthquake hit!

6 Cats may feel very early vibrations or sense the increase in static electricity that occurs before a quake. Whatever they're sensing, it's one more reason to pay attention to your cat.

---

seizure—a short time when someone passes out and cannot control their shaking bodies

flail—to wave your arms and legs in a wild manner

disorder—a medical condition that keeps a part of your body from working like it's supposed to

chemical—involving reactions between different substances

vibration—a continuous slight shaking movement

static electricity—electricity in the air

IN DEFENSE OF DOGS ... DOGS SAVE BABIES

7   Two-week-old Troy Sica was taking a nap in a back bedroom while his mother, Pam Sica, warmed his morning bottle in the kitchen. The baby's dad was in the shower, and the family dog, a golden retriever named Bullet, was quiet.

8   Suddenly Bullet appeared in the kitchen, barking and leaping off the floor. Extremely agitated, he insisted that the baby's mother follow him.

9   When she arrived at the bedroom where Bullet had led her, she was horrified at what she saw. Lying where she'd left him, Troy was in serious trouble. He was struggling to breathe and had turned blue. Pam quickly dialed 911. Emergency workers arrived fast, were able to get the baby breathing, and rushed him to the hospital. He was diagnosed with pneumonia. They treated him and today he's a healthy toddler, thanks to Bullet's heroic behavior.

10   How did the dog know something was wrong? "He sensed that Troy wasn't breathing," says Dr. Marty Becker, a vet from Bonners Ferry, Idaho. "He went to tell the leader of his pack—Mom."

IN FAVOR OF FELINES ... CATS SAVE TEENAGERS

11   Simba was acting strangely. The cat was inside the house, body-slamming the door that led out to the garage. He was meowing loudly. Trying to figure out what her cat's problem was, Leone Shannon opened the door. To her horror, smoke filled the garage where her 15-year-old son, Sam, was napping! She screamed to wake Sam and get him out into fresh air. Firefighters who arrived on the scene said that Sam had been very close to suffocating from smoke inhalation. Later that night, Simba enjoyed a hero's dinner of fish.

SO ... WHICH IS SMARTER ... A CAT OR A DOG?

12   Actually, this is a trick question and there's no simple answer. The "guard dog" from the beginning of this story didn't sound an alarm during the robbery because she knew the intruder, who was a frequent visitor to the house. Socks, a shy outdoor cat, tends to stay away from visitors and did not know the intruder. The Robbs think that during the robbery, Socks was somehow upset by the prowler and so yowled.

13   Dogs and cats have different abilities. Each species knows what it needs to know in order to survive. "For that reason, we can't design a test that is equal for both animals," says Dr. Beaver. "When people ask me which is smarter, I say it's whichever one you own!"

Source: *National Geographic Kids*

---

agitated—very upset

pneumonia—a disease of the lungs in which people have a lot of trouble breathing

4. Making Content Connections You have read an article
comparing cats and dogs. Work with a partner. Complete this chart.

Points of Comparison	Cats	Dogs
How do we know they are intelligent?	*They can flush toilets.*	
What special talents do they have?		
What physical characteristics make them special?		
What motivates them?		

5. Expanding Your Vocabulary

❶ Cross out the adjective in each row that *doesn't* belong. Use your
dictionary for help.

FUNNY	witty	humorous	~~boring~~	amusing
SKILLED	able	adept	expert	fumbling
TALENTED	accomplished	inept	able	agile
OBSERVANT	slow	perceptive	insightful	keen
CLEVER	astute	quick-witted	dull	shrewd

❷ Work with a partner. Use your dictionary to choose the best word
from above to complete each sentence. Be ready to talk about your
choices with your classmates.

1. Yo Yo Ma plays the cello beautifully. He is a(n) _____
   musician.
2. Senator Lee makes big promises to the voters. He is a(n)
   _____ politician.
3. My grandmother loves to watch reruns of "I Love Lucy." She
   thinks it's really _____.
4. Chipper barks when I put on my jacket. He is very
   _____. He knows when it's time for a walk.
5. Juan is a good problem solver. He is a(n) _____
   young man.
6. Marco has published 20 books. He is a(n) _____
   writer.

G WRITING CLINIC

Comparison and Contrast Essays

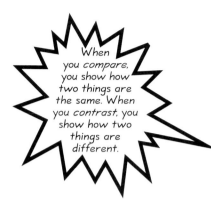

When you compare, you show how two things are the same. When you contrast, you show how two things are different.

1. Think about It Talk with a partner. What are examples of things besides dogs and cats that you might find compared in books, magazines, or the newspaper? Think to yourself. Then share.

2. Focus on Organization Work with a partner. Compare and contrast two very popular pets—dogs and cats.

❶ Take out a sheet of binder paper. Write a sentence like this. Use your own names and tell what item of clothing you will compare or contrast.

❷ Next, brainstorm a list of ten (or more) things that describe the two species. Look back at the article you have read.

Dogs	Cats
Mammals … canines … related to wolves	Mammals … felines … related to lions
Dense fur … sometimes spotted	Fine, fluffy fur … often striped
Work for praise	Work for food
Very "social" …like other dogs and people	Independent … happy to be alone
Very strong sense of smell	Very strong sense of hearing

❸ Look at your lists. Decide whether you will describe how dogs and cats are the same or how they are different—or both.

❹ Choose three points of comparison—you decide. Make a chart like this.

Points of Comparison	Dogs	Cats
Appearance	Dense fur	Fine, fluffy fur
Daily habits		
Amazing abilities		

❺ Now write your mini-essay. Make an outline, using this planner.

Introduction: *Dogs and cats are popular pets. They are alike in some ways and different in others.*

Three or more sentences that describe dogs:

1. *Dogs can be taught to do tricks.*

2. _____

3. _____

Three or more sentences that describe cats:

1. *Like dogs, cats can be taught to do tricks—if you reward them with food.*

2. _____

3. _____

❻ Turn your outline into a mini-essay. Use words and phrases that help your reader know that things are the same or that they are different.

Words that compare	Words that contrast
like	unlike
in the same way	on the other hand
also	but

2. Focus on Style
Writers often use similes that compare someone or something to an animal using the words *like* or *as*.

Bertha is as strong as an ox.

❶ Match each adjective to the animal.

1. strong   a. rabbit
2. quiet   b. fox
3. sly   c. ox
4. slow   d. peacock
5. scared   e. mouse
6. quick   f. tortoise
7. pretty   g. lion
8. brave   h. cat

❷ Write three sentences using similes.

H **WRITER'S WORKSHOP**   Comparison and Contrast Essays

Imagine that your class is writing a book of essays called, "The Truth about..." Your essay will examine the traits of two subjects by comparing them.

1. Getting It Out

❶ Brainstorm ideas for two subjects you might compare. Here are some *possible* ideas—

- school cafeteria food vs. fast food
- Americans vs. people in another country

- soccer vs. football
- music adults like vs. music kids like

- two best friends
- You decide what to compare!

"Vs." is an abbreviation of "versus." It shows that you are contrasting two people or things.

❷ Decide what you will compare. Ask yourself:

1. What is my purpose? Do I want to make people laugh? Do I want to convince them that one thing is better than another? Do I want them to learn more about the subjects I am comparing?

2. Is there a good reason to compare the two subjects? Are they alike in certain ways? Are the different?

❸ Describe each subject you will compare. Make a chart like this.

Subject #1: _____ *Carlos* _____	Subject #2: _____ *Juan* _____
Doesn't like school very much	*Loves school*

2. Getting It Down

❶ Decide whether you will describe how the two subjects are the same or how they are different. Choose three points of comparison to help you organize your writing. Make notes, using a chart like this.

Points of Comparison	Subject #1: _____Carlos_____	Subject #2: _____Juan_____
1. Attitude toward school	Doesn't like	Loves
2.		
3.		

❷ Turn your notes into an outline. Use a planner like this.

What I am comparing: _Two people I know who are "opposites" but still best friends_

Why: _I want to make others wonder how these two can be good friends_

Subject #1: _Carlos_

1. _Dislikes school_

2. _____

3. _____

Subject #2: _Juan_

1. _Loves school_

2. _____

3. _____

❸ Now turn your outline into an essay. Write two or three paragraphs. Make sure each paragraph has a topic sentence.

3. Getting It Right

❶ Read what Rafael wrote, comparing his two "best friends" Carlos and Juan.

> *"Best friends" are kids who think the same way and who like the same things, right? Not necessarily! Meet Carlos and Juan. They may be best friends, but they're as different as pizza and peanut brittle!*
>
> *Ask Carlos what he likes best about school, and he'll say, "Lunch." He never opens a book or studies for a test or turns in his homework. What does he like to do in his free time? Play sports? "No way! I hate sports," Carlos says. "I prefer working on my bug collection." And what about music? "Classical," says Carlos. "Beethoven, Brahms, and Bach. They're my favorites."*
>
> *Now meet Juan. Unlike Carlos, Juan loves school. He's his school's "Student of the Month." "Someday I plan to go to Harvard," he says. Juan is also Kennedy's star athlete. "Soccer, basketball, and baseball," Juan explains. "I love them all." As for music, Juan says, "I'm a hip hop addict."*
>
> *Pizza and peanut brittle? You can't have one without the other!*

Speech bubbles (left margin):

- Rafael's introduction tells us what he will compare. Why is the comparison interesting?
- Rafael uses vivid descriptions... Pizza and peanut brittle—that's clever!
- Rafael begins by describing Carlos. What are the three points of comparison?
- Next, he describes Juan. You can see how the points of comparison are the same.

--- MINI-LESSON ---

Using Contractions:
You can use contractions to make a piece of writing sound informal and natural:
Contraction: *They're my best friends.*
No contraction: *They are my best friends.*

■ ■ ■

❷ Now take a careful look at what *you* have written. Use these key questions to help you review and revise your work.

Question to Ask:	How to Check:	How to Revise If You Need to:
1. Does my introduction tell what I am comparing and why this is interesting?	Circle the two things you are comparing. Underline the words that tell why it is interesting.	Add information to your introduction.
2. Do I discuss each point of comparison for each subject?	Highlight the sentences that discuss each point of comparison in a different color.	Add information to make sure that you discuss each point for each subject.
3. Do I use descriptive language to "paint pictures"?	Put a check mark (✓) next to words and phrases that are descriptive.	Add more details to your description.

4. Presenting It Share your work with your classmates.

❶ Read your essay aloud. Read slowly and speak clearly.

❷ Ask if anyone has any questions.

❸ Ask for feedback from your classmates.

❹ As you listen to each presentation, take notes. Use a chart like this.

Carlos	Juan
Does not like school!	Loves school… "Student of the Month"…

❺ After you have heard a presentation, volunteer to restate what you heard. Practice using language that compares.

1. On Assignment Idioms are expressions that mean something different from the words they contain. They make comparisons— although sometimes you have to think really hard to see the comparison.

❶ Help your classmates make a class dictionary of animal idioms. Choose an idiom from the list below.

- Write the idiom at the top of the page.
- Write a definition of the idiom.
- Draw a funny picture that shows the meaning of the words in the idiom.
- Write a sentence using the idiom that describes the picture.

Someone's bark is worse than his or her bite.

have a cow

be raining cats and dogs

beat a dead horse

kill two birds with one stone

take a cat nap

cry wolf

Curiosity killed the cat.

It's a dog-eat-dog world.

be an eager beaver

get on your high horse

go ape

be in the dog house

It's a dog's life.

let the cat out of the bag

look like a cat that swallowed the canary

make a pig of yourself

monkey business

play cat and mouse with someone

put the cart before the horse

seem a little fishy

be the straw that broke the camel's back

have your tail between your legs

throw someone to the wolves

be a wolf in sheep's clothing

Be raining cats and dogs = Be raining very hard

It was raining cats and dogs all day yesterday.

❷ Gather all your classmates' pages and attach them together to make a book.

SHARED READING In her autobiography, *Fifth Chinese Daughter*, writer Jade Snow Wong compares her own upbringing with that of a classmate, Stella Green—

LET'S TALK

1. What are the points in comparison in the passage?
2. Who are you more like—Jade Snow or Stella Green?
3. How do you think you might learn more about yourself by comparing your life to that of a friend or classmate?

...There was good to be gained from both [Chinese and American] cultures if she could find the right combination. [Jade] studied her neighbor in class, Stella Green, for clues.

Stella had grown up reading Robert Louis Stevenson, learning to swim and play tennis, developing a taste for roast beef, mashed potatoes, sweets, aspirin tablets, and soda pop, and she looked upon her mother and father as friends. But it was very unlikely that she knew where her great-grandfather was born, or whether or not she was related to another strange Green she might chance to meet.

Jade Snow had grown up reading Confucius, learning to embroider and cook rice, developing a taste for steamed fish and bean sprouts, tea, and herbs, and she thought of her parents as people to be obeyed. She not only knew where her ancestors were born but where they were buried, and how many chickens and roast pigs should be brought annually to their graves to feast their spirits. She knew all of the branches of the Wong family, the relation of each to the other, and understood why Daddy must help support the distant cousins in China who bore the sole responsibility of carrying on the family heritage by periodic visits to the burial grounds in Fragrant Mountains. She knew that one could purchase in a Chinese stationery store the printed record of her family tree relating their Wong line and other Wong lines back to the original Wong ancestors.

Source: *Fifth Chinese Daughter* by Jade Snow Wong

ABOUT THE AUTHOR

Jade Snow Wong was born in San Francisco in 1922. Her autobiography, *Fifth Chinese Daughter*, was published in 1950. She has written other books, including *The Immigrant Experience* and *No Chinese Stranger*. She is also an accomplished potter.

How to Make Really Neat Stuff

Read...

- Instructions for making your own microscope and stethoscope. Learn how to assemble a skateboard.

Link to Literature

- Two how-to poems: "How to Be a Shark" and "How to Say I'm Sorry."

Objectives:

Reading:
- Following written instructions
- Strategy: Using text features, rereading
- Literature: Responding to a how-to poem

Writing:
- Writing instructions for making, doing, or fixing something
- Organizing instructions in a chronological sequence
- Using visuals and formatting to support writing
- Choosing a "writer's voice" that is appropriate to audience

Vocabulary:
- Learning prefixes that denote number
- Learning collocations: Nouns that take specific verbs

Listening/Speaking:
- Listening to instructions
- Giving oral instructions
- Paraphrasing instructions

Grammar:
- Using the articles *the* and *a/an*

Spelling:
- Doubling consonants when suffixes are added

BEFORE YOU BEGIN

Talk with your classmates.

1. Look at the picture. What are Juan and Carlos trying to do?
2. Give the picture a caption: "How to build _____"
3. What do you think Carlos is reading? Why do you think he looks confused?

For help with listening and taking notes, complete Mini-Unit Part A on page 222.

A CONNECTING TO YOUR LIFE

1. Tuning In Listen to Juan teach his friend Carlos how to make something.

a.

b.

c.

d.

e.

What is Carlos learning to make?

☐ a party hat   ☐ a flying kite   ☐ a paper airplane

2. Talking It Over Look around you. Many of your classmates know how to do things you don't know how to do. Do a "People Search." Find someone who can tell you how to...

make a submarine sandwich

make a kite
(that stays in the air!)

build a campfire

assemble a skateboard

make an article of clothing

make a paper party hat

Read the title of this unit. What do you think the unit is probably about? Check (✓) the correct answer.

_____ 1. It's about what to wear to the beach.

_____ 2. It's about how to read and write instructions for doing things.

_____ 3. It's about how to write the rules for games and contests.

_____ 4. It's about how to repair bicycles.

B GETTING READY TO READ

1. Learning New Words Read the definitions below.

instrument—a tool used in work such as science or medicine

microscope—an instrument that makes very small things appear large enough to be seen

magnify—to make something appear larger than it is

cell—the smallest part of a plant or animal that can exist on its own

bacteria—very small, one-celled living things, sometimes causing disease

stethoscope—an instrument used by doctors to listen to sounds within a person's body, like the heart or breathing

prepared slide—a small glass plate with a specimen to be examined under a microscope

Complete each sentence with a vocabulary word from above.

1. The doctor placed the _____ on my chest, then asked me to breathe deeply.
2. Tran's grandfather wears reading glasses that _____ the print on the page.
3. My dentist uses a special _____ to examine my teeth.
4. When you cut yourself, _____ sometimes get in the wound and cause an infection.
5. When you look at a droplet of water under a _____, you can see tiny creatures swimming around in it.
6. My biology teacher has a set of _____ of different types of cells.
7. Red blood _____ carry oxygen throughout the body.

3. Talking It Over Talk with a partner. Tying your shoes is simple, right? It's something you do without even thinking. Write instructions for making or doing something simple—something you do every day!

How to brush your teeth

How to use chopsticks

How to tie your shoelaces

Share and compare your instructions. Which set is easiest to write? Why?

| C | READING TO LEARN | How-to Instructions |

1. Before You Read Look at the pictures on pages 116–118. Work with a partner. List the words that you think you will find in the two reading passages. Be ready to say why.

 2. Let's Read Learn how to make several scientific tools. Use the illustrations to help you understand the instructions for making each.

Make a Microscope

Zacharias Jansen made some of the first eyeglasses in the 1500s and is credited with inventing the first compound microscope around 1590. Anton van Leeuwenhoek later created microscopes in the 1600s that could magnify objects more than 270 times.

Leeuwenhoek called the tiny objects he saw "invisible animals," which later became known as bacteria. He studied other life forms, such as mites, lice, and fleas. His findings led him to inspect with his microscope the blood of fish, birds, tadpoles, mammals, and humans. He was the first to identify red blood cells.

Create a tool straight out of history.

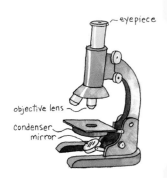

eyepiece

objective lens

condenser
mirror

A compound microscope

What You'll Need:

* Paper punch
* Thin piece of cardboard (a postcard or file card)
* Aluminum foil
* Needle
* Toothpick

* Petroleum jelly
* Glue
* Eyedropper
* Distilled water
* Scissors
* Flashlight or other light source

credit with—to recognize someone as the person who did something important

mite—a very tiny insect

lice—(*plural of* **louse**) very tiny insects that live in the hair of people and animals

tadpole—a small creature that matures into a frog

petroleum jelly—a mixture used in lubricants like Vaseline

What You'll Do:

Step One: Punch a quarter-inch hole in the cardboard. Cut and glue a piece of foil on the card to cover the hole. Do not get any glue over the hole. Gently poke the needle through the foil. Make the pinhole round and smooth; the more round the hole, the better your microscope will work.

Step Two: With the tip of a toothpick, carefully spread a thin layer of petroleum jelly just around the hole on both sides of the foil. Make sure to keep the hole open, free of jelly. With an eyedropper, squeeze a drop of clean distilled water into the pinhole. The petroleum jelly should hold the water in the pinhole. You may have to tap the card gently to get the water in the hole.

Step Three: Point the flashlight upward. Place the object you want to study over the light. Look at the object through the water drop.

Study things around the house. Onion skin, salt, sugar, a strand of human hair, the tip of a pencil and insect parts are good. Ask to borrow a few prepared slides from your science or biology teacher.

Source: *Boys' Life*

Make Your Own Stethoscope

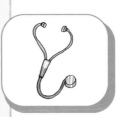

When you go to the doctor, he or she often uses an instrument to listen to your heart and lungs. This gadget the doctor uses is a binaural stethoscope. (Binaural simply means it works with both ears.) Apparently the first stethoscope was simply 24 sheets of paper rolled up tightly. Rene Laennec was a young French doctor who first used this "paper" stethoscope in 1816 to examine a young mademoiselle for modesty reasons. Before Laennec invented the stethoscope, it was customary to listen to the heart beat by putting an ear to the patient's chest. Doctor Laennec was so impressed by his simple paper listening device he went on to make others in his home workshop using a wood-turning lathe. Since it was so simple, Laennec first called the listening aid "le cylindre" which simply means "the cylinder." However, he changed the name to "stethoscope" which came from the Greek words for "I see" and "the chest." Laennec's stethoscopes were monaural since only one ear at a time was used.

The author's homemade monaural stethoscope is really simple, but it works really great! It probably works a lot better than Doctor Laennec's paper stethoscope!

modesty—being shy about showing your body   lathe—a tool for shaping wood

What You Need:

* cardboard tube from a used roll of paper towels

* a piece of aluminum foil

* duct tape

* scissors

Making It:

Keep an eye on the illustrations while you follow these steps.

(1) Wrap aluminum foil over one end of the cardboard tube that came from a used roll of paper towels.

(2) Use scissors to neatly cut the ends of the foil so your "stethoscope" looks better.

(3) Wrap duct tape over the ends of the foil. Hint: Make sure the foil is pulled tightly over the tube's opening.

1.

2.

Using Your Stethoscope

Press the stethoscope's open end against the chest of a person, about where you think their heart is. Press your ear against the stethoscope's foil end. You should clearly hear a heart beat. If you can't, try another place on the person's chest.

Sometimes it is quite important to listen to a person's breathing, especially if they have asthma or a bad cold. Stethoscopes come in handy here too! To hear breathing sounds, place the open end of your stethoscope on the back of the person, preferably near the center of the upper back. When the lungs are clear and not filled with fluid, you should hear very little. However, if there is fluid present, you will likely hear a wheeze either when they inhale or exhale (or both). If wheezing is present, that person should rest, and if a parent thinks it's wise, have a doctor examine the person.

Source: *Boys' Quest*

Inhale means to breathe in. What do you think exhale means?

duct tape—a type of cloth tape used for heating ducts, or pipes

asthma—an illness that causes difficulty in breathing

wheeze—to breathe with difficulty, making a whistling kind of sound

3. Unlocking Meaning

❶ Identifying the Purpose Choose the sentence that describes the main purpose of the two sets of instructions. Check (✓) the correct answer.

_____ 1. to describe two important events in medical history

_____ 2. to explain how medical equipment is made

_____ 3. to explain how to make an object using common household materials

_____ 4. to make you want to be a scientist or doctor

❷ Finding Details Work with a partner. One of you will be the "explainer," the other the "recorder." Retell the instructions for making a microscope.

Explainer

Recorder

• Read the instructions one more time, jotting down notes to help you remember.

• Tell your partner the instructions, using your own words.

• Record the instructions.

• Reread the instructions, checking to see if they are correct.

Now, reverse your roles, retelling the instructions for making a stethoscope.

Explainer

Checker

❸ Think about It Work with a partner. Learn more about magnification. Examine a tiny object under a microscope

• Draw a picture of what you think the object will look like when it is magnified.

• Now look at the object under the microscope. Draw a picture of what it really looks like.

• Share your two drawings with classmates.

❹ Before You Move On Work in a small group. Suppose that you wanted to make a solar oven that uses the sun's rays to cook food out of a pizza box. Using common items from the kitchen, how might you do that? Write instructions for your oven.

D WORD WORK

1. Word Detective Match the word on the left with the definition on the right. Think of other words that begin with the same prefix to help you guess.

1. **uni**cycle   a. a shape with three sides
2. **bi**lingual   b. able to speak two languages
3. **tri**angle   c. a train with one track
4. **hex**agon   d. half round
5. **multi**lingual   e. a shape with six sides
6. **mono**rail   f. able to speak many languages
7. **semi**circular   g. a cycle with just one wheel

2. Word Study Prefixes change the meaning of words. These common prefixes all refer to number or amount.

PREFIX	MEANING	EXAMPLES
mono-, uni-	one, single	**mono**gram, **uni**corn
bi-	two, double	**bi**focals, **bi**ceps
tri-	three, triple	**tri**athalon, **tri**logy
multi-	many	**multi**millionaire, **multi**lingual
inter-	among, between	**inter**state, **inter**national
semi-	half	**semi**soft, **semi**sweet

SPELLING:
To do this activity, go to page 237.

3. Word Play Complete the sentences below with the correct prefixes.

1. Juan speaks two languages. He is _____*bi*_ lingual.
2. André won the _____final tennis match. I hope he wins the finals.
3. Tran's ten-speed _____cycle was stolen. He forgot to lock it.
4. Oprah Winfrey is very wealthy. She is a _____millionaire.
5. Joe had an accident. He hit another car in the _____section.
6. The magazine comes out twice a month. It is published _____monthly.

E GRAMMAR
Using the Correct Article: *the* or *a/an*

1. Listen Up Listen to the mini-dialogs. If both speakers use correct English, point your thumb up 👍. If one speaker makes an error, point your thumb down 👎.

2. Learn the Rule Knowing when to use the articles *the*, *a*, and *an* is important—and sometimes tricky. Learn the main rules, then do Activity 1 again.

USING THE CORRECT ARTICLE: *the* or *a/an*

1. Use **the** with a definite noun. A noun is definite when both the speaker and listener (or writer and reader) are communicating about the same specific thing. Nouns are definite when—

   a. the noun has already been mentioned.
   A really vicious dog barked at me. Then, when I started to run, <u>the</u> dog chased me.

   b. a superlative or ranking adjective makes the noun specific.
   Juan is a really popular boy. He's <u>the</u> most popular boy in school.

   c. the noun describes a unique person, place, or thing—the only one of its kind.
   <u>The</u> moon revolves around <u>the</u> earth.

   d. the situation or the context makes the noun's identity clear to everyone.
   After school, I'm going to <u>the</u> library.

2. Use **a/an** with an indefinite noun. A singular noun is indefinite when it is part of a group of several others of the same kind. Use *an* with a noun or adjective that begins with a vowel sound.

   There are three cars parked in front of Brian's house. One car is <u>a</u> new Honda.
   Mr. Ruiz only has <u>an</u> allergy to cats, but he won't let Zaida have <u>an</u> animal of any kind.

---

3. Practice the Rule Complete the instructions below. Use *the*, *a*, or *an* in the blanks.

How to Make _____ Campfire

Begin by choosing _____ best spot for your fire. Make sure your fire is _____ safe distance from _____ tents.

Find _____ right fuel for your fire. _____ three main types of natural fuel are tinder (material that burns easily, such as shavings whittled from _____ stick), kindling (larger material such as twigs), and firewood (dry branches that will be _____ main fuel of your fire).

Arrange the wood in the shape of _____ teepee over _____ tinder. Light the tinder and add kindling as needed. Add larger branches last. Never leave _____ fire unattended.

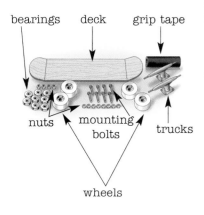

bearings deck grip tape

nuts mounting bolts trucks

wheels

F **BRIDGE TO WRITING**   How-to Instructions

1. Before You Read You know what a skateboard is, but have you ever taken a really close look at one? Look at the diagram at the left. Circle the words that are new to you.

2. Words to Know Read the definitions below.

metal file—a tool used to file down, or reduce, a metal object

power drill—an electrical tool used to make holes

awl—a pointed tool for making holes in something soft

nutdriver—a tool used to screw a nut to a bolt or screw

safety knife—a short, very sharp knife that retracts, or goes back, into its handle

mounting hardware—a metal device used to attach one object to another

Match each item on the left with the correct task on the right.

1. metal file
2. power drill
3. awl
4. nutdriver
5. safety knife
6. mounting hardware

a. adding another hole to a leather belt.
b. tightening a wobbly, or loose, table leg
c. cutting up a cardboard box
d. attaching a curtain rod above a window
e. smoothing off a sharp edge on a piece of metal
f. making many round air holes in a birdhouse

READING STRATEGY

Rereading:
When you read technical material, you can slow down, then re-read difficult parts—sometimes three or four times—until you understand them.

■■■

---

3. Let's Read Imagine that you wanted to assemble, or put together, a skateboard. As you read, ask yourself: Would I be able to follow these instructions?

Skateboard Assembly

So, you're ready to get your first skateboard? A decision you've made so that you too can ride the rolling urban landscapes of the world. Well, you have two choices: get a complete skateboard, which comes already set up and ready to ride, or get all the components and set it up to your own specs. The second choice may seem a bit more daunting, but in reality it's a no-brainer. And, you have the freedom of choosing and customizing your set up—exactly how you want it. What can be better than that? The following are instructions on setting up your new board properly and effectively. If you are under 15, get your Mom or Dad to help you out.

urban—found in a city

component—one of several parts of a machine

specs—(*short for* **specifications**) the details of how something should be made

daunting—making you feel a lack of confidence

Remember that " means inches.

Tools Needed

1. Metal file
2. Safety knife with fresh blade
3. Phillips screwdriver
4. Awl
5. $3/8"$, $1/2"$, $9/16"$ nutdrivers
6. Optional power drill

Griptape

This is the gritty sticker-backed material that helps your shoes grip the board while riding. This goes on your deck first—obviously, on the top of the board (duh). It usually comes in full-length sheets and various colors and designs. Pull the backing off the grip tape sheet and place it on the top of your board. It doesn't matter if it is crooked, but make sure it goes over all edges. Then place your board on the ground (carpet if you are worried about scratching the underside) and walk all over it, making sure the grip tape is stuck on good. Now put the board up on your bench or workspace.

OK, here comes the trade secret. Take your file and firmly file an outline of the board right onto the deck's edge. Do not file through the tape to the deck, just remove the gritty stuff. This gives you a guideline to cut the excess off, and also makes it easy to cut. Grab the safety knife, holding the blade 45 degrees to the edge, and come up from the bottom side of the grip (diagram 1a). Cut along the line you just filed and trim the excess tape off. Be careful not to file and trim so deep that you cut into the board. Once you've cut off the excess grip, give the board a light "run over" with the file to secure any raised edges. Success! We are ready to move on to the next step.

Truck Mounting

Use an awl (or whatever else will fit through a mounting hole) to poke through the grip tape where the truck holes are (on the board) so you can install the mounting hardware that holds the trucks on. Be careful not to poke yourself. Now grab the board and put it between your legs, or just hold it or have a friend hold it. Take the mounting bolts and push them through the truck holes on the board, four per truck (do one truck at a time). Slide the optional riser pads onto the bolt ends, then do the same with the truck. Make sure the truck bushings and kingpins are facing each other towards the middle of the board when they are both mounted (diagram 1b). This is very important, because if you put the trucks on backwards, they will turn in the opposite direction that you want them to, and that wouldn't be good. Secure them with locknuts and tighten them down snug with the screwdriver and the $3/8"$ nut driver. Repeat this process with the other truck. Wheels up next!

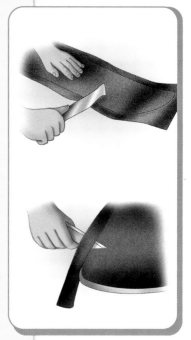

Diagram 1a.

Diagram 1b.

gritty—rough, like stone

trade secret—a tip known only by experts

excess—a larger amount of something than is needed

optional—not required to do if you don't want to

Diagram 1c.

Wheel Assembly and Mounting

OK, you're almost there. The most difficult part of assembling wheels is getting the bearings into the wheel without damaging the delicate shields, or coverings, on the bearings. There are two bearings and a spacer per wheel. Drop one of the bearings on the truck axle, followed by a spacer, and press the bearing into the wheel using the leverage between your hand and the truck (diagram 1c). Do the same for the other bearing. Most quality trucks have two thin washers on each axle. These are mounted on the outside of the bearings to achieve a good bearing seat and minimize friction. Axle washers minimize friction even more by allowing less of the bearing to come in contact with the washer. After the washers are in place and the wheel is installed, follow it all with a nylon ½" aircraft lock nut. Tighten it down snug and then back the nut off until you get non-binding roll with minimum play—just a little bit jiggly.

Ready to Skate?

OK, you are just about ready to roll. Give the deck a quick check for any missed nuts and bolts. Sometimes, when a board is brand new and you place the board on a flat surface, not all of the wheels will sit flat. Three wheels may touch but the other might be floating a bit. This is normal, and the problem will vanish once the truck cushions are worked in and relaxed. Another minor problem you may face is that new wheels don't spin very freely. Once the board is used and the bearings settle in the wheels, they will spin free and true…

One Last Thing to Do

Stickers! Get them out and start plastering that puppy. Or, if you don't like stickers, skip it. It's your board—your personal form of expression. Now it's time to go get crazy. Ride on, fellow wood pusher.

Source: skateboard.com

leverage—lifting power

non-binding—allowing free movement

plaster—to stick things like decals all over the surface of something

puppy—(*slang*) a way of referring to an object you like

4. Making Content Connections Talk with a partner. Think of something you have put together rather than buying already assembled. What was the experience like? Complete the chart below.

	My object: _____	Partner's object: _____
1. What materials did you use to do the job?		
2. What were the steps?		
3. What problems did you have, if any?		
4. What was the end result?		

4. Expanding Your Vocabulary Learn to use "how-to" verbs. Match each verb to its object. Some verbs have more than one possible object. Then write a short sentence using each verb and object. You can use your dictionary.

1. set up
2. assemble
3. refurbish
4. mend
5. construct
6. manufacture
7. patch
8. troubleshoot

a. an old, run-down house
b. a new building
c. a cracked ceiling
d. an automobile
e. a model airplane
f. a VCR
g. a computer problem
h. a broken vase

G WRITING CLINIC   How-to Instructions

1. Think about It Examples of how-to instructions might include—

- ☐ instructions for setting up a VCR
- ☐ an anti-tobacco poster
- ☐ a collection of short stories
- ☐ directions for fixing a leaky toilet
- ☐ a guide for installing software
- ☐ a history textbook

2. Focus on Organization Good instructions—in other words, instructions that others can follow—have certain characteristics:

Your introduction tells the reader what you are going to explain...

So, you're ready to get your first skateboard? Well, you have two choices: get a complete skateboard, which comes already set up and ready to ride, or get all the components and set it up to your own specs ... The following are instructions on setting up your new board properly and effectively.

Tools Needed

1. Metal file
2. Safety knife
3. Phillips screwdriver

4. Awl
5. Nutdrivers
6. Optional power drill

Next, you list the tools and supplies that are needed...

Griptape

This is the gritty sticker-backed material that helps your shoes grip the board while riding. This goes on your deck first ... Pull the backing off the grip tape sheet and place it on the top of your board. It doesn't matter if it is crooked, but make sure it goes over all edges. Then place your board on the ground (carpet if you are worried about scratching the underside) and walk all over it, making sure the grip tape is stuck on good. Now put the board up on your bench or workspace.

OK, here comes the trade secret. Take your file and firmly file an outline of the board right onto the deck's edge. Do not file through the tape to the deck, just remove the gritty stuff. This gives you a guideline to cut the excess off, and also makes it easy to cut. Grab the safety knife, holding the blade 45 degrees to the edge, and come up from the bottom side of the grip (diagram 1a) .... Success! We are ready to move on to the next step ...

Then, you provide the instructions—in time order. Use signal words and phrases to help guide your reader through the directions...

Provide important tips...

Ready to Skate?

OK, you are just about ready to roll. Give the deck a quick check for any missed nuts and bolts. Sometimes, when a board is brand new and you place the board on a flat surface, not all of the wheels will sit flat. Three wheels may touch but the other might be floating a bit. This is normal, and the problem will vanish once the truck cushions are worked in and relaxed. Another minor problem you may face is that new wheels don't spin very freely. Once the board is used and the bearings settle in the wheels, they will spin free and true.

One Last Thing to Do

Stickers! Get them out and start plastering that puppy. Or, if you don't like stickers, skip it. It's your board—your personal form of expression. Now it's time to go get crazy. Ride on, fellow wood pusher.

Use subheadings and boldface to help your reader...

Try to think of problems others might have as they follow your instructions...

Conclude with a sentence or two that has to do with use...

3. Focus on Style When you write, ask yourself: Who is my audience? Your "writer's voice"—that is, the words you use and your tone—should match your audience.

❶ Look again at the last paragraph of the skateboard instructions. Who is the audience for these instructions?

☐ teenagers   ☐ adults   ☐ older adults

What words tell you this? What is the tone of the writing—formal or casual?

❷ Work with a partner. Reread the instructions on pages 122–124. Make a list of at least five examples of informal words and phrases and casual tone.

The writer uses a sentence fragment here—just like in conversation.

So, you're ready to get your first skateboard? A decision you've made so that you too can ride the rolling urban landscapes of the world. Well, you have two choices: get a complete skateboard, which comes already set up and ready to ride, or get all the components and set it up to your own specs. The second choice may seem a bit more daunting, but in reality it's a no-brainer. And, you have the freedom of choosing and customizing your set up—exactly how you want it. What can be better than that?

"No-brainer" is an example of slang, meaning "something that is so easy you don't need to think about it."

H | WRITER'S WORKSHOP   How-to Instructions

Imagine that your class is putting together a manual of how-to instructions. Write a set of instructions for the manual.

1. Getting It Out

❶ Decide what you will explain. Brainstorm a list of things you know how to do—

Set up a VCR

Build a birdhouse

Make a model airplane

Operate a manual can opener

Use a video camera

Make a skateboard quarterpipe

Make a blouse

Build a solar oven

❷ Choose your topic. Explain something that...

- has a result
- is something that most other kids probably don't know how to do
- involves three or more steps to get to the result
- is something you know how to do

❸ Make a list of the materials, tools, and supplies you will need. Here is part a list of things you would need to make a skateboard quarterpipe.

Jigsaw, or saw for cutting curves

Handsaw

Five-foot piece of string

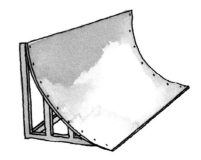

❹ List the steps in time order. Here is part of Juan's chart.

Steps	Things that can go wrong	Words to explain
1. Sketch slope for quarterpipe on plywood.	Be sure that your string is tight.	slope
2. Make the sides for the ramp.	Make sure that each side is exactly the same!	
3. Make frame from plywood.		

❺ Think about problems other people might have with each step. Make notes to yourself on your chart, so that you won't forget to discuss what can go wrong.

❻ Identify technical words or phrases that you might have to explain or illustrate.

❼ "How-to" instructions are almost always easier to understand if you use a diagram, picture, or flowchart. Look again at the skateboard diagram.

- Tell a partner how the illustration helps you understand the instructions.

- Why is the diagram a good one?

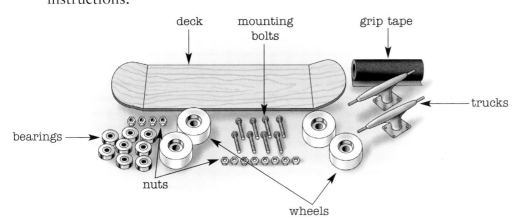

deck   mounting bolts   grip tape   trucks   bearings   nuts   wheels

Plan on using at least one illustration in your instructions.

2. Getting It Down

❶ Turn your timeline into instructions. Use a planner like this one.

How to _____

Introduction: _____

Materials:

1. _____

2. _____

3. _____

Instructions:

1. _____

2. _____

3. _____

Great introduction! Juan tells us what is going to explain.

Juan's audience is other kids. He talks to the reader like a friend.

He lists the materials.

❷ Here are Juan's instructions for making a skateboard quarterpipe—

He provides detailed steps, and they are in order. He uses transition words.

How To Build A Skateboard Quarterpipe

Are the older kids hogging all the public skateboard ramps around town? Here's a simple way to build your very own quarterpipe.

Materials:

Jigsaw, or saw for cutting curves	Pencil
Handsaw	8 six-foot lengths of 2" × 4" lumber
Five-foot piece of string	3 6' × 4' sheets of plywood
Pushpin or nail	

First, sketch out the slope of your quarterpipe. You will need a piece of string, a pushpin, and a pencil. Lay a sheet of plywood on the ground. Attach the pushpin to one end of the string and then push it into the ground, near the plywood. Attach the pencil to the other end of the string. Holding the string tight, swing the pencil in an arc along the surface of the plywood to draw the slope.

Next, make the sides to the ramp. Using the jigsaw, cut along the traced line. Cut out two identical pieces of plywood.

From here on, it's pretty much bang-bang-bang. Cut four-foot lengths from the 2×4s. 12 should be enough. Nail one length on each corner of your plywood. Then along the bottom and the back edge bang in 2×4 crossbeam supports every 18 inches or so. On the ramp, nail a 2×4 every foot or so. Make certain that the 2×4s are flush with the lip of the plywood. This will give better support and make for a smoother ride. This is your completed frame.

Take a piece of plywood and gently arch it along your ramp. Nail down the edges. If you moisten the wood, it will bend and curve easier.

Your quarterpipe is done! Use the remaining lumber and plywood to build a table top for the back side of the ramp. You can ride over the lip and onto the table top—just like Grandma used to do!

Source: *The Portland Mercury*

MINI-LESSON

Using Commas with Transition Words:
Use a comma after a signal or transition word at the beginning of a sentence:

First, sketch out the slope.

3. Getting It Right Take a careful look at what you have written.
Use this guide to help you revise your work.

Question to Ask...	How to Check...	How to Revise...
1. Does my introduction identify what I am going to explain?	Underline your introduction.	Add a sentence or two that identifies the task and tells why it is important.
2. Do I list the materials that the reader will need?	Reread your instructions, putting a check mark (✓) next to each item needed.	Add anything you have forgotten to your list.
3. Do I list each step? Are the steps in time order?	Put a number next to each step.	Add steps or reorganize the order of steps.
4. Do I include at least one visual that helps the reader understand my explanation?	Put a star (★) next to your visual(s).	Add a diagram, flowchart, photo, or hand-drawn picture.
5. Overall, are my instructions easy to follow?	Put yourself in your reader's shoes. Try to follow the instructions, as you read them to yourself.	Add illustrations, more steps or details, or transition words (*first, next ...*).

4. Presenting It

❶ Share your instructions with your classmates. Begin by telling them what you will explain or teach them.

❷ Teach your classmates key terms. Show pictures or actual objects, writing each word on chart paper or on the board.

❸ Present each step slowly and clearly. Show your classmates a drawing or other visual, if that will help them understand.

❹ Ask for volunteers to repeat each step in your directions as you present them.

1. On Assignment Diagrams can help us understand objects and how they work.

❶ Learn more about diagrams. Sometimes a diagram is *two-dimensional*. The object that is pictured has only height and width (or length). This is an example of a cross-sectional diagram of a volcano. It's as if the volcano were sliced opened with a knife.

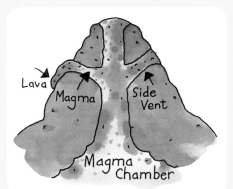

❷ Many diagrams are *three-dimensional*. They show height, width (or length), and depth. Three-dimensional diagrams are often used to show the parts of an object and how they work together.

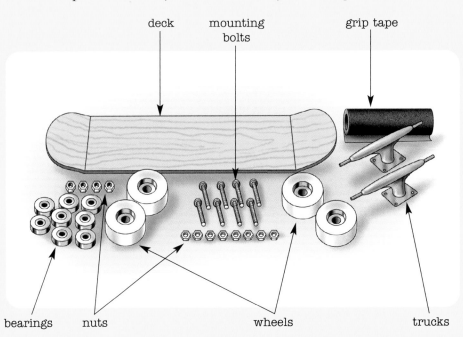

❸ Choose a simple object in your life. Make an exact diagram that shows the parts of the object. You may wish to use graph paper, so that the parts of the object are to scale. Label the important parts.

2. Link to Literature

🎧 **SHARED READING** A how-to poem gives instructions on how to be something or how to do something. Read these two poems.

LET'S TALK Answer the questions.

1. Find the "instructions" in each poem. Share with a partner.
2. "How to Be a Shark" is an amusing poem. Why is it funny?
3. Which poem do you like best? Why?

JUST FOR FUN Write your own how-to poem. Be sure that it has at least three steps.

How to Be a Shark

Get born with a full set of
self-replicating razor-sharp teeth
Swim in the oceans for
400 million years,
175 million years before the
dinosaurs,
(but who's counting)
Devour fish, or squid, or seals
And don't worry
if you break a tooth
on a bone
Because you'll grow 30,000
new ones in a lifetime
Lift up your nose and smell
prey two miles away,
Roll back your eagle eyes
take a bite
But don't eat humans
yuck,
they taste bad
even with ketchup

—Barry Lane

Source: *51 Wacky We-Search Reports*
by Barry Lane

How to Say "I'm Sorry"

The first thing you do
is make quick conversation.
The weather's beautiful.
How's the kids?
Fine, thanks.
What did you call
me over here for?
It couldn't have been
to say how nice a day
it has been.
Well, the truth is
I wanted to tell you,
I wanted to tell you,
well, you know what
I want to say,
don't you?
No, I don't,
so please
by all means
spit it out.
I wanted to say
I'm sorry
sorry for everything.
Oh, is that all!
I forgave you
right after you did it.
You should know
by now at least,
good friends know
when something's wrong
but thanks anyway
for saying, "I'm sorry."

—Julie Schmitz

Source: falcon.kcsd.K12.or.us

What Were the 1960s Like, Grandpa?

Read...

■ Oral histories about the lives of two ordinary people—a man who grew up poor in the Appalachian Mountains and a farm girl who played professional baseball during World War II.

Link to Literature

■ Two tall tales told by American frontiersman, Davy Crockett.

Objectives:

Reading:
■ Reading two types of oral histories: Interviews and narratives
■ Strategy: Questioning the author
■ Understanding written dialect
■ Literature: Responding to tall tales

Writing:
■ Writing an oral history
■ Note taking: Recording exact words
■ Avoiding run-on sentences and fragments

Vocabulary:
■ Recognizing common roots
■ Understanding dialect differences

Listening/Speaking:
■ Interviewing others/listening for information
■ Understanding regional dialect speech
■ Listening for details

Grammar:
■ Talking about repeated actions in the past/past ability: *would, used to,* and *could*

Spelling:
■ Spelling words with *-ie-* or *-ei-*

Mother and children in California, 1936

Pictures can tell us about the past—things that even words cannot express. Study the photograph for a minute or two, then talk with your classmates—

1. Describe what you see in the picture. Talk about the woman and her children.

2. What does the picture tell you about the era, or time period from the past? Help your teacher make a list of your ideas.

3. What can photographs tell us about times past?

A CONNECTING TO YOUR LIFE

1. Tuning In Listen to a high school girl interview her grandmother. Take notes. What did you learn about her grandmother's life? Share with a partner.

2. Talking It Over Work in a small group. Imagine you wanted to know more about what life was like in the past—and how it was different from your own life. Choose one photograph. Make a list of questions you might ask that person.

A 1960s hippie

Two 1950s brothers

1940s schoolgirls

A 1930s farm boy

Read the title. What do you think the unit is probably about? Check (✓) the correct answer.

_____ 1. It's about how to write a report about the 1960s.

_____ 2. It's about grandparents and their grandchildren.

_____ 3. It's about learning about a time in the past by interviewing someone who lived during that era.

_____ 4. It's about learning about hippies and the harmful effects of drugs.

B GETTING READY TO READ

1. Learning New Words Read the definition for each important event or period in our history.

a. **World War I**—a war fought from 1914 to 1918, in which Great Britain, France, Russia, Belgium, Italy, Japan, the United States, and other allies, or partners, defeated Germany and its European allies

b. **The stock market crash of 1929**—the day that many stocks, or shares in companies, lost all or most of their value, or worth

c. **The Great Depression**—a long period throughout the 1930s when businesses had trouble selling their products and many people had very little money

d. **The New Deal**—new government programs that President Franklin D. Roosevelt introduced during the 1930s to help people without jobs and to help the U.S. economy improve

e. **World War II**—a war fought from 1939 to 1945, in which Great Britain, France, the Soviet Union, the United States, China, and other allies defeated Germany, Italy, and Japan

f. **Pearl Harbor**—an attack by the Japanese on an American naval base in 1941 that made the U.S. decide to join World War II

Write the letter of each event or period above in the correct blank below.

1. Many people lost their jobs and, for many years, struggled to survive. What was this terrible time in our history called? _____ c _____

2. This military location in Hawaii was attacked on December 7. What is its name? _____

3. France and Japan fought on the same side in this war. Which war was it? _____

4. Congress approved President Roosevelt's plan to improve the economy. What was the plan called? _____

5. The Allies defeated Germany for a second time in this war. Which war was it? _____

6. People lost billions of dollars on this terrible day. What was the event? _____

2. Talking It Over Work in a small group. Imagine that you are historians studying family life in an earlier period—the 1970s, for example. You plan to interview someone who is still alive and can remember the period.

- Choose a period of time to study.
- Make a list of ten questions you would ask the person. Compare your questions with your classmates' questions.

C READING TO LEARN Oral History

1. Before You Read Look at the Web page. What do you think you might find in the archives, or information about the past? Read and find out.

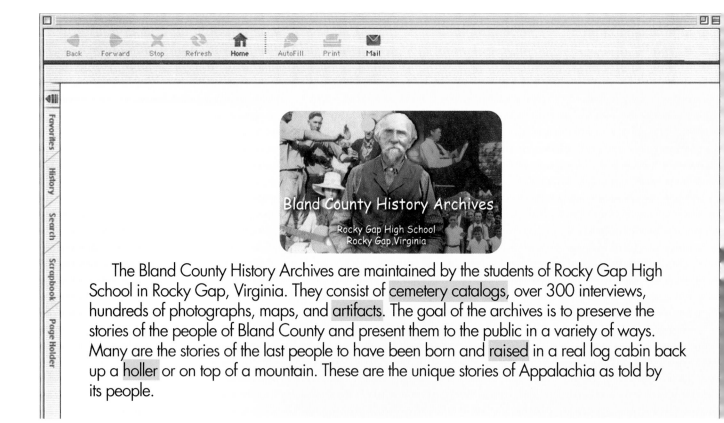

Bland County History Archives
Rocky Gap High School
Rocky Gap, Virginia

The Bland County History Archives are maintained by the students of Rocky Gap High School in Rocky Gap, Virginia. They consist of cemetery catalogs, over 300 interviews, hundreds of photographs, maps, and artifacts. The goal of the archives is to preserve the stories of the people of Bland County and present them to the public in a variety of ways. Many are the stories of the last people to have been born and raised in a real log cabin back up a holler or on top of a mountain. These are the unique stories of Appalachia as told by its people.

cemetery catalog—a list of people buried in a graveyard

artifact—an object made or used a long time ago

raised—brought up

holler—(*dialect*) a small valley between mountains (a word used only in the Appalachians)

2. Let's Read In 1995, Betina Looney interviewed her grandfather. He was born in 1920. As you read, jot down questions you would ask Mr. Looney.

READING STRATEGY
Questioning the Author:
Questioning the writer as you read can help you understand what he or she is telling us.

Betina:	What is your name?
Wallace:	Wallace Randolph Looney
Betina:	Where and when were you born?
Wallace:	I was born up Wolf Creek...was born in a log house, and a doctor came on a horse to deliver me in 1920. I weighed under three pounds.
Betina:	Who [were] your mother and father?
Wallace:	My mother was Vergas Territory Short, my father was John Harrison Looney.
Betina:	What did they do for a living?
Wallace:	They farmed on a farm, raised cattle and sheep.
Betina:	What were your chores around the house?
Wallace:	Well, we cut wood, wood for a cook stove, wood for a heatin' stove, and carried it in the house.
Betina:	What was your house like?
Wallace:	We lived in a log house with three rooms and a fireplace...
Betina:	How was your house heated?
Wallace:	Well, we had a fireplace, a wood cook stove we cooked on, and the fireplace— my mother would cook taters in it and roast them for us to eat...
Betina:	What was your favorite meal?
Wallace:	Sausage, gravy, and corn bread, and brown beans.
Betina:	Where did you go to school?
Wallace:	I went to school up Wolf Creek, to a one-room schoolhouse...
Betina:	What did you study?
Wallace:	We studied spelling, arithmetic, history, and English.
Betina:	How did the teachers make the students behave?
Wallace:	They would draw a ring in the corner of the blackboard and make them stand there with their nose

When people talk, they sometimes change the –ing ending to -in'. The apostrophe takes the place of -g.

Wallace Looney speaks a dialect of English typical of people who live in Appalachia. He sometimes uses different words and nonstandard grammar.

A one-room schoolhouse has one teacher who teaches a class of students at all grade levels!

tater—(*dialect*) a potato

in that ring on one foot for fifteen to twenty minutes. The other punishment was to make them sit in after school.

Betina:	Did you ever get into trouble at school?
Wallace:	NO, I never even got a whippin'.
Betina:	Did you graduate?
Wallace:	No, I went through the sixth grade and then quit.
Betina:	Do you remember what year that was?
Wallace:	1936.
Betina:	Do you remember World War I?
Wallace:	No, I don't!
Betina:	Do you remember when the stock market crashed?
Wallace:	Yeah, I remember a little bit about it.
Betina:	What was it like during the Great Depression?
Wallace:	Well, our family couldn't get ahold of money. We had to wear patched clothes, and we couldn't get nothing to eat unless we raised [it]. We had to can a lot of stuff—fruit, berries. We lived like that.
Betina:	How did you feel about President Franklin Roosevelt and his New Deal?
Wallace:	Well, I think President Roosevelt done a pretty good job. That's when we started making money and having automobiles to ride in, and I think things picked up good.
Betina:	Do you remember where you were when you heard that the Japanese had bombed Pearl Harbor?
Wallace:	Yeah, I lived up Wolf Creek with my dad, and it was announced on the radio. There was another guy there, and my dad told him to listen—said something's gonna happen ...
Betina:	What kind of shape is the country in today in your opinion?
Wallace:	Well, it's in pretty fair shape.
Betina:	Have things changed for the better or the worse?
Wallace:	Better.
Betina:	Why?
Wallace:	Because we didn't have anything when we was kids, and they have more today than we had.
Betina:	Thank you.

Source: bland.k12.va.us

sit in—(*dialect*) to stay after

whippin'—(*dialect*) a punishment of being hit with a switch, or thin branch from a tree

can—to preserve food in jars or cans

3. Unlocking Meaning

❶ **Finding the Main Idea** Check (✓) the correct answer. Wallace Looney's interview helps us...

_____ 1. learn about the role of American women in the last century.

_____ 2. learn what daily life was like in a part of America in the 1930s and 40s.

_____ 3. learn more about World War I.

_____ 4. learn how to make Appalachian food.

❷ **Finding Details** We learn from his interview that Wallace Looney...

- grew up in a rural, or country, area
- had little money.

Find three details in Wallace's oral history that support each idea. Make a chart.

Lived in a rural area	Did not have very much money
Went to a one-room schoolhouse.	

❸ **Think about It** Talk with a partner. Imagine that you are historians. You want to find out about some period in the past. Besides books, make a list of primary sources, or original types of information, you might look for...

- photographs
- interviews with people who lived at the time (oral histories)
- newspapers from the era

❹ **Before You Move On** Write down one more question that you would like to ask Wallace Looney about his life as a young person.

D WORD WORK

1. Word Detective Knowing common roots, or the part of a word that carries its main meaning, can help you guess what new words mean. Read the definition of each root.

-aqua-—water	**-derm-**—skin
-bio-—life	**-phone-, -phono-**—sound
-biblio-—book	**-therm-**—heat

Complete each sentence with the correct root.

1. Carlos is interested in plants and animals. His favorite subject is ____*bio*logy.
2. I think I have a temperature. Where's the _____ometer?
3. Maria loves to talk to her friends. Every night, she spends hours on the tele_____.
4. When you write a report, you should put a list of sources, or _____graphy at the end.
5. When the doctor gives you a shot, she uses a hypo_____ic needle to go through the skin.
6. Ms. Vasquez' students are studying marine animals. They are going on a field trip next week to the _____rium.

2. Word Study Learn the meanings of common roots. For each root, write one more example.

SPELLING:
To do this activity, go to page 238.

ROOT	EXAMPLE	ROOT	EXAMPLE
-simil- ("same")	facsimile ("fax")	-mater- ("mother")	maternal
-man- ("hand")	manual	-scrib-, -script- ("write")	manuscript
-nym-, -onym- ("name")	synonym	-geo- ("earth")	geography
-dent- ("tooth")	dental	-spect- ("see")	spectator

3. Word Play Work with a partner. Here are three very common roots. Choose one root, then make a list of as many words as you can think of with the root.

-meter- ("measure")　　　-graph- ("writing")　　　-log- ("word")

E GRAMMAR — Repeated Actions or Ability in the Past: *would, used to,* and *could*

1. Listen Up Listen to these sentences. Point your thumb up 👍 if the sentence sounds correct. Point your thumb down 👎 if it sounds wrong.

👍👎 1. When I was little, my mother will read to me every night.

👍👎 2. When we lived in Los Angeles, we used to go to the Dodgers game every weekend.

👍👎 3. In the past, Maria would always do her homework. Now she rarely does it.

👍👎 4. Juan can play the piano by the time he was five years old.

2. Learn the Rule Learn how to express habitual action or ability. Then do Activity 1 again.

REPEATED ACTIONS OR ABILITY IN THE PAST: *would, used to,* and *could*
1. When you want to tell about things you did repeatedly in the past, use *would*—especially in written narratives: *In the summer, we <u>would</u> go swimming every day.*
2. You can also use *used to* to express past habit—especially in speech: *Juan's mother <u>used to</u> tie her son's shoes. Finally, he learned to do it himself.*
3. When you want to express past ability, use *could*:   *When I was young, I <u>could</u> speak German perfectly. Now I can't remember a word!*

3. Practice the Rule Complete each sentence, using *would, used to,* or *could*.

1. Here in the U.S. Stefan takes the bus to school every day. When he lived in Poland, he ___used to___ walk.
2. I _____ talk by the time I was a year and a half old.
3. My family hardly ever goes on vacation to Hawaii anymore. When I was younger, we _____ go every year.
4. Today, you pay two or three dollars for a loaf of bread. Years ago, a loaf of bread _____ cost 25 cents.
5. Every night, my father _____ bring my mother flowers when he came home.

F | BRIDGE TO WRITING   Oral History

1. Before You Read Look at the poster and the photograph of "Rosie the Riveter." Write three words to describe her. Now learn more about "Rosie."

1   When World War II came, there were more factory jobs than there were workers to fill them. This was because so many soldiers went overseas to fight, and there were not enough men to do the work.

2   America's women were suddenly needed to do the "heavy lifting!" For years working women had been limited to sewing clothing, putting together watches and other low-paying jobs in light-manufacturing. Now the government had to convince America that women could build airplanes, battle ships, and military equipment.

3   The woman in the poster to the right helped show people that women could do anything men could do! The woman was called "Rosie the Riveter." Women who worked the factories became known as "Rosies." You could tell who Rosie was by her blue-jeans, her red bandana and her big attitude.

4   In 1995, ninth graders at South Kingstown High School in Rhode Island interviewed women who had lived during World War II. They wanted to know what they remembered about the time and what life was like. Their interviews form a collection of oral histories, "What Did You Do in the War, Grandma?"

Source: stg.brown.edu

2. Words to Know Read the sentences below. Try to guess what the underlined words mean.

1. Alex Rodriguez works for the New York Yankees. He is a <u>professional</u> baseball player.

2. Maria has a piece of paper that promises the government will pay her $100. Her parents bought her a government savings <u>bond</u> when she was a baby.

3. Juan hopes to go to Stanford, but his family doesn't have the money. Because Juan is a good student, the university may give him a <u>scholarship</u>.

4. When you leave paper in water a long time, it falls apart. The water makes it <u>disintegrate</u>.

5. Tran's parents make about $75,000 a year. They have a good <u>income</u>.

6. During World War II, the government could force men to join the army. Millions were <u>drafted</u> during that war.

7. Sandra was greedy. She went to jail for cheating on her taxes. Greed was her <u>downfall</u>.

Match each word or phrase on the left with the correct definition on the right.

1. professional
2. bond
3. scholarship
4. disintegrate
5. income
6. draft
7. downfall

a. to officially order someone to join the military

b. the money you earn from working

c. the cause of a sudden loss of money, happiness, or health

d. doing a job, sport, or activity for money

e. a promise the government makes to pay back money it has borrowed

f. to become weaker and be destroyed

g. money that is given to someone to pay for his or her education

3. Let's Read Read the first paragraph of the interview with Wilma Briggs. As you read, figure out why her opinions about women were *not* at all what the interviewer expected!

READING STRATEGY
Questioning the Author:
Questioning the writer as you read can help you understand what he or she is telling us.

What Did You Do in the War, Grandma?
A Farm Girl Plays Professional Baseball
Interviewed by Ben Tyler

1   *Wilma Briggs is an elementary school teacher. Her feelings about women in the family were not what I had expected, considering her unusual career for the time as a professional baseball player.*

2   I was born in 1930 and grew up on a farm in East Greenwich. There were 11 living children in my family. We had a 60 acre dairy farm, and a lot of work to do. Not a lot of money, but a lot of food. We had our own garden, grew our own food, and played a lot of baseball.

3   We didn't get a daily newspaper, only the Sunday paper. The kids just didn't do much reading other than the comics and the sports section. We knew there was a war—my father was an air raid warden. We had blackouts where they would have the practice air raids, and he'd go out and stop traffic. That's about as close as I came to the war. None of my brothers were old enough to be in it.

4   We would get up at 6:30 and go to the barn before breakfast. We had probably 35 milking cows, and we milked by hand. It was only my father, my two older brothers, and myself. We all milked, or the boys would milk and my father and I would feed, which meant I swept out in front so that it was clean for the grain to be put down.

air raid warden—someone with the job of warning the community when an air attack in coming

blackout—an occasion when all lights are turned off in a city during an air attack

When we got home from school, we'd have to clean the barn. Homework was a problem. When I got home I had farm work to do, which meant if I didn't get homework done in school, it didn't get done.

5 But we fit everything around baseball as much as we could because that was our hobby. We had baseball equipment because my father had a team. All the neighborhood kids came to our house to play, which was convenient for us because sometimes they helped us finish up the work so we could play earlier.

6 *Did your family make a lot of money from the farm?*

7 (Laughs.) Farmers never make a lot of money. They were always, you know, underpaid for everything. We never had much money, but we never knew that as kids. I thought that we were rich. Most kids didn't have horses. And we had sleds and bicycles and ice skates and that kind of thing. But we hardly ever went anywhere. Once a year we'd go to Fenway Park or something like that, or we'd get a treat to go out for ice cream. We didn't go to the movies very often. Some kids went regularly. We went, if we were lucky, once a month. We had only one family car …

8 *What type of clothing did you wear?*

9 Well, I wore dungarees, even to school. I wore them every day because we didn't have a lot of money. My mother and father had to buy dungarees for the boys and I'd say, "Well, get me some too." I was wearing them in the barn. And we wore the same style clothes working as we did to school. By the time I got to high school and started playing basketball, and was on the gym team—I needed slacks anyway, so I wore slacks or dungarees to school, and I got away with it. I was the only girl that did, but then I was the only girl who played on the boys' baseball team, too.

10 Had it not been for the war, I never would have played professional baseball. That started because of the war. People didn't have money to go places. Phil Wrigley of the Chicago Cubs was certain that all the men would be drafted, and the major league ballparks would be empty. That's the reason he started that league, the All-American Girls' Professional Baseball League.

11 So, because of the war, I got that chance. That league started in 1943, and I joined it after high school in 1948. Had it not been for the war, that part of my life would never have come to pass …

12 *How did the war change your life?*

13 I think our whole country changed after the war when all the "Rosie the Riveters" continued to rivet when the war was over. I really believe that's one of the major problems in our world today. I think that was the beginning of the downfall of the family. The family unit started to disintegrate right after the war when Rosie kept riveting. Families found out that they could have two incomes. And now, 45 years later, parents need those two incomes to survive. Because of that, nobody's home. The kids know their baby-sitter better than they know their parents. They know their teacher better than they know their parents. Everybody seems to be going in a different direction. And I really think that all happened because Rosie was needed to rivet during the war, but when the war was over, she didn't stop.

Source: stg.brown.edu

Fenway Park—a baseball park in Boston

dungarees—(*old fashioned*) denim pants

4. Making Content Connections Work with a partner. Imagine that you are both 50 years old. Thinking back, what would you say about your life today? Make a chart.

	You	Your Partner
My family and what they were like	Both my parents worked.	
What I did for fun	Hung out at the mall.	
What school was like		
A funny story I'll never forget		

5. Expanding Your Vocabulary Imagine that you are interviewing someone. Do you know how to use just the right words and phrases? For each situation, find the question that does *not* belong and cross it out.

1. You begin the interview.
   a. Could you begin by telling me about yourself?
   b. I appreciate your agreeing to talk with me.
   c. ~~The next time we talk, you can tell me more.~~

2. You want to let the person know you don't understand what they said.
   a. I disagree with you.
   b. I'm sorry. I didn't get that.
   c. I'm confused. Could you repeat that?

3. You want the person to clarify a point.
   a. I have a slightly different idea about that...
   b. So what you're saying is that...
   c. I'm a little confused. Could you say more about that?

4. You want to let the person you are interested in what they are saying.
   a. That's totally fascinating!
   b. Does what I've just said make sense?
   c. I'd like to hear more about that.

5. You want to get the interview back on track.
   a. Thank you for your time.
   b. Returning to what you said earlier ...
   c. How did we get onto that?

6. It's time to end the interview.
   a. Thank you very much for talking with me.
   b. Could you begin by telling me about yourself?
   c. It was a pleasure to listen to your stories.

G WRITING CLINIC

Oral History

1. Think about It What is the main purpose of an oral history?

- ☐ To entertain others by telling funny stories
- ☐ To teach others how to live their lives better
- ☐ To describe or explain a time in the past

2. Focus on Organization Oral histories can be *interviews*, or they can be *narratives*, or stories.

❶ Talk with a partner. Compare the interview and the narrative. Which do you prefer reading? Be ready to say why.

> *An interview states each question and answer.*

> *The person's exact words are quoted.*

Betina:	What is your name?
Wallace:	Wallace Randolph Looney
Betina:	Where and when were you born?
Wallace:	I was born up Wolf Creek where the Boy Scout camp is now...was born in a log house, and a doctor came on a horse to deliver me in 1920. I weighed under three pounds.
Betina:	Who [were] your mother and father?
Wallace:	My mother was Vergas Territory Short, my father was John Harrison Looney.
Betina:	What did they do for a living?
Wallace:	They farmed on a farm, raised cattle and sheep.

> *A narrative is in story form. The interviewer often begins with a short introduction.*

> *Information is broken into chunks—each a different paragraph.*

I interviewed my grandfather, Wallace Randolph Looney, about growing up in Rocky Gap. He was eager to tell his story.

My name is Wallace Randolph Looney. I was born in 1920 up Wolf Creek, where the boy scout camp is now. I was born in a log house. A doctor came on horse to deliver me. I weighed less than three pounds.

My mother was Vergas Territory Short and my father was John Harrison Looney. We lived on a farm, and the family raised cattle and sheep for a living.

❷ Go back to Betina's interview with her grandfather on pages 138–140. Choose one section of the interview. Rewrite the section as a narrative, using complete sentences. Correct the grammar, if you need to.

3. Focus on Style

❶ People don't always talk in complete sentences. Sometimes they leave out the subject, verb, or some other part, in casual speech.

In writing, a sentence like this is called a fragment.

> *"Went to a one-room school house there on Silver Creek."*

And, sometimes they run two or more sentences together.

> *"There wasn't a bus that run to Hollybrook School it was five miles away and I remember the last year that I was at Silver Creek school when I was in the seventh grade and there were two boys who walked that five miles to school all year."*

And, a sentence like this, when written, is called a run-on.

❷ When you write, always avoid using fragment sentences and run-on sentences. Read the sentences below. Write *F* if a sentence is a fragment. Write *R* if a sentence is a run-on.

___F___ 1. Because he didn't want to go to school.

_____ 2. Maria felt sleepy, she went to bed, she forgot to turn off the lights.

_____ 3. When the teacher looked at me.

_____ 4. Raining all night with thunder and lightening.

_____ 5. I ran into Tran he is leaving for a trip to Vietnam tomorrow.

_____ 6. You should hear Juan sing he is really good.

_____ 7. My computer keeps doing weird things, because it keeps shutting down, I don't know what to do.

_____ 8. Tran told a funny joke, no one could stop laughing.

_____ 9. Ms. Valdez is one of my favorite teachers. Even though she is strict.

_____ 10. Lori kept falling asleep in class. From staying up too late the night before.

H WRITER'S WORKSHOP   Oral History

Your class will develop a collection of oral histories about what life was like for teenagers in the "old days" or the past! You will interview someone *at least 40 years old*—an adult who remembers what life was like then.

1. Getting It Out

❶ Begin by deciding who you will interview.

A parent

A community member

A teacher

A neighbor

❷ Get ready for the interview. Decide on the questions you will ask. Write ten good questions that require more than a "yes" or a "no" answer.

AVOID: Did you ever do things with friends for fun? (gets only yes/no answers)

ASK: What did you do with friends to have fun? (gets information)

Personal information	Family life	Relations with parents
Where were you born?	What was it like being the oldest child?	What did you parents used to nag you about?
Chores	Friends and fun	School
What were the chores you liked/disliked most? Why?	When did you start dating?	What was school like?

❸ Set up a time for your interview. Choose a quiet place.

❹ If you can, use a cassette tape recorder. If you can't do that, schedule several shorter interview sessions so that you can ask all of your questions and have time to write down the answers.

❺ Interview the person.

- Begin by asking basic personal questions.

When and where were you born?

Why were you born in Peru? What did your father do for a living?

- Ask questions that begin with *Wh*-question words and phrases like "describe..." and "let's talk about..."

What did you and your friends do for fun?

Describe what it was like speaking two languages...

Let's talk about what school was like...

- Ask follow up questions. Ask a final question that causes the person to think about their life.

Could you tell me more about...?

If you could be a teenager again, what would you do differently?

- Record or write down the person's exact words

My favorite group was the Beatles. I remember when...

"My favorite group was the Beatles. I remember when..."

- Thank the person for talking with you.

Thank you for talking with me.

2. Getting It Down Draft your oral history.

❶ Begin by introducing the interviewee, or the person you interviewed, to the reader. Here is what Lori wrote.

> *I interviewed Ms. Susana Garvin-Ponce, the Director of Multilingual Programs for our school district. Ms. Ponce was born in 1950 in Peru. Ms. Ponce's parents were Americans. Her father was a geologist who worked for a large American company that did business in Latin America. When she was 4, the family moved to Torreon Coahuila, Mexico, where she lived until she was 18.*

> *Lori begins by telling about Ms. Ponce's family and where she grew up.*

❷ Decide whether you will write up the oral history as an interview or as a narrative.

> *Ms. Ponce began by sharing what it was like to grow up speaking two languages. For as long as I can remember, I spoke both English and Spanish. I spoke English at home—even though my parents were bilingual—and spoke Spanish with my friends and at school. My parents sent me to a bilingual school. In the morning, my classes were in English and in the afternoon in Spanish.*

> *Lori decides to present her oral history as a narrative. Narratives are easy to read.*

❸ Write the interviewee's story in the first person, using the subject pronoun "I." Use the person's exact words as much as possible.

> *Ms. Ponce talked about dating.*
> *We never went out alone on boy-girl dates. Instead, our social life revolved around the home. Our parents would always arrange for kids to come to the house for parties, and I would meet boys that way. One time, when I was 16, an older boy Jorge asked me to the movies. My sister went along with us. Jorge's four brothers also went along. We took up almost the entire row in the movie theater!*

> *Lori's questions get Ms. Garvin-Ponce to open up. She provides details that help the reader understand how different it was to be a teenager in Mexico than in the U.S.*

— MINI-LESSON —

Using Apostrophes to Show Possession:
Use an apostrophe to show possession. When the possessor is singular, add 's. When the possessor is plural ending in -s, just add an apostrophe.

Jorge's brothers' wives also went along. The Ramirez boys' dog is very friendly.

❹ Remember to group the same kind of information together—and in logical order—so that your oral history is easy to follow.

❺ End with an interesting question and response that will stay in the reader's mind.

3. Getting It Right Take a careful look at your interview. Use this guide to revise what you have written.

Ask Yourself	How to Check	How to Revise
1. Did I begin by asking personal questions?	Put a star (★) next to the part or parts that introduce the person.	Add information about the person's age, family, or where they were raised.
2. Did I ask questions that were open-ended and got the person to provide interesting details?	Did the person answer more than "yes" and "no"?	Ask the person follow-up questions that begin with words like *what, why, who, when,* and *how.*
3. Was each question correctly formed?	Ask a neighbor to read your questions.	Correct the word order in the question. Add a helping verb, if you need to.
4. Did I record the person's exact words?	Ask the person you interviewed to read his or her oral history.	Make changes, as needed, in the answers or narrative.
5. Overall—does the person's oral history help people know what it was like to be a teenager at an earlier time?	<u>Underline</u> passages that provide information that is new, surprising, or interesting.	Consider asking the person follow-up questions that add more information.

4. Presenting It Choose one section of the oral history to share with your classmates.

❶ If you wrote the oral history as an interview, consider asking a classmate to read aloud the response to the questions you ask.

What was the chore you disliked the most?

Milking the cows! I had to get up at 3:30 every morning—even when it was snowing.

❷ As you listen to others share, listen for details that show how life for teenagers was different than it is today. Jot down notes, then share with your classmates.

I BEYOND THE UNIT

1. On Assignment Writers often show that a character speaks a dialect, a kind of English that people only speak in a certain place. The writer does this by purposely misspelling words to look like they're pronounced.

❶ Work with a partner. *Lil* (= Little) *Abner* was a popular comic strip in the 1950s. Read the strip and find five words that are examples of dialect. Write each of these words correctly.

EXAMPLE: *Say: "thar"   Write: "there"*

❷ Here is how certain everyday words are often misspelled in literature, advertisements, comic strips, etc. Say each word aloud, then match the word to the correct spelling.

1. fer		a. sort of
2. yer		b. give me
3. 'em		c. going to
4. gonna		d. come on
5. kinda		e. for
6. sorta		f. your
7. c'mon		g. kind of
8. gimme		h. them

❸ Listen carefully to how English speakers pronounce words when they are outside of class, talking to friends. Make a list of words that you often hear pronounced differently than they are spelled. Share your list with your classmates.

2. Link to Literature

SHARED READING Davy Crockett is a famous American frontiersman who was known for the tall tales, or exaggerated stories, he told about himself. Read along, as you listen to the audio or CD.

LET'S TALK Answer the questions.

1. Find examples of exaggerations in each of Davy's tall tales.

2. Why are these tales fun to read? Which one do you like best? Why?

3. Find example of Davy's use of dialect. Why does dialect make his tall tale interesting?

"When I was only three years old, I out-wrestled a big old bear. That bear wandered into the kitchen one day and started to eat up the jam. So I grabbed him in a bear hug with my mighty twelve-inch arms, and I squeezed and I squeezed and I squeezed until that bear just fell down, ker-plunk! Just like that, wasn't nothing to it. So my folks knew right then that I was cut out to be a wild frontiersman, a ring-tailed roarer who's part horse and part alligator with a bit of snappin' turtle thrown in."

"Now when I was still just a wee lad, my pa gave me my first rifle. We all had to have a rifle back then just to survive out in the woods, 'cause there were all kinds of critters running around that wanted to eat us. So we'd eat them first. And we'd use their skins to make our clothes. I called my rifle Old Betsy, and in no time at all I got to be a powerful keen shot. Fact is, I got to be such a good shot, that the critters all heard about my reputation, and when they'd see me a-coming, they'd just surrender. Sometimes I'd come home with a whole bag full of meat on my shoulders—enough to feed my family for a whole month—on account of so many animules would surrender."

Source: activated-storytellers.com

ABOUT THE AUTHOR

Davy Crockett (1786-1836) was a well-known American frontiersman from Tennessee. He served in the army and later in Congress. Often known as "America's first comic superman," he was a skilled storyteller whose tall tales captured the spirit of the western frontier. He died at the Alamo in 1836, fighting for Texan independence.

ker-plunk!—the sound something very heavy makes when it falls

ring-tailed roarer—(*19th-century dialect*) a wild and uncontrollable boy

snappin' turtle—(*dialect*) a type of turtle with very powerful jaws.

wee—little; young

critter—(*dialect*) creature

keen—very good at something

animule—(*dialect*) an animal

Pro or Con?

Read...

- Two short persuasive essays from *New York Times Upfront*— "Should Students Be Allowed to Use Cell Phones?" and "Should the U.S. Halt Human Space Flight?"

Link to Literature

- An entertaining persuasive speech about the wooden baseball bat, delivered by a member of Congress to the U.S. House of Representatives.

Objectives:

Reading:

- Reading persuasive essays on two different issues
- Strategies: Reading like a writer, questioning the author
- Literature: Responding to a persuasive speech

Writing:

- Writing a persuasive essay
- Arguing and supporting a position
- Writing strong conclusions

Vocabulary:

- Recognizing word families: Related nouns, verbs, and adjectives
- Learning adjectives that describe peoples' attitudes and reactions

Listening/Speaking:

- Listening to a discussion of an issue
- Stating an opinion
- Presenting arguments to support your opinion
- Giving a short speech to persuade

Grammar:

- Using factual and contrary-to-fact conditionals

Spelling:

- Spelling words that end in *-ant* and *-ent*.

BEFORE YOU BEGIN

Talk with your classmates.

1. Look at the picture. What seems to be happening? Write a caption for the picture.
2. Could this happen at your school? Why or why not?
3. Should cell phones be allowed at school? What do you think?

A CONNECTING TO YOUR LIFE

1. Tuning In Should parents get report cards? Is this a good idea—or a crazy one? Listen to the conversation. As you listen, write down the main points each person makes. What do you think?

2. Talking It Over We are often asked to take a stand on interesting questions. Complete the survey below. Check (✓) your answer.

	Definitely Yes	Probably	Probably Not	Definitely No
1. Are school uniforms a good idea?	❑	❑	❑	❑
2. Do sports stars make too much money?	❑	❑	❑	❑
3. Should music CDs warn kids about bad language on the cover?	❑	❑	❑	❑
4. Should college be free?	❑	❑	❑	❑
5. Should the voting age be lowered to 16?	❑	❑	❑	❑
6. Should schools ban junk food?	❑	❑	❑	❑
7. Should pets be cloned?	❑	❑	❑	❑
8. Should student athletes be suspended if their parents misbehave at games?	❑	❑	❑	❑

Choose a question to which you answered "definitely yes." Find a classmate who answered "definitely no" to the same question. Then list three reasons explaining why each of you answered the way you did.

Read the title. What do you think the unit is probably about? Check (✓) the correct answer.

_____ 1. It's about topics or questions most people agree on.

_____ 2. It's about topics or questions people often disagree about.

_____ 3. It's about topics or questions that are silly.

_____ 4. It's about professional athletes.

B GETTING READY TO READ

1. Learning New Words. Read the definitions below.

argument—a reason you give to explain why something is right or wrong.

issue—a subject or problem people discuss

position—an opinion about a subject

valid—based on strong reasons or facts

independent—able to do things on your own

prohibit—to make something illegal or against the rules.

susceptible—likely to be affected by a problem or illness

confiscate—to take away someone's property, usually as punishment

Complete the sentences with the vocabulary words above.

1. Should students have to take PE? That is an interesting _____ *issue* _____ to debate.
2. Juan's _____ is that students should not have to take PE.
3. What are the _____ for and against making students take PE?
4. Many schools _____ skateboards on campus.
5. If students wear hats in class, the teacher _____ them.
6. Having a job often makes students feel more _____.
7. Lori is _____ to colds in the winter.
8. We listened to the debate. Both speakers made several _____ points.

2. Talking It Over Work in groups of three or four to complete the chart below. Think of three important school rules and discuss why the rules are important.

School Rules	Why These Rules Are Important
1.	1.
2.	2.
3.	3.

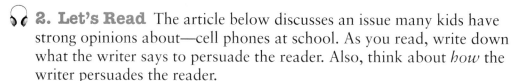

C READING TO LEARN   **Persuasive Essays**

1. Before You Read Many people own a cell phone. Why are cell phones so popular? Share with a partner.

2. Let's Read The article below discusses an issue many kids have strong opinions about—cell phones at school. As you read, write down what the writer says to persuade the reader. Also, think about *how* the writer persuades the reader.

Should Students Be Allowed to Use Cell Phones in School?
*As cell phones **pop up** everywhere, some schools are prohibiting them. But others say the phones are useful in emergencies.*

YES

1   I found out about the terrorist attacks of Sept. 11 while I was in school. My first impulse was to pull my cell phone out of my purse to call my father. He was in Boston at the time, and when I heard that two of the hijacked planes came from Boston's Logan Airport, I was terrified. Never have I let out such a great sigh of relief as when I heard his voice on the other end of the line.

2   More than 40 percent of American teenagers own cell phones. For many of them their use is a specific one: safety. We teenagers are getting more independent as we get older, and often the only way that our parents can be immediately assured of our whereabouts and our safety is by calling us.

3   Nevertheless, some school boards have decided that cell phones do more harm than good. School officials say that along with causing distractions in an educational environment, cell phones have also been used in illicit acts such as drug dealing and making bomb threats. Still, why should thousands have to pay the price for the illegal actions of a few? If a phone rings during class, the teacher has every right to confiscate it, but to forbid the very presence of cell phones is ridiculous.

Remember that the prefix il– means "not."

pop up—to appear suddenly

impulse—a sudden desire to do something

whereabouts—the area where someone is

distraction—something that takes your attention from what you are doing

illicit—against the law or what most people approve of

presence—the fact that someone or something is in a particular place

4   We are living in unpredictable times. The horrors of Sept. 11 and the Columbine school massacre ought to show us that we are highly susceptible to danger, even during the school day. The only way that we can have the slightest peace of mind is by knowing that our loved ones are just a call away, and no school board should take that away from us.

—Nneka Ufere, 16
Atlanta, Georgia

So do the prefixes *un-*, *in-*, and *im-*

NO

1   Everyone has seen it before: You're taking notes in class, and all of a sudden, you hear it—a [cell phone] starts blaring out of someone's backpack over the silence of an attentive class. Chaos ensues, and the teacher struggles to re-establish order. My position on this issue might be unpopular with my peers, but I do not believe cell phones should be allowed in school.

2   To begin with, I would like to ask what use cell phones are in a school environment in the first place. Chances are, most students are in the same building, and can find each other at lunch or after school. If a student needed urgently to reach a classmate, the calling student would probably tell a teacher first anyway. I understand the need for a channel of communication between students and parents, but really. Parents can easily call the office and get directed to the student's classroom. Those little black phones that the teachers have in their rooms? Believe it or not, they do serve a purpose.

3   The most common argument for cell phones in school is that if you play a sport, you'll need a cell phone to get a ride home; and this is actually a valid point. For this one purpose, I think coaches should be able to sign permission slips that allow cell phones at school if they are turned off and not brought out of the student's backpack.

To begin with is a transitional phrase that helps organize ideas in order of importance. "First," "more important," "most important," and "Last" can also be used to arrange ideas from most to least important.

4   I believe my concerns about cell phones in school are shared by most teachers and school administrators. The bottom line is that cell phones are distracting in school, and in all cases but possibly one, entirely unnecessary in a learning environment.

—Eric Huntley, 15
Saginaw, Michigan

Source: *The New York Times Upfront Online*

massacre—the killing of many people at one time, in one place

peace of mind—when you are not worried

blare—to make a loud, unpleasant noise

ensue—to happen as a result of something

peers—other students your age

channel (of communication)—a way (of communicating)

administrator—a person who is in charge of the school

3. Unlocking Meaning

❶ **Finding the Main Idea** These sentences state Nneka's arguments for allowing cell phones. Write the number of the paragraph or paragraphs where each argument is found.

Paragraph(s)

   2   1. When teenagers have cell phones, parents worry about them less.

_____ 2. Teenagers need cell phones mostly for safety reasons.

_____ 3. Banning cell phones won't stop teenagers from misusing them.

_____ 4. All teenagers shouldn't have to suffer because a few teenagers misuse cell phones.

These sentences state Eric's arguments for not allowing cell phones. Write the number of the paragraph or paragraphs where each argument is found.

Paragraph(s)

_____ 1. In certain situations, cell phones should perhaps be allowed at school.

_____ 2. Cell phones disrupt the classroom and get in the way of learning.

_____ 3. Students don't need cell phones while they are at school.

❷ **Finding Details** Choose the best ending for each sentence. Check (✓) the correct answer.

1. Nneka mentions September 11 as an example of a time when...

      _____a. she was scared because she didn't have her cell phone.

      _____b. her cell phone allowed her to talk with her family.

      _____c. her cell phone was useless.

      _____d. her cell phone allowed her to save lives.

2. According to Nneka, more than 40 million teenagers...

      _____a. own cell phones.

      _____b. misuse their cell phones.

      _____c. keep their cell phones in their backpacks.

      _____d. have had their cell phones confiscated by a teacher.

3. Nneka admits that some teenagers misuse their cell phones by...

      _____a. using them to cheat on tests.

      _____b. calling their parents at work.

      _____c. using their phones in class to talk to friends.

      _____d. doing things that are illegal.

4. Eric says that his position on cell phones might be unpopular because he knows that...

      _____a. lots of kids agree with him.

      _____b. lots of kids disagree with him.

      _____c. cell phones are cool.

      _____d. most teachers carry cell phones, too.

5. Eric argues that if parents really need to communicate with their child, they can...

      _____a. call another student's cell phone.

      _____b. call the main office at school.

      _____c. ask the police to come to school.

      _____d. have their child call them on a pay phone.

6. Eric would allow students who play sports to have cell phones if...

      _____a. they were top atheletes.

      _____b. they were kept in the coach's office.

      _____c. they were turned off and left in their backpacks.

      _____d. they lived a long way from school.

❸ **Think about It** Work with a partner. Think of one more argument for each position—pro and con. Write down your arguments. Then share with classmates.

❹ **Before You Move On** Work with your classmates. Imagine you are the principal. Write rules for the use of cell phones at your school.

D WORD WORK

1. Word Detective Words that look alike, or almost alike, often belong to the same word family. Read the list of nouns. For each noun, write a verb that is in the same word family. You can use your dictionary.

1. education _____educate_____
2. prediction _____
3. permission _____
4. communication _____
5. satisfaction _____
6. distraction _____

2. Word Study Members of a word family look similar, but they have different but related meanings and different jobs in a sentence.

NOUN	VERB	ADJECTIVE
distraction	distract	distracting
Cell phones can be a distraction.	*Cell phones can distract others.*	*Cell phones can be very distracting.*

SPELLING :
To do this activity, go to page 238.
■ ■ ■

3. Word Play Work with a partner. Complete the word family chart below. You can use your dictionary. Then choose a word family and write a sentence for each word in the family.

Noun	Verb	Adjective
economy	*economize*	economical
expense	expend	
exploration		exploratory
law		legal
	embarrass	embarrassing

E GRAMMAR · Factual and Contrary-to-Fact Conditionals

1. Listen Up Listen to these sentences. Point your thumb up 👍 if the sentence sounds correct. Point your thumb down 👎 if it sounds wrong.

👍👎 1. If I didn't have homework, I would go to the movies.

👍👎 3. If I hadn't overslept, I wouldn't have been late to class.

👍👎 2. If you hadn't talked in class, you will not have detention.

👍👎 4. We'll go swimming tomorrow if the weather is nice.

2. Learn the Rule Learn the rules for using conditionals. Then do Activity 1 again.

FACTUAL AND CONTRARY-TO-FACT CONDITIONALS

1. When a sentence expresses a real (factual) situation in the present, use the present tense in both clauses. When the sentence refers to the future, use the present tense in the "if" clause and the future tense in the main clause:
   Present: *If a cell phone <u>rings</u> in class, the teacher <u>is</u> right to take it away.*
   Future: *If Maria <u>gets</u> an A on next week's test, she <u>will shout</u> for joy.*

2. When a sentence expresses an *imaginary* (often unlikely) situation in the present or future, use the past tense in the "if" clause and *would* or *could* in the main clause. Use *were* instead of *was* for this type of conditional:
   If a student <u>needed</u> to call someone, he <u>could</u> use the phone in the office.   *If it <u>were</u> warmer, I <u>would</u> go swimming.*

3. When a sentence refers to the past, use the past perfect tense in the "if" clause and *would/could have* + past participle in the main clause:
   If a student <u>had needed</u> to call someone, he <u>could have used</u> the phone in the office.
   If Juan <u>had earned</u> enough money last summer, he <u>would have bought</u> his own car.

3. Practice the Rule Complete the sentences below with the verbs in parentheses.

1. If I study hard, I (get) _____ an A.
2. If I (study) _____ harder, I would get more A's.
3. If I had studied harder, I (get) _____ an A.
4. I would not have been angry if you (tell) _____ me the truth.
5. If my brother were in this situation, he (know) _____ what to do.
6. If I knew how to cook, I (make) _____ a fancy dinner.

F BRIDGE TO WRITING   **Persuasive Essays**

1. Before You Read Read the paragraph below about the space shuttle Columbia accident. Talk with a partner. Is it a good idea for humans to go into space?

> History is filled with tales of brave men and women traveling into the unknown. Explorers have always taken risks in the search for knowledge. The world was reminded of those risks on February 1. Seven courageous explorers lost their lives as the space shuttle Columbia was returning to Earth. After traveling 6 million miles through space, Columbia broke apart minutes before it was due to land. Some people are now asking if humans need to go into space.
>
> Source: "A Terrible Loss," *TIME For Kids*, Feb. 14, 2003, Vol. 8, No. 7, p. 2. Used with permission from TIME For Kids Magazine.

the unknown—a place no one has ever been

explorer—someone who travels to places no one has ever visited

risk—the chance something bad might happen

courageous—brave

2. Words to Know Read the sentences below. Try to guess what the underlined words mean.

   a. Juan never wastes time. He uses his time <u>efficiently</u>.
   b. Lourdes spends very little money. She lives very <u>economically</u>.
   c. My computer is always crashing! It is <u>unreliable</u>.
   d. Stefan looks for information on the Internet to write his reports. It's an excellent tool for doing <u>research</u>.
   e. Apollo XII landed on the moon in 1968. It was a daring <u>expedition</u> into space.
   f. Angela is running for mayor because she has many ideas for our city. She has a <u>vision</u> for the future.
   g. Computers have caused a <u>revolution</u> in how we live.

Match each word or phrase on the left with the correct definition on the right.

1. efficiently   a. dependable
2. economically   b. the study of a subject to learn new facts
3. reliable   c. an idea or dream of what could happen
4. research   d. a complete change in how we do things
5. expedition   e. using time, money, or effort effectively
6. vision   f. a carefully planned trip, especially to a
7. revolution   dangerous place
                          g. carefully, without wasting money

2. Let's Read Read two sides of the debate about human space flight. As you read, write down three questions you would ask each writer if you had the chance.

READING STRATEGY
Questioning the Author:
When you read a persuasive essay, challenge the writer's ideas by asking questions. This will help you understand better what the writer is trying to say.

Should the U.S. Halt Human Space Flight?

YES

1   Anything we want to do in space we can do more efficiently, more economically, and more safely with automated spacecraft than with astronauts. It is now impractical and unsafe to send humans into space.

2   The space shuttle is the world's most sophisticated launch vehicle, but also the most expensive, the most fragile, and the most unreliable. Seven astronauts died in the Columbia accident and another seven died when the Challenger exploded in 1986. The shuttle will never achieve the vision of sending humans to Mars.

3   Whatever we are trying to do in space costs 10 times as much if we send astronauts along for the ride. The primary mission of all human space flight is getting the crew back alive, and so we burden the spacecraft with life-support equipment and we limit where it can go. Nothing that astronauts contribute can compensate for the weight and safety penalties imposed as a result.

4   For the past 25 years, NASA has been trying to re-create the golden age of the Apollo program, which aimed to send a man to the moon—and did so six times between 1969 and 1972. Since then, the world has undergone a computer revolution. Technology has taken over many human activities on Earth, from manufacturing to surgery. Only the space program—supposedly the center of our most visionary science and technology—remains wedded to the idea of keeping people in jobs that machines do better. NASA should turn its considerable talents to developing a safer and more reliable launch vehicle. Until then, we should stop risking people's lives by sending them into space.

—Alex Roland History professor, Duke University

automated—done or controlled by machines

sophisticated—well made, complicated

launch vehicle—something that takes people into space

fragile—very delicate

primary mission—the most important purpose

life-support—what is needed to keep a person alive

compensate—to make up for a lack in another area

penalty—a disadvantage or drawback

imposed—caused by a situation

golden age—the time when something was at its best

manufacturing—making things in factories

remain wedded to—to be unwilling to change something

considerable—large and noticeable

Space Shuttle Columbia

The National Air and Space Administration (NASA) is the government agency, or office, that runs the space program.

NO

1   I was a teacher when men first landed on the moon in 1969, and I remember how it moved my students and this country. It is now more than 30 years since the last American left the surface of the moon and returned to Earth. And we haven't ventured outward since then. That's 30 years too long! America's human space-flight program is adrift, with no clear vision or goals beyond the completion of the International Space Station.

2   I want NASA to establish a phased series of goals over the next 20 years, including human visits to asteroids that cross the Earth's orbit, establishing a research and living facility for humans on the moon, and human expeditions to the surface of Mars and its moons. Astronauts are key to this expanded exploration.

3   An astronaut is today's Christopher Columbus, who sailed into the unknown and discovered the Americas. The knowledge we gain from having actual people exploring can never be replaced by robots. Our ability to send humans into space and have them return gives us amazing information about ourselves and our universe. Robots are useful, but humans can do things that robots can't.

4   The real obstacle we face in overcoming the drift in the nation's human space-flight program is not technological and it's not financial—it's the lack of commitment to get started.

5   The lesson from the Columbia accident is not that humans don't belong in space. Instead, we should honor the memory of the lost astronauts by pushing our exploration of space further.

—Congressman Nick Lampson
Democrat of Texas

Source: *The New York Times Upfront Online*

venture—to risk going somewhere or doing something new

adrift—not having any plan or purpose

phased series—actions that are planned and happen one after the other

asteroid—one of a group of small planets between Jupiter and Mars

facility—a place used for a particular purpose

robot—a machine that moves and does the work of humans

universe—all of space, including the planets and stars

obstacle—something that gets in the way

overcome—to succeed in dealing with a problem

drift—a movement somewhere without a plan or purpose

financial—related to money

commitment—a promise to do something

3. Making Content Connections You have read two articles about two interesting issues, or topics. Work with a partner. Compare the articles. Complete the chart below.

	Cell Phones	Humans in Space
What is the question?	*Should students be allowed to use cell phones in school?*	
What are the reasons for answering *yes*?		
What are the reasons for answering *no*?		
What is your own answer to the question? Do you agree?		

4. Expanding Your Vocabulary

❶ Adjectives can describe ideas. Cross out the word in each row that *does not* go with the word in capital letters. You can use your dictionary.

RIDICULOUS   absurd   senseless   ~~ingenious~~   preposterous
INTELLIGENT   brilliant   idiotic   masterly   shrewd
RECKLESS   foolhardy   reasonable   irresponsible   careless
ORIGINAL   creative   imaginative   laughable   innovative
UNWISE   imprudent   foolproof   short-sighted   ill-advised

❷ Write five sentences, using one word from each row in the sentences.

EXAMPLE: *Banning junk food at school is an absurd idea.*

G WRITING CLINIC

1. Think about It When you want to *persuade* someone, you want them to...

☐ have the same opinion as you do

☐ follow your directions or instructions

☐ like you a lot

2. Focus on Organization

❶ Look again at Eric's essay on cell phones.

Eric's introduction identifies the issue and states his thesis statement, or position.

Eric's knows his audience. He admits how many students will feel!

In the body of his essay, Eric provides reasons *for his position and support for each reasons. Eric states the* most important reason *first, in his introduction.*

He tries to appeal to the common sense of his readers.

Eric is smart. He anticipates, or tries to figure out, what others might argue... and then offers his own idea.

Eric's conclusion summarizes his arguments. *He also identifies* experts, *or people with special knowledge on the subject, who agree with his position.*

Should Students Be Allowed to Use Cell Phones at School?

NO.

1   Everyone has seen it before: You're taking notes in class, and all of a sudden, you hear it—a [cell phone] starts blaring out of someone's backpack over the silence of an attentive class. Chaos ensues, and the teacher struggles to re-establish order. My position on this issue might be unpopular with my peers, but I do not believe cell phones should be allowed in school.

2   To begin with, I would like to ask what use cell phones are in a school environment in the first place. Chances are, most students are in the same building, and can find each other at lunch or after school. If a student needed urgently to reach a classmate, the calling student would probably tell a teacher first anyway. I understand the need for a channel of communication between students and parents, but really. Parents can easily call the office and get directed to the student's classroom. Those little black phones that the teachers have in their rooms? Believe it or not, they do serve a purpose.

3   The most common argument for cell phones in school is that if you play a sport, you'll need a cell phone to get a ride home; and this is actually a valid point. For this one purpose, I think coaches should be able to sign permission slips that allow cell phones at school if they are turned off and not brought out of the student's backpack.

4   I believe my concerns about cell phones in school are shared by most teachers and school administrators. The bottom line is that cell phones are distracting in school, and in all cases but possibly one, entirely unnecessary in a learning environment.

❷ Join the debate on cell phones! What is your position? Work with a partner who agrees with you. Make a chart like the one on this page.

- Write a sentence that states your position
- Think of one reason for your position
- Provide support for your reason

Here is the chart that Graciela and Suanna made.

Our position: Students should be able to use cell phones at school.
One reason: You might have a family emergency.
Support:
  Personal experience or example: Last year, Graciela's father was in an accident. Her mother was able to call her.
  Fact: Very few students misuse their cell phones. Only two students in the school were sent to the office for misusing cell phones last year.
  What experts say: Our principal says that cell phones are OK as long as the ringer is turned off.

3. Focus on Style Your conclusion wraps up your ideas rather than simply coming to a sudden stop. An effective conclusion helps you accomplish your purpose.

❶ Reread Nneka's conclusion, or final paragraph. How does her conclusion strengthen her essay?

- It gives the reader good advice.
- It attempts once more to convince the reader.
- It shows the reader how smart she is.

❷ Work with a partner. Reread Eric's essay *except for the last paragraph*. Write a new conclusion for Eric's essay. Try one or more of these ideas:

- Restate Eric's position and summarize the reasons he gives.
- Restate his ideas a different way, using synonyms.
- Encourage the reader to take action.
- Try one more time, in a new way, to convince the reader.
- Leave your reader with an idea that makes him or her think.

❸ Now look at Eric's final paragraph. Compare the conclusion you have written with Eric's. Which is more effective?

H WRITER'S WORKSHOP   Persuasive Essays

Imagine that you have been invited to write a "pro" or a "con" essay for the *New York Times Upfront* magazine.

1. Getting It Out

❶ Choose an issue that interests you. Here are two possible issues.

Should Classrooms Have Security Cameras?

1   In recent years, preventing violence in schools has become a top concern among U.S. lawmakers, educators, parents, and students. Now the school district of Biloxi, Mississippi, has installed surveillance cameras in all classrooms. Many students and teachers say that the cameras help them feel safer. Others believe they are an invasion of privacy.
2   Biloxi officials say that the cameras have led to fewer fights and disruptions, freeing students to concentrate on their schoolwork.
3   But critics charge that a camera surveillance system creates an environment of suspicion and mistrust.
4   What do you think?

Should Schools Require Kids to Volunteer?

1   Lots of teens in the U.S. help out in their communities. Some hold car washes or bake sales to raise money for worthy causes. Others volunteer in soup kitchens or hospitals.
2   Most of these efforts come from the heart. But many schools now require kids to perform community service. In Maryland it's even the law—a student must log 75 hours of community service in order to graduate from high school.
3   What do you think? Should schools require kids to volunteer?

Source: Junior Scholastic

---

surveillance—the activity of watching a person or place that could be related to a crime

invasion of privacy—a situation where people try to find out about your personal life when it is none of their business

suspicion—a lack of trust

mistrust—a feeling among people that they do not trust each other

worthy—good enough to deserve attention or support

come from the heart—to be sincere

Here are some other questions to think about—

- Should schools be year-round?
- Should a student athlete be suspended if the parents misbehave at a game?
- Should people clone their pets?
- Should music CDs warn kids about bad language on the cover?

❷ Choose an issue, or question. Brainstorm reasons that people might have a "pro" opinion or a "con" opinion. Make a chart like the one below.

OUR QUESTION: *Should schools have a four-day week?*

Pro	Con
It would save money on lights and heating.	

❸ Choose a position on the issue. List three reasons for your position. Then think about what you might say to support each reason.

- Think of your own experiences
- Talk to other kids or adults to get their ideas
- Learn more about the issue

My position: *School should be year-round.*

Reason #1: *Students learn more.*

Reason #2: *Students who fall behind can catch up easier.*

Reason #3: *Students who play sports can practice all year long.*

- Students don't forget what they have learned.
- Less time needed for review
- Test scores are higher.

-
-
-

-
-
-

CONNECT TO THE WEB. CHECK IT OUT:

Read what others have to say about important issues—

www.scholastic.com/juniorscholastic

http://teacher.scholastic.com/upfront/

http://teenink.com

2. Getting It Down

❶ Make an outline like the one below.

Title (Question): *Should School Be Year-Round*

Introduction (the issue/my position): _____

Body:

   Reason 1: *Kids learn more*

   Support: *Higher test scores* .

   Reason 2: *Kids who fall behind can catch up easier*

   Support: _____

   Reason 3: *Sports practice and games*

   Support: _____

Conclusion: _____

❷ Draft your essay. Here is part of what Tomás wrote.

Tomás identifies the issue and states his position in the introduction.

He gives three reasons.

And he supports each reason with facts and examples.

Should School Be Year-Round?

This year, our school switched from a traditional calendar to a year-round calendar. We still go to school for the same number of days, but instead of having a long summer vacation, we take a three week break after each ten-week session. A lot of kids moan and groan, but I believe that year-round schools are a great idea!

The biggest advantage to year-round schools is that kids learn more. When kids have a long summer vacation, they forget what they've learned. Teachers spend as much as six weeks on review each fall, according to our principal. Also, research shows that test scores are higher in year-round schools.

Another advantage is that kids who fall behind have time to catch up during our three-week break. Our school has an "inter-session" tutoring program for these kids, and teachers say that the program is working.

Finally, kids who are on sports teams especially like year-round schools because they practice and play games all year long and...

MINI-LESSON

Using Commas after Adverbs:

Place a comma after an adverb that introduces a sentence:

Also, research shows that test scores are higher.

Finally, kids on sports teams like year-round schools.

∎∎∎

3. Getting It Right Look carefully at your review. Use this guide to revise your paragraph.

Ask Yourself	How to Check	How to Revise
1. Does my introduction grab the attention of the reader?	Do I describe an experience my reader can relate to?	Write about a personal experience that supports your position.
2. Does my introduction identify the issue and state my position?	Put a star (★) in front of the thesis statement.	Add a sentence that clearly states your opinion.
3. Do I provide at least three reasons and do I support each reason?	Circle each reason and underline the support you provide.	Add reasons and/or support. Add facts, examples, or the words of experts.
4. Does my conclusion summarize my arguments?	Put a wavy line under your summary.	Add words, as needed, to summarize each reason.

4. Presenting It Instead of reading your essay aloud, give a persuasive speech, based on your essay.

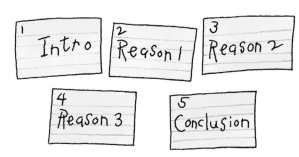

❶ Write your main ideas on note cards. Use just words and phrases. Put your introduction on one card. Put each reason—and the support for it—on a separate card. Put your conclusion on another card.

❷ Practice giving your speech to a friend, using your note cards. Use your note cards to help you remember, but try not to read from the cards.

❸ Begin by telling your audience, in everyday words, what the issue is and why it is important to you. Clearly state your position on the issue.

❹ Present each reason and support it. Present the most important reason first. Use natural, everyday language. Look at your audience—not at your note cards—and speak in a voice everyone can hear.

❺ Conclude by summarizing your arguments. Then ask for feedback.

1. On Assignment Hold a "four corners" debate.

❶ As a class, decide on an interesting issue to debate. Here are some possibilities.

- There should be separate schools for boys and girls.
- Students should wear uniforms to school.
- Junk food should be banned at school.

❷ Hang four signs up in your classroom, one in each corner. They should read "Strongly Agree," "Agree," "Disagree," and "Strongly Disagree." Decide how you feel *personally* about the issue. Then go to the appropriate corner.

a.

Strongly Agree

b.

Agree

c.

DISAGREE
Disagree

d.

Strongly Disagree

❸ Talk in your corner group.

- Choose a person to take notes.
- Discuss the reasons you strongly agree, agree, disagree or strongly agree.
- Decide who will share your ideas with the class.

❹ After listening to each group share its ideas, decide if you want to stay in the same corner or move to another corner! Be ready to share why you moved—or stayed in the same corner.

One-Minute Speech to the U.S. House of Representatives Congressman Richard Durbin

SHARED READING Read the "one-minute" speech by former Congressman Richard Durbin, which he delivered in 1989.*

LET'S TALK Answer the questions.

1. What are Congressman Durbin's purposes in making the speech? Use your own words.

2. What points does he make?

3. How does he feel about baseball? What makes his speech entertaining? Find examples.

*The U.S. House of Representatives has a rule that allows members to make one-minute speeches on any topic.

> The congressman has fun with words. The word "ping dinger" sounds like the noise an aluminum baseball bat makes when it hits a ball.

ABOUT THE AUTHOR

Richard Durbin has served as senator from Illinois since 1996. He was first elected to the House of Representatives in 1982. His interests include improving health care, protecting consumers, and gun safety. He is an avid baseball fan.

1 Mr. Speaker, I rise to condemn the desecration of a great American symbol. No, I am not referring to flag burning; I am referring to the baseball bat.

2 Several experts tell us that the wooden baseball bat is doomed to extinction, that major league baseball players will soon be standing at home plate with aluminum bats in their hands.

3 Are we willing to hear the crack of a bat replaced by the dinky ping? Are we ready to see the Louisville Slugger replaced by the aluminum ping dinger? Is nothing sacred?

4 Please do not tell me that wooden bats are too expensive, when players who cannot hit their weight are being paid more money than the President of the United States.

5 Please do not try to sell me on the notion that these metal clubs will make better hitters.

6 I do not want to hear about saving trees. Any tree in America would gladly give its life for the glory of a day at home plate.

7 I do not know if it will take a constitutional amendment to keep our baseball traditions alive, but if we forsake the great Americana of broken-bat singles and pine tar, we will have certainly lost our way as a nation.

---

desecration—the action of damaging something that is highly respected

extinction—the state of no longer existing, like dinosaurs

dinky ping—a little "pinging" sound

Louisville Slugger—a type of baseball bat

constitutional amendment—an addition to the U.S. Constitution

pine tar—a substance used to help the batter hold the bat

I Can't Put It Down!

Read...

- Teens' book reviews of *Harry Potter and the Sorcerer's Stone, When I Was Puerto Rican,* and *Seabiscuit.*

Link to Literature

- "Books Fall Open," a poem by David McCord.

Objectives:

Reading:

- Reading book reviews: Fiction and nonfiction
- Recognizing elements of fiction (including plot) and nonfiction
- Strategies: Overviewing, sorting out main ideas from details
- Literature: Responding to a poem

Writing:

- Reviewing a fiction or a nonfiction book
- Varying the beginning of sentences
- Writing a tongue-in-cheek book review

Vocabulary:

- Recognizing word families
- Learning names of types of fiction novels

Listening/Speaking:

- Listening for main ideas and details
- Discussing a favorite book
- Presenting a book review to classmates

Grammar:

- Using the present perfect tense

Spelling:

- Spelling words that end in *–able* or *–ible*

BEFORE YOU BEGIN

Talk with your classmates.

1. Look at the pictures. What are Shawna and her mother both reading?
2. Looking at the cover, what can you tell about the story?
3. Make up a short story about Leo and his flying bicycle and tell it to a partner.

A CONNECTING TO YOUR LIFE

1. Tuning In. Listen to Juan and Lori describe their favorite books. Guess which book each one is talking about.

a.

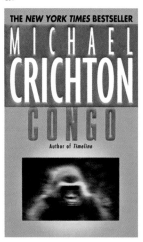

b.

c.

ANNE FRANK — THE DIARY OF A YOUNG GIRL

d.

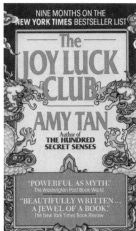

e.

f.

2. Talking It Over If you could read one of these books, which one would you read? List three reasons, then share with a partner.

Read the title. What do you think the unit is probably about? Check (✓) the correct answer.

_____ 1. It's about books that students had to read in school.

_____ 2. It's about books that students loved to read.

_____ 3. It's about books that were made into movies.

_____ 4. It's about very long books.

B GETTING READY TO READ

1. Learning New Words Read the sentences below. Try to guess what the underlined words mean.

1. Juan likes to read books with imaginary stories. His favorite <u>novel</u> is *Harry Potter and the Sorcerer's Stone*.

2. Ron Weasley and Hermione Granger are people in the Harry Potter books. They are important <u>characters</u> in each book.

3. The book is mostly about Harry Potter. He is the book's <u>protagonist</u>.

4. Harry Potter books are about imaginary people, places, and events. They are works of <u>fiction</u>.

5. J.K. Rowling has written several books all about Harry Potter. *The Sorcerer's Stone* was the first book in the <u>series</u>.

6. The *Chamber of Secrets* was written after *The Sorcerer's Stone*. It continues the Harry Potter story. It is a <u>sequel</u> to the first book.

Match each word or phrase on the left with the correct definition on the right.

1. novel   a. the main person in a book, play, or movie
2. character   b. books and stories that are not about real events
3. protagonist   c. a set of books with the same characters or on the same subject
4. fiction   d. a long written story with characters and events
5. series   e. a book that continues the story of a previous book
6. sequel   f. a person in a book, play, or movie

2. Talking It Over Work in groups of three or four. Think of a story everyone has read. Then complete the chart below.

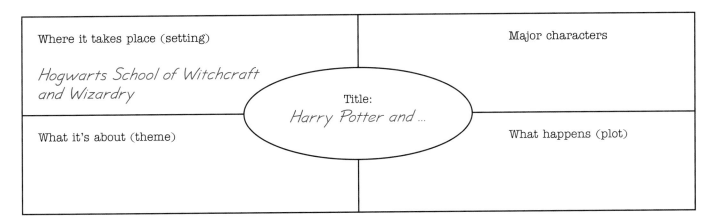

Where it takes place (setting)		Major characters
Hogwarts School of Witchcraft and Wizardry	Title: *Harry Potter and …*	
What it's about (theme)		What happens (plot)

C READING TO LEARN

1. Before You Read Look at the book cover. What kind of boy do you think Harry Potter is?

2. Let's Read Read the first sentence of each paragraph in each review. What do both girls think of the book? As you read, write down the reasons that each girl gives for her opinion of the book.

READING STRATEGY

Overviewing:
You can get an idea of what an article is about by reading the first sentence of each paragraph.

Harry Potter and the Sorcerer's Stone by J. K. Rowling

Review by Cassandra A. – Scituate, MA

1   The new craze that has captured the hearts of children everywhere has recently drawn me in, too. I'm not referring to Pokemon but to J. K. Rowling's premier children's novel, *Harry Potter and the Sorcerer's Stone.* It reeled me in at the first chapter and kept my undivided attention through to the astonishing and creative conclusion. Overall, I was very impressed by Rowling's talent at creating a captivating child's dream world.

2   As a young girl, I enjoyed novels full of zest, and Rowling's work is certainly full of that. Her unforgettable characters and delightful ability to create a fantasy world that is easy to picture are two of the best characteristics of her writing. Harry, an orphan child of two witches who, as a baby, remarkably saved himself from being murdered by the evil Lord Voldemort, makes a fabulous protagonist. When, at age 12, Harry starts receiving mysterious letters from another realm, the story really comes to life. The reader is transported to the magical, mystical world of Hogwarts, the school for young witches. Harry encounters many challenges he must

Use the picture of Harry to predict what a sorcerer is. As you read, see if your prediction is correct.

Notice how the present tense is used to summarize the plot.

---

craze—a popular new fad or fashion

Pokemon—a popular video game and cartoon

reel in—to pull in or interest someone

zest—a feeling of enjoyment

orphan—a child whose parents have both died

realm—a place ruled by a king or queen

mystical—having magical powers people cannot understand

overcome to live up to his role as the powerful warlock who defeated Voldemort as a mere baby. It is not a surprise that Voldemort returns to take his revenge. Rowling creates an imaginary world that would attract any kid, filled with magic, dragons, secrets, friendship, evil adversaries and, of course, the boy who conquers it all.

3   *Harry Potter and the Sorcerer's Stone* is well worth the short time it takes to read it. You will be thoroughly entertained and also probably gain a great deal of useful creative-writing knowledge. I am looking forward to reading the two sequels. I recommend this book to anyone who wants to take a thoroughly enjoyable trip into a child's world of imagination, adventure, and the heroism of one small boy.

Source: teenink.com

warlock—a boy or man with magical powers

take revenge—to do something to punish or harm someone who has harmed you

adversary—an enemy

Harry Potter and the Sorcerer's Stone

Review by Gina B. – Chesterland, OH

1   Adults seem to have lost their ability to imagine. Reading fiction should be a way to regain a bit of imagination and the childlike aura of giddy expectation, but not many authors have successfully created books that children and adults can enjoy.

2   The world of fiction changed when J. K. Rowling released *Harry Potter and the Sorcerer's Stone*, the first installment of the Harry Potter series. This book introduces the shy, quirky Harry Potter, whose life has not been easy. He lives with his Uncle Vernon, Aunt Petunia and cousin Dudley, none of whom even come close to being civil to him.

aura—a feeling other people get about someone

giddy expectation—a happy, excited sense that something good will happen

installment—one of several parts of a story that are published at different times

quirky—unusual or strange

civil—polite, but not quite friendly

What is most amazing ... tells you that a really important idea is coming.

You can guess the meaning of "adversity" by reading the whole paragraph. What does the word mean?

The Little Prince is a famous children's book that many adults enjoy because of its message.

3   Potter's life changes when he receives a very special letter, and so he comes to attend Hogwarts School of Witchcraft and Wizardry. While his adventures will entertain, his self-discovery will sober readers.

4   What is most amazing, however, is how connected readers are to Potter and the other characters, like his wisecracking sidekick Ron or the kindhearted headmaster Professor Dumbledore. Why can an adult relate to this book that is about children? It is simple: If an adult has a memory of her childhood, then *Harry Potter and the Sorcerer's Stone* will bring it back.

5   Harry Potter intrigues the young for a completely different reason. Children can easily relate to other children, and even more so to those who have some adversity to overcome—for all children have problems. It may be a bully, their appearance, or even something as serious as the death of a parent, but children (and adults) can work out some of their own issues by reading this enchanting story.

6   The language Rowling uses does not talk down to her young audience, and so she is able to keep her adult readers. True, the vocabulary she uses may force some to pick up a dictionary, but no one has complained.

7   Her tone is what makes Rowling famous. Reading Harry Potter and the Sorcerer's Stone is like talking to a childhood friend you haven't seen for years. It is, without a doubt, the most definitive piece of children's literature since *The Little Prince* by Antoine de Saint-Exupéry.

8   *Harry Potter and the Chamber of Secrets* and *Harry Potter and the Prisoner of Azkaban*, the second and third books, do not quite live up to *Harry Potter and the Sorcerer's Stone* in terms of its universal appeal, but are nonetheless worth reading.

9   Rowling, once a struggling single mother, wrote *Harry Potter and the Sorcerer's Stone* when she was down on her luck and out of money. Now she is one of the most sought-after creative fiction writers and is raking in the profits, which just goes to show that the adult who holds onto her inner child—her imagination—wins the race!

Source: teenink.com

sober—to make someone feel serious

wisecracking—always making funny, slightly unkind remarks

bully—a person who picks on people who are weaker

talk down to—to talk to someone as if you are smarter or more important than they are

tone—the general feeling of a piece of writing

definitive—considered the best and unable to be improved

universal appeal—the quality of being liked by everyone

rake in the profits—to make a lot of money

3. Unlocking Meaning

❶ Finding the Main Idea Compare the two reviews. Complete the chart below.

	Cassandra	Gina
What is the reviewer's reaction to, or opinion about, the book?		
What are the main reasons each reviewer likes the book?		

❷ Finding Details Read the sentences below. If the information is found in Cassandra's review, write C. If the information is found in Gina's review, write G. If the information is in both reviews, write B.

   B   1. The author of *Harry Potter and the Sorcerer's Stone* is J. K. Rowling.

_____   2. Rowling wrote her first Harry Potter book when she was a poor, single mother.

_____   3. *The Sorcerer's Stone* is the first in a series of Harry Potter books.

_____   4. Harry attends Hogwarts School, a school for witches.

_____   5. When he was just a baby, Harry saved himself from Lord Voldemort.

_____   6. Harry's best friend is named Ron.

_____   7. *The Little Prince* is similar to *Harry Potter* because it appeals both to children and adults.

_____   8. *The Chamber of Secrets* and *The Prisoner of Azkaban* are sequels to *The Sorcerer's Stone*.

❸ Think about It Talk with a partner. Which review most makes you want to read *Harry Potter and the Sorcerer's Stone?* Write three reasons, then share with classmates.

❹ Before You Move On Think of a book you enjoyed. Write a magazine advertisement that makes others want to read the book.

D WORD WORK

1. Word Detective Words that look alike can sometimes belong to the same word family. Read the list of verbs. For each verb, write a *noun* that is in the same family. You can used your dictionary.

a. enjoy   *enjoyment* _____

b. differ   _____

c. define   _____

d. astonish   _____

e. disappoint   _____

f. expect   _____

2. Word Study Members of a word family look similar, but they have related but different meanings and different jobs in a sentence.

VERB	NOUN	ADJECTIVE
enchant	enchantment	enchanting
Harry Potter enchants both children and adults.	*Harry Potter lives in a world of enchantment.*	*Harry Potter lives in an enchanting world.*

— SPELLING: —
To do this activity, go to page 239.

3. Word Play Work with a partner. Complete the word family chart. Use your dictionary for help. Then choose two word families and write a sentence for each word in the families.

Verb	Noun	Adjective
introduce	*introduction*	introductory
	discovery	discovered
connect		connected
	imagination	imaginative
create	creation	
entertain		entertaining

E GRAMMAR   Present Perfect Tense

1. Listen Up Listen to these sentences. Point your thumb up 👍 if the sentence sounds correct. Point your thumb down 👎 if it sounds wrong.

👍 👎 1. I saw five movies so far this year.

👍 👎 2. We have already eaten dinner.

👍 👎 3. The weather has been terrible yesterday.

👍 👎 4. It has rained all day.

2. Learn the Rule Learn how and when to use the present perfect tense. Then do Activity 1 again.

THE PRESENT PERFECT TENSE
The present perfect is used to express several time-related situations:
1. An event that happened at an unspecified or unknown time in the past. If you know the exact time it happened in the past, use the simple past tense.
Juan has read two Harry Potter books.   *Mr. Chan has moved into a new apartment.*
2. A repeated activity or experience in the past that will probably happen again
Juan has visited Mexico many times.   *Dad has made pancakes every Sunday morning since he was a teenager.*
3. A situation that began in the past and still continues into the present
Harry's life has not been easy. (It's still not easy.)   *I haven't seen Maria for many months. (I still haven't seen her.)*

3. Practice the Rule Each of these sentences is in the wrong tense. Rewrite each sentence using the correct tense.

1. Juan was in New York since last Wednesday.
2. I have been to Disneyland last year.
3. I love my grandparents' house. They lived there for 20 years.
4. Stop bothering me! I didn't finish my homework yet.
5. Lori has taken science in the seventh grade.
6. My father is late. He didn't come home from work yet.
7. My parents have gotten married when they were both eighteen.

F BRIDGE TO WRITING

Response to Literature: Book Reviews

1. Before You Read Think of a work of nonfiction—a book about real people, things, facts, or events—that you enjoyed reading. Share with a partner.

2. Words to Know Read the sentences in the box. Try to guess what the underlined words mean. Then read the numbered sentences. Choose the sentence from the box that goes with each numbered sentence and write it on the line.

> Everyone admires her <u>spirit</u>.
> Many people have read her <u>autobiography</u>.
> Her description is filled with <u>sensory detail</u>.
> It is a powerful <u>medium</u> of communication.
> She explains things with <u>clarity</u>.
> She has <u>insights</u> into how her students learn.
> She has a strong sense of cultural <u>identity</u>.

1. Television reaches into the homes of hundreds of millions of people each day. *It is a powerful medium of communication.*

2. Lori is proud of her culture and her heritage.
   _____

3. Maria wrote a description of the sights and sounds of her city.
   _____

4. It is always easy to understand Ms. Johnson's lessons.
   _____

5. Juan's grandmother is fighting to conquer her illness.
   _____

6. Mr. Perez is an experienced teacher.
   _____

7. Miss Jane Pittman told many interesting stories about her own life.
   _____

3. Let's Read Read two reviews of non-fiction books. Ask yourself—based on each review—which book you would rather read.

---READING STRATEGY---
Sorting Out Main Ideas From Details:
Use a two-column note-taking chart to help you see the difference between main ideas and supporting details. This will help you understand the organization of a reading better.
■ ■ ■

When I Was Puerto Rican
by Esmeralda Santiago

Review by Jennifer K. —Saratoga, CA

1 This is a delightfully woven story of immense passion and unconquerable spirit. In this extraordinary autobiography, Santiago, an immigrant to New York from rural Puerto Rico, tells the story of her trials and triumphs, defeats and heartaches in a unique concoction of vivid sensory detail.

2 Santiago grew up in what her mami calls "savage" conditions, dutifully obeying her parents as they constantly move. Her greatest relocation occurred when a "metal bird" flew her, her mother and two of her siblings to the rough city of New York.

3 This book is the account of the maturing of an extraordinary woman who overcame barriers formed by hate, prejudice, cultural differences, puberty and heartaches to rise triumphantly.

4 Using words as her medium, Santiago paints a beautiful picture of her life. I smelled the spices and herbs emanating from the special Puerto Rican dishes her mami prepared. Mesmerized, I watched as her abuela delicately stitched her needlework. We laughed together and cried together, and I allowed my spirit to run free with hers. Santiago writes with such clarity and fierceness that it is impossible for any person not to see, feel and understand what she went through in her remarkable journey.

5 Santiago's unique style is easy to follow. When I read the book, I was immediately hooked and could not stop until I read the last word. The stories are interesting and full of insight. She addresses fears and trials of all people. I especially related to her conflicts with her cultural identity. Anyone who has lived in between two cultures can relate to her story. Santiago wrote: "When I returned to Puerto Rico after living in New York for seven years, I was told I was no longer Puerto Rican ... In writing the book I wanted to get back to that feeling of Puertoricanness I had before I came here. Its title reflects who I was then, and asks, who am I today?"

6 Santiago's book provides a sense of hope. She is transformed from a confused and frightened child into a spirited woman full of courage and hope. Her success in life—acceptance into New York City's High School of Performing Arts and graduating from Harvard with highest honors—proves she is capable of achieving her dreams.

> The word dutifully contains the smaller word "duty". What does the word mean?

> Jennifer uses the Spanish words mami (mom) and abuela (grandmother) to help "paint the picture."

> Esmeralda makes up a new word to mean "what it is like to be Puerto Rican" by adding the suffix -ness.

unconquerable—not able to be defeated

concoction—an unusual mixture

sibling—a brother or sister

account—a description of things that have happened

puberty—the time when you change from a child to an adult

emanate from—to come from or out of something

mesmerized—totally interested in or absorbed by something

transformed—changed into something different

7 Santiago proves her strong will and the courage to do whatever it takes are adequate tools to break barriers and achieve the impossible. Through her book, she shares the remarkable journey of her life and shines hope into all of our hearts.

Seabiscuit by Laura Hillenbrand

Review by Rachel S. —Williamsville, NY

1 When I received this as a present, I was skeptical. But don't let the name of this true story fool you—you're in for a great ride with Seabiscuit.

2 Trainer Tom Smith, who understands horses better than people, first sees Seabiscuit as a mean, underfed horse at the lowest levels of racing. But when jockey Red Pollard signs on with Smith and owner Charles Howard, they forge an unforgettable trio that turns Seabiscuit into a star. Seabiscuit attracted crowds comparable to those of today's Superbowls, shattered over a dozen track records and had more media coverage in 1938 than FDR or Hitler.

3 The reader is carried on Seabiscuit's back through four years of disappointment, horror and exuberance. The book is not suspenseful, but it is exciting. I always wanted to know what would happen next, who Seabiscuit would race, if he would win or lose, and if Pollard would be injured again.

4 Hillenbrand's descriptions of the races had me jumping around in my seat. This was the first book I read about racing, and not only did I enjoy it, but I learned a lot.

5 Tom Smith's constant war with the press and Pollard's wickedly crude humor put a sharp edge on an already amazing book. There are no words to describe the experiences and emotions this book depicts. It is impossible not to fall in love with the raggedy horse who became one of the fastest and most famous racing horses of all time.

Here is an example of imagery.

Source: teenink.com

underfed—not having enough to eat

forge—to form a strong relationship

comparable to—similar to

shatter—to break something completely

exuberance—a feeling of being very happy and full of energy

crude—offensive or rude

raggedy—in poor condition

3. Making Content Connections

❶ Work with a partner. Compare the two reviews. Complete the chart below.

	When I Was Puerto Rican (Jennifer's review)	**Seabiscuit** (Rachel's review)
What is the book about?		
What is each reviewer's opinion of the book?		
What reasons does each reviewer give for liking the book?		

❷ Discuss which review each of you likes best. Make a list of reasons.

4. Expanding Your Vocabulary

Read the definitions of different types of novels below. Then make a list of the last three to five novels you have read or movies you have seen in English or another language. What type were they? Compare your lists in small groups.

adventure—a type of story that involves survival in a strange, often harsh or exotic, land

fantasy—a type of story often set in imaginary lands where the natural and the supernatural meet. The hero often has magical powers.

horror—a type of story that involves the unknown, the forbidden, or the supernatural. A horror story can frighten the reader and often involves ghosts, werewolves, and vampires.

mystery—a story about a crime, often a murder. A detective usually solves the crime.

science fiction—a type of story that takes place on another planet or in the future

thriller—a story with an exciting plot and lots of action and suspense. The hero usually defeats an evil villain.

western—a story about life on America's frontier, usually involving conflict between cowboys and outlaws

young adult—a type of story with a main character in the 12 to 16 age range

G WRITING CLINIC

Response to Literature: Book Reviews

1. Think about It Why do you think many people like to read book reviews? Discuss your ideas with a partner.

2. Focus on Organization

❶ Take another look at excerpts from Jennifer's review of *When I Was Puerto Rican.*

The **adjectives** *Jennifer uses tells us her reaction, or what she thinks of the book.*

Jennifer begins by introducing and summarizing the book. Her introduction grabs your attention.

Jennifer gives us **reasons** *for liking the book.*

She provides lots of **details** *and* **examples.**

Jennifer ends her review by summarizing the book and her reaction to it.

When I Was Puerto Rican by Esmeralda Santiago

1 This is a delightfully woven story of immense passion and unconquerable spirit. In this extraordinary autobiography, Santiago, an immigrant to New York from rural Puerto Rico, tells the story of her trials and triumphs, defeats and heartaches in a unique concoction of vivid sensory detail ...

2 This book is the account of the maturing of an extraordinary woman who overcame barriers formed by hate, prejudice, cultural differences, puberty and heartaches to rise triumphantly ...

3 Using words as her medium, Santiago paints a beautiful picture of her life. I smelled the spices and herbs emanating from the special Puerto Rican dishes her mami prepared. ... We laughed together and cried together, and I allowed my spirit to run free with hers. Santiago writes with such clarity and fierceness that it is impossible for any person not to see, feel and understand what she went through in her remarkable journey.

4 Santiago's unique style is easy to follow. When I read the book, I was immediately hooked and could not stop until I read the last word. The stories are interesting and full of insight. ... Anyone who has lived in-between two cultures can relate to her story. Santiago wrote: "When I returned to Puerto Rico after living in New York for seven years, I was told I was no longer Puerto Rican ... In writing the book I wanted to get back to that feeling of Puertoricanness I had before I came here. Its title reflects who I was then, and asks, who am I today?"

5 Santiago's book provides a sense of hope. She is transformed from a confused and frightened child into a spirited woman full of courage and hope. Her success in life—acceptance into New York City's High School of Performing Arts and graduating from Harvard with highest honors—proves she is capable of achieving her dreams.

6 Santiago proves her strong will and the courage to do whatever it takes are adequate tools to break barriers and achieve the impossible. Through her book, she shares the remarkable journey of her life and shines hope into all of our hearts.

❷ Book reviews give reasons and details that support the writer's reaction. Look carefully at Jennifer's review. How does she support each reason? Make your own chart, based on the one below. Use your own words to complete it.

Reasons	Details
Her descriptions are incredible.	*She describes what it was like growing up. Her words make you think you were there.*
Her stories show insight.	
Her stories inspire the reader.	

3. Focus on Style

❶ Good writers vary the way they begin sentences. One way to do this is to move part of the sentence to the beginning:

> Santiago paints a beautiful picture of her life, using words as her medium.
> Using words as her medium, Santiago paints a beautiful picture of her life.

❷ Rewrite each sentence by reversing the beginning and the end. Write your answers on a separate piece of paper.

EXAMPLE: *Chipper shows that he's happy by wagging his tail.*
By wagging his tail, Chipper shows that he's happy.

1. Maria walks to school to save money.
2. Stefan must do his homework if he wants to improve his grade.
3. The president reveals new details about his childhood in his new autobiography.
4. She touches our hearts through her book.
5. Mr. Perez enjoyed books about sports as a boy.
6. The story gets really exciting when another dead body is found.
7. Juan stays healthy by eating lots of fruits and vegetables.
8. Brian cleaned his room to please his mother.

H **WRITER'S WORKSHOP**   Response to Literature: Book Reviews

Write your own review of a favorite book. Perhaps you will send your work to teenink.com, a Web site with student-written reviews.

1. Getting It Out

❶ Choose a book to review. It might be fiction or nonfiction. Select a book that...

- you have already read
- you had a strong reaction to—either positive or negative
- other kids might like to read

❷ Begin by thinking about why you liked or disliked the book. Brainstorm your ideas.

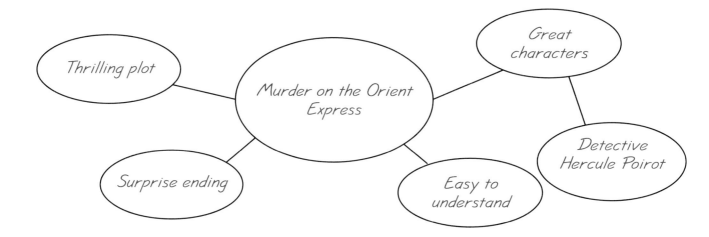

❸ Think about the possible elements, or aspects, of the book you might focus on. Here are some possible elements:

If the book is fiction...	If the book is nonfiction...
• where it takes place (setting) • the characters (how interesting or real they are) • what happens in the story (plot) • how believable, exciting, suspenseful, funny, etc. the plot is • how the story ends (climax) • the language the author uses • the style of the writing • the words and thoughts of the charaters • the theme, or meanings in the story • how the story affected you • what you "learned about life" from reading the book	• what it is about (topic or subject) • how the book is organized—the main parts or chapters • how interesting it is to read • how the book connects to your life • how informative the book is • the style of writing • how easy it is to understand • how the book helped you • what you learned from the book

❹ Evaluate the book. Focus on just two or three major reasons you like or dislike the book. Gather support—details, examples, and quotes. Organize your ideas by making a chart like the one below.

Book: Murder on the Orient Express	
Reasons	*Details, examples, quoted passages, etc.*
exotic setting	*unusual, "exotic" setting...takes place on the Orient Express...trapped in the snowy mountains on the way to Istanbul, Turkey*
interesting characters	*Detective Poirot ... good sense of humor ... conceited ... brilliant mind*
complicated plot	*lots of twists and turns*

WRITING

2. Getting It Down

❶ Plan and organize your review. Make an outline like the one below.

1. Introduction

   Grabbing the reader's attention: *Do you like murder, mystery, suspense ...*

   Summary of the book or story: *Poirot is on the Orient Express. A gangster is murdered.*

   My reaction: *A spine-tingling adventure ... !*

2. Body

   Reason 1: *Exotic setting*

   Details: *Orient Express ... snowbound*

   Reason 2: *Interesting characters*

   Details: *Poirot–vain, brilliant*

3. Conclusion:

   Summary of my reaction:

❷ Draft your review. Here is Hamed's review.

— MINI-LESSON —
Formatting Titles:
The titles of books are usually italicized in print. In handwriting, they are underlined:

Murder on the Orient Express.

■■■

He summarizes the plot.

He gives reasons for his reaction and supports each reason.

His conclusion summarizes his opinion and makes a recommendation to the reader.

He states his reaction to the book.

> Murder on the Orient Express
> by Agatha Christie
>
> Do you like murder, mystery, suspense, and excitement? If you do, you'll want to read Murder on the Orient Express. Written in a lighthearted manner, this thrilling mystery takes the reader on a spine-tingling adventure on a train called the Orient Express.
>
> While Detective Poirot is traveling on the Orient Express, a gangster is murdered and it is up to Poirot to find the killer. Poirot, aware that the killer is still on the train, begins interviewing the passengers. Each has an alibi and seems unlikely to have committed the vicious crime, but with Poirot's brainpower, there is a surprising conclusion.
>
> Agatha Christie entertains the reader with delightful and memorable characters–especially Detective Poirot. He is vain and conceited. He's also observant. One of the things he's observed over the years is that he's the world's greatest detective ...
>
> Christie tells an intricate story. As she adds each detail and clue, readers find themselves trying to play detective. The plot is filled with twists, turns, and sudden revelations ...
>
> My only disappointment was that the book ended too soon! I was so eager to find out who did the murder that I read it very quickly. I recommend this book to anyone who enjoys mysteries. So grab a copy and see if you can discover the killer on the Orient Express!

3. Getting It Right Look carefully at your review. Use this guide to revise your review.

Ask Yourself	How to Check	How to Revise
1. Does my introduction grab the reader's attention?	(Circle) the words that are meant to get the reader interested.	Begin your introduction with a question to the reader or with a scene from the book.
2. Do I summarize the book for my reader?	Put a star (★) before the sentence or paragraph that summarizes the book.	If the book is fiction, tell where the story takes place, who the main characters are, and what happens to them. If the book is non-fiction, tell the most important ideas.
3. Do I state my reaction to the book?	Underline the sentence that tells your reaction.	Tell the reader, overall, why you liked or disliked the book.
4. Do I provide reasons for my reaction? Do I support each reason?	Put a number next to each reason. Put a wavy line under the sentences that support each reason.	Give more reasons or add examples or quoted words from the book that support each reason.
5. Does my conclusion summarize my reaction and offer a recommendation to the reader?	Put a check mark (✔) next to the sentence that summarizes your reaction and an ✗ next to your recommendation.	Work on your conclusion so that the reader really wants to read (or avoid) the book.

4. Presenting It Share your book review with your classmates.

❶ Introduce the book to your classmates. Provide a short summary. Let others know your reaction to the book.

❷ Read the rest of your review aloud. Read slowly and speak clearly.

❸ Ask for feedback from your classmates.

You really got my attention, right from the start!
You did a great job summarizing the plot!

I can hardly wait to read the book!

1. On Assignment

We say that Jennifer's review is "tongue-in-cheek" because she writes as though she is *serious*, but her review is really meant as a joke!

❶ Read Jennifer's review of *The Commonwealth of Massachusetts Driver's License Manual*. Find examples of Jennifer's "tongue-in-cheek" style.

Driver's License Manual
Jennifer C., Holyoke, MA

I recently read a wonderfully informative piece of literature: *The Commonwealth of Massachusetts Driver's License Manual* by Jerold A. Gnazzo, William F. Weld, and Thomas C. Rapone. I like this book in that it aided me in attaining my driver's permit, and will aid me as I prepare for my license.

Most of this book is numbingly boring and predictable; there's no action at all. Pages 58 through 75, however, offer exciting, educational questions and answers that are fun for the whole family. Question number 26 on page 63 just sent shivers up my spine: "Q: How do you sober up quickly? A: You can't." It's mind-blowing.

I wholeheartedly suggest this manual for anyone applying for a driver's permit or license, or persons in need of something with which to squish pesky spiders. Considering this book as an option when in search of actual reading material, however, is strongly discouraged.

Source: teenink.com

sober up—to recover from the effects of drinking alcohol

wholeheartedly—completely

mind-blowing—(*informal*) making you feel very surprised

❷ Work with a partner. Write your own "tongue-in-cheek" review of a book. Consider reviewing...

the phone book.

the student handbook.

a grammar book.

the dictionary.

a textbook.

your choice!

❸ Read your review aloud to your classmates.

Books Fall Open
David McCord

Read the poem, "Books Fall Open." As you read, think about whether you feel the same way about reading as the poet does.

LET'S TALK Answer the questions.

1. According to the poet, what do books do for you? Use your own words.
2. Can you think of a book you've read that has taken you "where you've never been"?
3. Have you ever read a book that changed your way of thinking?
4. Does the poem make you want to read the book? Why or why not?

ABOUT THE AUTHOR

Poet David McCord was born in New York City in 1897. He is best remembered for the poetry he wrote for children. Of the more than 40 books McCord wrote or edited, his most popular include *Far and Few: Rhymes of the Never Was and Always Is* (1952), *All Day Long: Fifty Rhymes of the Never Was and Always Is* (1966), and *One at a Time* (1978). He died in 1997.

Books fall open,
you fall in,
delighted where
you've never been;
hear voices not once
heard before,
reach world on world
through door on door;
find unexpected
keys to things
locked up beyond
imaginings.
What might you be,
perhaps become,
because one book
is somewhere? Some
wise delver into
wisdom, wit,
and wherewithal
has written it.
True books will venture,
dare you out,
whisper secrets,
maybe shout
across the gloom
to you in need,
who hanker for
a book to read.

Source: *One at a Time* by David McCord

delver—someone who is searching for information

wherewithal—the money and ability to do something

venture—to risk going somewhere

gloom—darkness

hanker—to have a strong desire for something

Unit **10**

The Perfect Storm

Read...

- Illuminating articles about nature's beasts: Ferocious hurricanes and vicious killer waves.

Link to Literature

- An old Hawaiian myth about the fire goddess Pele.

Objectives:

Reading:

- Reading articles that explain a process
- Recognizing the organization of cause and effect writing
- Strategies: Flagging new information and questions, summarizing
- Literature: Responding to a myth

Writing:

- Feature articles: Explaining a process
- Writing powerful introductions
- Making a labeled flow diagram

Vocabulary:

- Recognizing common Greek and Latin prefixes
- Learning earth science terminology

Listening/Speaking:

- Listening to a firsthand account of a disaster
- Giving an oral presentation
- Listening to an oral presentation and taking notes

Grammar:

- Using clause connectors

Spelling:

- Spelling words with *s* or *c*

BEFORE YOU BEGIN

Talk with your classmates.

1. Look at the photograph. What appears to be happening?
2. Imagine that this photograph were on the front page of your local newspaper. Write a headline.
3. Have you or has a family member ever experienced a frightening natural disaster? What sights and sounds can you recall? Share with your classmates.

A CONNECTING TO YOUR LIFE

1. Tuning In Listen to Mieko describe a tsunami. Take notes as you listen. Then write a short paragraph that describes this terrifying event.

2. Talking It Over

Match each picture of a natural disaster to its cause from the list below.

a. an underwater earthquake

b. a release of stress in the earth's crust

c. a change in temperature or movement

d. a buildup of gases and molten rock

e. a severe rainstorm or hurricane

f. high winds that spin around rising warm air

_b_ 1. Earthquake

_____ 2. Avalanche

_____ 3. Flooding

_____ 4. Tornado

_____ 5. Tsunami

_____ 6. Volcanic eruption

Talk with a partner. Which disaster would be the most terrifying to live through? Why? List three reasons.

Read the title of this unit. What do you think the unit is probably about? Check (✓) the correct answer.

_____ 1. It's about how events of nature are caused.

_____ 2. It's about why rain is important.

_____ 3. It's about the ideal type of rainstorm.

_____ 4. It's about the frightening experiences people have had.

B GETTING READY TO READ

1. Learning New Words Read each sentence. Try to guess what the underlined words mean. Then read the numbered sentences. Choose the sentence from the box that goes with each numbered sentence and write it on the line.

They are all in the <u>tropics</u>.

A <u>degree</u> is equal to 1/360 of the distance around the outside.

<u>Latitude</u> gives the location of a place north or south of the equator.

It has a very simple <u>molecule</u>.

They are located in the northern <u>hemisphere</u>.

It has a very damaging effect on the <u>environment</u>.

It moves in a <u>clockwise</u> direction.

1. North America and Europe are north of the equator.
   They are located in the northern hemisphere.

2. You tighten a screw by turning it to the right.
   _____

3. Pollution ruins the air and water.
   _____

4. Venezuela, Nigeria, and Indonesia are all located along the equator.
   _____

5. A circle is divided into equal units of measure.
   _____

6. The surface of a globe is divided by imaginary lines.
   _____

7. Water is made of two atoms of hydrogen and one of oxygen.
   _____

2. Talking It Over Work with a partner. There are many processes—related events that happen again and again in the same order—in nature. What does the flow diagram tell us about the water cycle? Write at least five complete sentences based on the diagram. Be ready to share your sentences.

EXAMPLE: *The sun's heat makes ocean water evaporate.*

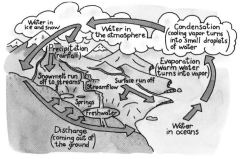

For help with making process diagrams, complete Mini-Unit Part B on page 224.

C READING TO LEARN

Feature Articles: Explaining a Process

1. Before You Read Talk with a partner. Look at the visuals on this page and the next page. What do they tell you about hurricanes?

READING STRATEGY
Flagging New Information:
Jot notes in the margin or on sticky notes to record your thoughts as you read.

2. Let's Read You are going to learn about how hurricanes develop, or are formed. Make a process diagram to help you understand how they develop. As you read, record your reactions to each paragraph on sticky notes or in the margin.

✓ = I knew this already.
☆ = This is new information.
? = I don't understand this.

Warm, Windy, and Wet

1   Dark clouds fill the sky. It's the middle of the day, but it looks like night. The wind howls. Rain pelts the ground so hard that holes form in the mud. Tree branches bend and crack. Whole trees are uprooted and crash down. Store windows break. The roofs of buildings sail through the air. Electric wires send out sparks and dangle dangerously from broken utility poles. Signs fly across highways. Water floods the streets. It is no time to be outdoors, that's for sure. You are in the middle of a hurricane—the largest, fiercest storm of nature. How do these storms start, and how can we protect ourselves from them? Read on.

2   Why don't hurricanes ever form in Kansas, Oregon, or Vermont? Why do they always start in the tropics? It's because an area of the tropics that lies between five degrees north and five degrees south latitude of the equator has ocean waters of at least 80°F (27°C) over a large area. This is the first ingredient needed for a hurricane to develop. The second ingredient is wind blowing westward off the continent of Africa.

3   Hurricanes feed on warm moist air rising from the Atlantic Ocean. Warm water evaporates (turns into water vapor) from the surface of the ocean and rises. As it rises, it cools. This causes the water vapor to condense (to become more dense or compact), forming cumulonimbus clouds. A cumulonimbus is a very large thunderstorm cloud that extends to a great height. Once these clouds form, the first stage of hurricane development has begun.

uproot—to pull a plant and its roots out of the ground

dangle—to hang

vapor—very tiny droplets of water that float in the air

Tropical Disturbance

4   When water condenses to form clouds, it releases its heat into the air. As air warms, it rises and is drawn into the cloud columns. The cloud columns grow larger and higher. Evaporation and condensation continue in a cycle. This creates a pattern of wind that circulates around a center (similar to that of water going down a drain). As the moving column of air encounters more clouds, it becomes a cluster of thunderstorm clouds, called a tropical disturbance.

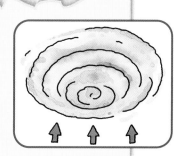

Tropical Depression

5   When winds inside the cloud mass reach between 25 and 38 mph (40 and 61 kph), weather forecasters call the storm a tropical depression. How do the wind speeds get this fast? Air molecules are in constant motion, pushing and pulling when striking objects. This push-or-pull force is called air pressure. At higher elevations, there are fewer air molecules, and air pressure decreases. Air flows from high- to low-pressure regions. This flow of air is called wind. The greater the difference between the high- and low-pressure areas, the stronger the wind. As the thunderstorm grows higher and wider, the air at the top of the cloud column is cooling and creating an area of low pressure. This area of low pressure draws more and more warm air up toward it. Winds in the storm cloud column spin faster and faster, whipping around in a giant circular motion.

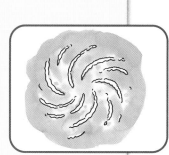

The earth's rotation affects how objects (like airplanes) move across the earth. In the northern hemisphere, they move toward the right. In the southern hemisphere, they move left. Winds and ocean currents behave the same way.

Tropical Storm

6   When wind speeds reach 39 mph (63 kph), the tropical depression is termed a tropical storm. This occurs when the winds move faster and begin twisting and turning around the eye, or calm center, of the storm. Wind direction is counterclockwise (west to east) in the northern hemisphere and clockwise (east to west) in the southern hemisphere. This is known as the Coriolis effect.

column—something with a long, narrow shape

circulate—to move around in a circle

cluster—a group of things of the same kind that are very close together

mass—a large amount of something

mph—(*abbreviation*) miles per hour

kph—(*abbreviation*) kilometers per hour

forecaster—someone who says what is likely to happen, especially with the weather

elevation—the height of something above sea level

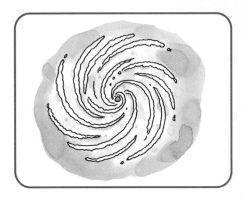

Hurricane

7   When wind speeds top 74 mph (119 kph), the tropical storm is officially called a hurricane. Now the storm is not only high (over 50,000 feet, or 15,200 meters) but also wide (about 125 miles, or 201 kilometers, in diameter). When air at the top of the spiraling column merges with high-altitude air currents that do not change much in direction and speed, the air goes in the opposite direction. However, some of the now-dry air is forced back down the center of the spiral—the relative calm of the eye. The eye, a low-pressure region, is anywhere from 5 to 30 miles (8 to 48 kilometers) wide. Trade winds from the western coast of Africa propel the hurricane's track from east to west.

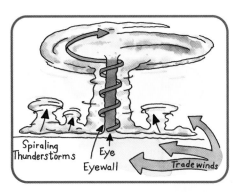

The End

8   Hurricanes weaken when they encounter land because warm ocean waters are no longer available to fuel their growth. Over land, during a time period of no more than two or three days, wind speeds decrease, so the storm is no longer called a hurricane. However, hurricanes can cause a lot of trouble before they turn out to sea again, or before they die out entirely.

Source: "Warm, Windy, and Wet," *Kids Discover*, June 2002, and "How a Hurricane Develops," *Kids Discover*, June 2002. Copyright © 2004 Kids Discover Magazine used by permission. All rights reserved.

spiraling—moving up or down, winding around a central point

altitude—the height of something above sea level or the earth's surface

encounter—to meet

3. Unlocking Meaning

❶ Finding the Main Idea Which statement tells what the selection is mostly about? Check (✔) the correct answer.

1. _____ how destructive hurricanes can be
2. _____ why hurricanes are so dangerous
3. _____ how hurricanes develop
4. _____ where hurricanes usually happen

❷ Finding Details

1. Put these stages of a hurricane in the correct order.

_____ Winds in the storm cloud begin swirling in a circular pattern.

_____ The storm is 10 miles high and 125 miles wide as it moves quickly toward land.

__/__ Cumulonimbus clouds form when warm water evaporates and condenses.

_____ The hurricane reaches land and wind speeds decrease, then stop blowing.

_____ Winds begin turning around the eye of the storm.

2. Read the sentences below. If the sentence is true, write *T*. If the sentence is false, write *F*.

__T__ 1. Hurricanes are the most powerful storms of nature.

_____ 2. They usually occur in the Midwestern states.

_____ 3. Hurricanes form over the icy waters of the ocean.

_____ 4. Clouds are formed when water evaporates, forming vapor.

_____ 5. Air pressure decreases at higher elevations because there are fewer air molecules.

_____ 6. A tropical storm is more dangerous than a hurricane.

❸ Think about It The storms that form in the Atlantic Ocean are called hurricanes, while similar storms in the Pacific Ocean are called typhoons. Typhoons are usually stronger than hurricanes.

Talk in a small group. Why do you think typhoons are so much more powerful than hurricanes?

❹ Before You Move On Work with a partner. Imagine that you live in an area where there are hurricanes. Make a list of safety ideas.

D WORD WORK

1. Word Detective Match each word on the left with the definition on the right. Think of other words that begin with the same prefix to help you guess.

1. **counter**attack   a. after high school
2. **con**current   b. a ship that can travel under water
3. **ex**hale   c. happening at the same time
4. **pre**view   d. to breathe out
5. **post**secondary   e. to go after an enemy that has struck you
6. **sub**marine   f. to see something before other people do

2. Word Study Prefixes change the meaning of words. Below are some common prefixes and their meanings.

PREFIX	MEANING	EXAMPLE
counter-	opposite, against	**counter**clockwise
con-	together, with	**con**dense
e-, ex-	out (of)	**e**vaporate, **ex**pel
pre-	before	**pre**cede
post-	after, later	**post**pone
sub-	under	**sub**terranean

> **SPELLING:**
> To do this activity, go to page 239.

3. Word Play Complete the sentences using the correct prefix.

| counter- | con- | ex-, e- |
| post- | sub- | pre- |

1. Everybody ___*con*gregates on the front steps after school.
2. After college, Juan plans to earn a _____ graduate degree.
3. When I watch foreign movies, I always read the _____ titles.
4. Tiffany bought a pair of _____ shrunk jeans. They're really tight.
5. Punishing a child too harshly can be _____ productive.
6. The ointment is for _____ ternal use only. You put it on your skin.

E GRAMMAR

1. Listen Up Listen to these sentences. Point your thumb up 👍 if the sentence sounds correct. Point your thumb down 👎 if it sounds wrong.

👍 👎 1. Juan is outgoing, while Carlos is shy.

👍 👎 2. Rosa hasn't talked to him unless he moved away.

👍 👎 3. Before you study hard, you'll get an A.

👍 👎 4. Whenever I eat strawberries, I get hives.

2. Learn the Rule Clause connectors help connect two related ideas. Learn more about the jobs clause connectors do, then do Activity 1 again.

CLAUSE CONNECTORS

1. Some clause connectors can express ideas about *time*—
   Connectors: before, as, as soon as, after, when, while, until, whenever, since
   Example: *Hurricanes can cause a lot of trouble <u>before</u> they die out.*

2. Some clause connectors can express *cause and effect*—
   Connectors: because, since, now that
   Example: *Hurricanes form in the tropics <u>because</u> the ocean waters are very warm.*

3. Some clause connectors can express a *condition or result*—
   Connectors: when, if, unless, even if, whenever, once
   Example: *<u>When</u> water condenses to form clouds, it releases its heat into the air.*

4. Some clause connectors can express *contrast or contradiction*—
   Connectors: while, whereas, although, even though, despite, though
   Example: *<u>Although</u> storms can turn into hurricanes, that does not always happen.*

3. Practice the Rule Circle the correct clause connector to complete each sentence.

1. Juan went to bed (if/(as soon as)) he finished his homework.
2. (Although/Because) she has a sore throat, Lori will stay home from school today.
3. Some dogs are friendly, (while/since) others are vicious.
4. You can't drive (unless/although) you have a license.
5. (Although/When) it rains, I like to stay indoors.
6. Stefan arrived at the party (because/before) anyone else got there.

Tsunami damage in Kodiak, Alaska, in 1964. This tsunami caused the death of 21 people and $30 million damage to property in and around Kodiak.

F BRIDGE TO WRITING   Feature Articles: Explaining a Process

1. Before You Read Look again at the photo at the left. What do you think causes a tsunami? Share with a partner.

2. Words to Know Read the sentences below. Try to guess what the underlined words mean.

a. In outer space, things float in the air. That's because there is no <u>gravity</u>.

b. Diet and exercise help your body grow strong. This is a basic <u>principle</u> of good health.

c. Earthquakes occur regularly in California. The entire state is an earthquake <u>zone</u>.

d. Our mountain cabin collapsed last winter. The <u>pressure</u> of the snowload caused the roof to give way.

e. In 1811, an huge earthquake shook the Mississippi Valley. The <u>energy</u> from the quake caused church bells to ring in Boston, nearly 1,000 miles away!

f. Stefan likes to hunt for things at the beach. He uses a metal <u>detector</u> to help him find coins buried in the sand.

g. Juan's father ran out of gas. He didn't notice that the gas <u>gauge</u> said *E*, or empty!

Match each word or phrase on the left with the correct definition on the right.

1. gravity
2. principle
3. zone
4. pressure
5. energy
6. detector
7. gauge

a. a part of an area that has something special about it

b. the physical force that something gives off

c. a piece of equipment that finds or measures something

d. the force that makes objects fall to the ground when dropped

e. an instrument used to measure the amount or size of something

f. force or weight that is put on something

g. a rule that explains the way something works

3. Let's Read Now read about why tsunamis occur. Once again, practice using sticky notes to help you think deeply about what you are reading and learning.

For help with reading and summarizing, complete Mini-Unit Part C on page 230.

READING STRATEGY
Summarizing:
Use your own words to summarize what you are reading. This will help you see if you understand.

In Rolls Nature's Killer Wave

1   What kind of monster is this? It rises from the sea and speeds across it as fast as a jet airplane. On reaching land, it can suck all the water out of a harbor. Then the fearsome creature may grow more than a hundred feet tall and flatten whole villages, tossing around buildings, boats, railroad cars—even, sadly, people.

2   This sea monster is a tsunami (tsoo-NAH-mee). That's the Japanese word for "great harbor wave." Though sometimes called "tidal waves," tsunamis have nothing to do with tides—the everyday rise and fall of the sea. Tides are caused by the pull of gravity between the moon and the earth. Tsunamis are not created by wind, either, as ordinary waves are.

3   Usually an undersea earthquake starts a tsunami's waves rolling across the ocean. If you've ever tossed a pebble into a pond, then watched ripples spread out over the surface, you've seen this principle at work. About four out of five tsunamis take place within an area known as the "Ring of Fire," a zone of frequent earthquakes and volcanic eruptions roughly matching the borders of the Pacific Ocean. The area includes the coasts of North and South America and Japan, as well as islands in the western Pacific.

4   Along the ring's edges, tectonic plates, or gigantic slabs of the earth's crust, grind together. But sometimes the plates get stuck. Huge pressure builds up as they struggle to move past each other. To picture this, imagine arm wrestling with someone. You both push hard, but no one budges. Finally one person's arm is whammed onto the table. Similarly, slabs of the earth's crust can suddenly come apart and slam into a new position. The jolt causes an earthquake.

5   If an earthquake lifts or drops part of the ocean floor, the water above it starts moving, too. This triggers a tsunami.

6   A tsunami can race across the ocean at more than 500 miles (800 kilometers) an hour. Oddly, in deep water its spreading waves are only a few feet high. In fact, if you were sipping soda on the deck of an ocean liner, the wave from a passing tsunami wouldn't even slosh the drink in your glass. Only when the waves come close to shore do their energy and height increase.

The writer uses imagery here—comparing a hurricane to a fearsome, or frightening, creature.

An underwater landslide can also cause a tsunami.

The article doesn't tell you this, but why do you think the waves become so high as they reach shore?

wham into/onto—(*informal*) to hit something very hard

trigger—to cause an event to happen

ocean liner—a ship that carries passengers

slosh—to move the liquid in a container from side to side

7   Often before a tsunami hits, there is a giant vacuum effect, and water is sucked from harbors and beaches. People are amazed to see the bare sea bottom littered with flopping fish and stranded boats. Waves are made up of crests, or high points, and troughs, or dips between crests. When a trough hits land first, the water level drops drastically. Usually another wave blasts ashore about 15 minutes later, then another and another—for two hours or more.

8   Tsunamis have killed more than 50,000 people in the past century. Japan has been the country hardest hit. [This article was written before the 2004 tsunami that killed more than 150,000 people in Southeast Asia and Africa.] To reduce the death toll in the future, scientists established the Pacific Tsunami Warning System, with headquarters in Hawaii. Its network of earthquake detectors and tide gauges detects quakes that may cause a tsunami.

9   We can't tame the tsunami. But we can learn when it's coming and escape the sea monster's fury.

Source: *National Geographic World*

tame—to change something from violent to gentle

Tsunami damage

3. Making Content Connections Work with a partner. The article tells us that tsunamis are both similar to and different from regular waves. Make a Venn diagram that compares and contrasts the two. Use the information in the article and at least one other source of information, such as the Internet or an encyclopedia.

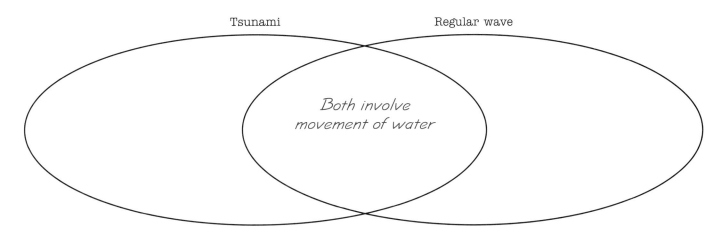

Tsunami   Regular wave

*Both involve
movement of water*

4. Expanding Your Vocabulary Complete the diagrams below with the words in the box.

magma	funnel
fault	downdraft
snow pack	plate
lava	side vent

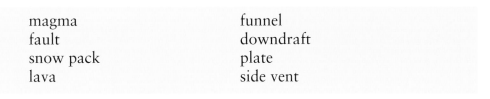

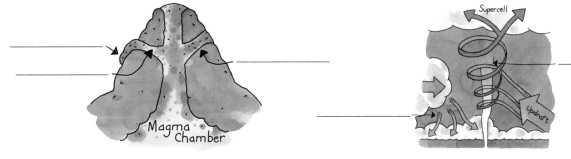

Volcano   Tornado

Earthquake   Avalanche

G WRITING CLINIC   Feature Articles: Explaining a Process

1. Think about It People write articles that explain how events in nature occur because they want to...

☐ show how smart they are.   ☐ save the planet from pollution.   ☐ share information with readers who are interested.

2. Focus on Organization Processes in nature are often complex, involving stages that have causes and effects that are linked like a chain.

❶ Read again how a hurricane develops.

> Each paragraph explains a stage in the development of a hurricane.

> The stages are arranged in logical order—each the cause of the stage that follows.

> Each paragraph includes **important details** that help the reader understand the process.

Hurricanes feed on warm moist air rising from the Atlantic Ocean. Warm water evaporates from the surface of the ocean and rises. As it rises, it cools. This causes the water vapor to condense, forming a very large thunderstorm cloud that extends to a great height ... the first stage of hurricane development.

The cloud columns grow larger and higher. Evaporation and condensation continue in a cycle. This creates a pattern of wind that circulates around a center (similar to that of water going down a drain). As the moving column of air encounters more clouds, it becomes a cluster of thunderstorm clouds ...

... As the thunderstorm grows higher and wider, the air at the top of the cloud column is cooling and creating an area of low pressure. This area of low pressure draws more and more warm air up toward it. Winds in the storm cloud column spin faster and faster, whipping around in a giant circular motion.

When wind speeds reach 39 mph (63 kph), the tropical depression is termed a tropical storm. This occurs when the winds move faster and begin twisting and turning around the eye, or calm center, of the storm ...

When wind speeds top 74 mph (119 kph), the tropical storm is officially called a hurricane ...

❷ Now make a chart that shows the stages of a tsunami and important details. Arrange the stages in logical order.

Stages of a Tsunami	Important Details
1. An undersea earthquake occurs, causing the ocean floor to lift or drop.	Earthquakes are caused by tectonic plates grinding against each other...
2.	
3.	

3. Focus on Style

❶ Look again at the introductions for both selections. How are they similar?

☐ They both state the author's opinion about the occurrence.

☐ They both involve the reader by painting a vivid picture of the event.

☐ They are both meant to entertain you.

Both introductions involve the reader by asking a question.

> Dark clouds fill the sky. It's the middle of the day, but it looks like night. The wind howls. Rain pelts the ground so hard that holes form in the mud. Tree branches bend and crack. Whole trees are uprooted and crash down. Store windows break. . . . You are in the middle of a hurricane—the largest, fiercest storm of nature. How do these storms start, and how can we protect ourselves from them?

> What kind of monster is this? It rises from the sea and speeds across it as fast as a jet airplane. On reaching land, it can suck all the water out of a harbor. Then the fearsome creature may grow more than a hundred feet tall and flatten whole villages, tossing around buildings, boats, railroad cars—even, sadly, people.

❷ Good introductions "hook" the reader. One way of doing this is by helping the reader visualize what the occurrence or event is like—by "showing, not telling." Compare these two introductions. Which one catches your attention more? Why?

> Volcanoes form when molten lava flows or erupts from a fissure, or narrow opening in the Earth's crust. Most volcanoes form from repeated eruptions, which, over the centuries, build up a cone.

> The rocky ground shakes and bulges upward. Then a powerful blast throws rock bombs, gas, and ash high into the sky. Fiery red lava pours from the Earth, and nearby fields of snow and ice melt, creating huge rivers of mud. An exploding volcano is an awesome sight and dangerous for those living nearby. Let's look more closely at how a volcano erupts by going inside its fiery underbelly.
>
> Source: *Volcano!* by Ellen J. Prager

❸ Work with a partner. Choose an introduction and rewrite it so that it grabs the reader's attention.

1. Most earthquakes last less than a minute yet they cause more damage than any other natural disaster. The worst earthquakes can kill thousands of people.

2. Tornadoes don't happen just anywhere. Weather conditions have to be just right for a tornado to form. This is how it happens.

3. Each winter, hundreds of skiers and mountain climbers are killed by deadly avalanches. In many cases, avalanches are caused by human beings.

H WRITER'S WORKSHOP — Feature Articles: Explaining a Process

Imagine that your class has been invited to submit short articles (350–400 words) to *National Geographic Kids*. Your article should include at least one visual. Your job is to explain a complex process in the world around us—one that has several stages.

1. Getting It Out

❶ Find a topic that interests you. Make a list of at least ten "how" and "why" questions.

> *How do tornadoes form? Why are they so deadly?*
>
> *Why does it rain?*
>
> *What causes an earthquake? Why do they happen?*
>
> *Why do the seasons change?*
>
> *Why do volcanoes erupt?*

❷ Choose your topic or research question. Ask yourself:

- Does it involve a process with stages or steps?
- Is it about our world?
- Is it a topic most kids don't know about and would be interested in learning about?

Do library research.

Ask an expert.

Search the Internet.

❸ Gather information about your topic.

- Look for sources that provide a detailed explanation and list the stages.
- Take thorough notes. Copy down important details you will need for later.
- Take the time to learn the meanings of words you don't know. Copy the definitions.
- Copy drawings or diagrams that will help your reader understand.

❹ Plan your article. Make a chart that shows each stage in the process and important details. Maria plans to write about why avalanches happen. Here is part of the chart she made.

Stages in the Process	Important Details
1. Snowflakes form …	–Each begins as a microscopic drop of water … –Joins with other droplets to form a snowflake –Snowflakes are hexagonal (six sides)
2. A snowpack forms …	
3.	
4.	
5.	

❺ Identify words that you will need to define. For example, Maria might want to define *hexagonal*. She can do that by adding a short definition right after the word.

The droplet joins together with almost a million other droplets to form a single hexagonal flake, or one that has six sides.

❻ Articles that explain a complex process often include visuals to help the reader understand—illustrations, photographs, or a flowchart. Look again at the visuals on hurricanes.

- Tell a partner how the illustrations help you understand the explanations.

- Why are the visuals effective?

Remember to use at least one visual in your article.

 CONNECT TO THE WEB. CHECK IT OUT:

For ideas of questions, go to Science Q&A: New York Times Learning Center—

http://www.nytimes.com/learning/students/scienceqa/

2. Getting It Down

❶ Turn your chart into words. Make an outline like the one below.

---

1. Introduction (identifying the process): _____

2. Stages in the process (explaining the process):

    a) Stage 1: _____

       ☐ Detail: _____

       ☐ Detail: _____

    b) Stage 2: _____

    c) Stage 3: _____

    d) Stage 4: _____

3. Conclusion: _____

---

❷ Draft your article. Here is what Maria wrote about avalanches.

> *Each paragraph describes a stage in the process.*

> *Maria provides details that make her explanation easy to understand.*

> *Her conclusion is missing. Her essay just comes to a sudden stop.*

> *Maria's introduction is awesome! It really grabs the reader's attention. Then she identifies the process she will explain.*

MINI-LESSON

Using Commas with Adverbial Clauses:
Set off adverbial clauses with a comma:
Some layers of snow pack lightly, while others pack tightly.

Avalanche!

At 9,000 feet, you're on the top of the world! Beautiful Squaw Valley lies below you. You push off. You cut a series of perfect turns. Suddenly you hear a thundering WHOOOSH sound! The snow drops below you, throwing you off balance. Then the slab you're skiing on starts to break apart. This isn't a scene from a disaster movie! It's an avalanche, and you're on the ride of your life!

Each year, hundreds of people die in avalanches. How is it that a tiny, delicate snowflake can turn into such a deadly killer? Let's find out.

Snow begins its life as a tiny ice crystal that joins together with other ice crystals to make snowflakes. Snowflakes start to change as soon as they touch the ground, forming a snow pack. Mild weather can turn the snowflakes into rounded grains, which then stick together to form a hard slab. When it is very cold, water vapors can slip to the deeper snow pack, forming a certain type of ice crystals that weaken it from below. The warmer temperatures of the ground then cause melting.

A heavy storm, strong winds, a change in temperature, or even the weight of a skier or snowboarder can cause a break in the snow pack. When the slope, or mountainside, is between 30 to 45 degrees, this means trouble.

There are two types of avalanches: loose snow and slab. Loose snow avalanches occur when loose, light snow tumbles down a mountain, spreading out as it moves. Loose snow avalanches are usually shallow and will often send a skier tumbling in the air. Slab avalanches are more deadly. They occur when a large, single layer of icy snow sits on top of a weaker layer of snow. When the weaker layer of snow breaks, the slab begins to slip, riding over an ice sheet or even bare ground at breathtaking speeds.

3. Getting It Right Take a careful look at what you have written. Use these questions to help you revise your work.

Questions to Ask ...	How to Check ...	How to Revise ...
1. Does my introduction grab the attention of the reader?	Ask a partner to give you feedback.	Begin with a description or pose an interesting question to the reader.
2. Do I identify the process I will explain?	Circle the words in your introduction that identify the process.	Add a sentence—perhaps a question—that identifies the process you will explain.
3. Do I explain each stage in the process in a logical sequence?	Number each stage in the margin. Ask yourself: Are the stages in time order?	Rearrange the information or add information if a stage is missing.
4. Do I provide enough details so that my explanation is clear?	Underline each detail.	Add details or remove details that are unnecessary.
5. Do the visuals I use help make my explanation clear?	Have a partner tell you, in his or her own words, what your visual says to others.	Add labels, arrows, or additional illustrations to your visual(s).

4. Presenting It Share your essay with your classmates. Take notes as you listen to other students. Use a chart like the one you used to organize information for your essay.

❶ Plan your presentation. Look at the checklist.

❷ Begin by showing your classmates a visual.

❸ Read your article aloud, referring to your visual.

❹ Invite your classmates to ask questions.

❺ As you listen to others, take notes. Volunteer to summarize the explanation, using your own words.

Presentation Checklist

❏ My introduction is interesting.

❏ I describe each stage in the process in logical order.

❏ My visuals are carefully drawn and labeled and are easy to understand.

❏ I use a loud, clear voice.

❏ I pause briefly after each stage.

❏ I look at the audience from time to time.

1. On Assignment Learn more about using visual information to explain a process. Practice making different types of flow diagrams.

❶ Some processes are explained best using a *linear* flow diagram, or one that shows stages in a one-way process. Work with a partner. Make a flow diagram that shows a linear process. Here are examples of questions:

- Where does bread come from?
- How does a plant grow?
- How do you catch the common cold?

❷ Other processes are explained using a *cyclical* flow diagram, or one that shows a process that happens over and over again. Now make a flow diagram that shows a cyclical process.

- What is the life cycle of a moth (or other animal)?
- What happens to recycled bottles?
- How does gossip travel?

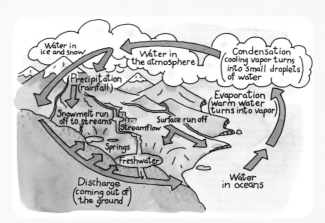

❸ Show your diagrams to classmates.

🎧 **SHARED READING** Hawaii is a land of myths and legends. Read this myth about Pele, the Goddess of Fire.

LET'S TALK Answer the questions.

1. Who is Pele? Where does she live?
2. Think of three adjectives that might describe Pele.
3. Why do you think ancient Hawaiians worshiped Pele?

The Puna Chief Who Boasted

There was once a Puna chief who could talk of nothing but his own district. Wherever he went he boasted of Puna. "Beautiful Puna," he chanted. "Its fields and its gardens are shining like a mat spread over the hillside and edged above by the forest."

"Be careful," people warned him. "Remember Pele! That goddess does not like boasting!"

"I fear her not!" the chief answered. "She lives above in the pit, tending her fires. Puna is safe from her evil." And he went on boasting:

"My country is beautiful Puna,
Land where all food plants are growing,
Land where bananas hang heavy,
Where potatoes burst from the earth,
Where sugar-cane stalks are the sweetest.
My country is sweet smelling Puna.
To the seaman who comes near our coast
The winds bear the fragrance of hala.
Birds gather over our trees
Drinking the nectar of blossoms.
My country is beautiful Puna."

A wise kahuna heard these words. "Alas!" he said. "Your boasting has angered Pele.

Return to your country. You will finds its beauty laid waste."

"Ho!" shouted the chief, "I do not fear your words! No harm can come to Puna!" But for all his shouting the chief was frightened. As quickly as wind and paddle could take him, he returned. He reached a point of land, beached his canoe, climbed a hillside, and looked toward his beautiful Puna.

Black smoke hung heavy over all his land. As he looked, wind lifted the smoke and he saw no fertile fields and gardens, but a waste of twisted lava. No flowers bloomed in the forest, only spurts of flame. No fragrance of hala was borne on the wind, but the bitter smell of smoke.

Pele had been angered by the chief's boastful words. Now he knew that no land below her fire pit was safe from her power.

Source: *Hawai'i Island Legends: Pikoi, Pele, and Others*
Image: © 2004 Herb Kawainui Kane, Artist

Puna—the district on the Big Island of Hawaii from north of Hilo to the Hawaii Volcanoes National Park and all the land south of that

boast—to brag

hala—a type of tree in Hawaii with nice-smelling flowers

kahuna—a Hawaiian priest or priestess

Mini-Unit: Note-Taking and Summarizing

Sometimes it's hard to understand and remember everything you hear or read at school. **Note-taking** and **summarizing** can help you do both.

A | LISTENING AND TAKING NOTES

Always take notes when you listen to your teacher describe or explain something (unless your teacher tells you to "just listen").

1. Talk It Over Talk with a partner. Add five examples to the list below of when you might take notes in class.

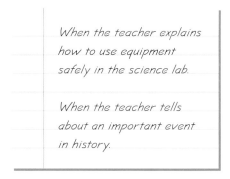

When the teacher explains how to use equipment safely in the science lab.

When the teacher tells about an important event in history.

2. Learn How to Do It Listening and note-taking is a six-step process. Read the steps below.

Step 1: Before class, make sure that you are *ready* to listen and learn. Do a quick check.

- I have done my homework and finished my assignments.
- I have reviewed yesterday's notes.
- I have my books and supplies.
- I intend, or *really mean*, to pay attention.

Step 2: Listen actively while others are talking. When you *listen*, you don't just hear words. You *think* about what the person is saying. You ask yourself questions.

- What am I learning?
- Why is this important or interesting to know?
- What do I need to remember?
- Do I understand what my teacher is explaining?

Step 3: Listen for "signal" words. They help you organize information.

First ... second ... third ... in addition ...furthermore ... finally... These signal that a **new idea** is coming.	*For instance ... for example ... picture this ... to illustrate...* These signal that an **example** is coming.	*Previously ... before ... at first ... as soon as ... following ... after...* These let you know **when.**

Step 4: As you listen, write down ideas that are important. Jot down details, examples, definitions, and important facts that support each idea—

- Use your own words.
- Indent examples, details, and facts under each idea.
- Leave a wide margin on both sides of the paper.

2 inches   2 inches

Grizzly bears are omnivores
  -Love to eat small mammals, fish, and birds
  -Also eat berries, roots, and other plants)

Step 5: After class, review and edit your notes. <u>Underline</u> or highlight the most important ideas. Put a question mark ? next to points you don't understand. Add your own comments to your notes. Fill in missing points or define terms you need to remember.

Additional Notes   *Questions and Ideas*

omnivore = eats both   *Grizzly bears are omnivores*
animals and plants   *-Love to eat small mammals, fish, and birds*   *Do grizzly bears*
                                   -Also eat berries, roots, and other plants)   *attack people?*

Step 6: Ask your teacher to explain the things you didn't understand.

Practice It Listen to the passage. Take notes, then review them. Compare your own notes with a partner's notes.

When you read your textbook or are working on a report, take notes as you read to help you understand and remember what you read.

1. Talk It Over Talk with a partner. How can note-taking help you when you read? Add three ways to the list below.

> *Helps you really think about what you are reading.*

2. Learn How to Do It *Graphic organizers* can help you take good notes. Remember to use your own words.

T-Charts

Use a **T-chart** when you are reading for **information**. Complete the T-chart below.

> Sharks are carnivores. They eat all kinds of flesh. Sharks prefer tuna, mackerel, and even smaller sharks for dinner, but they will eat swimmers if the conditions are right.
>
> Sharks have very sharp senses of vision, hearing, and smell to help them find food. They can see seven times better than humans and can hear sounds over two miles away. About two-thirds of a shark's brain is used for smell, so if there is even a tiny amount of blood in the water, a shark will smell it—even if it's almost a mile away!
>
> Instead of bones, sharks have something called cartilage. Bones are hard and don't bend. Cartilage is flexible, allowing sharks to bend so their heads can reach their tails. The cartilage also allows sharks to turn very quickly. All this makes them better hunters. Humans have cartilage too, but only in places like our ears and noses.

Ideas	*Details, Examples*
Sharks are carnivores (meat eaters)	*They mostly eat smaller fish (tuna, mackerel, sharks)*

Venn Diagrams

Use a **Venn diagram** when the reading is **comparing and contrasting** two things (describing how two things are the **same or different**). Make your own Venn diagram comparing alligators and crocodiles, based on this selection.

In many ways, alligators and crocodiles are similar. They are both large reptiles that live in water and on land. They both lay eggs. They both have huge teeth and powerful jaws.

But they are also different in many ways. The biggest difference between alligators and crocodiles is the shape of their heads. The crocodile's skull and jaws are long and narrow. The alligator's snout is flat and round. Alligators and crocodiles both have thick, bumpy skin but alligators tend to be darker in color.

Another difference between crocodiles and alligators is their choice of homes. Alligators live in rivers, lakes, and swamps. On the other hand, crocodiles prefer coastal, salt water habitats.

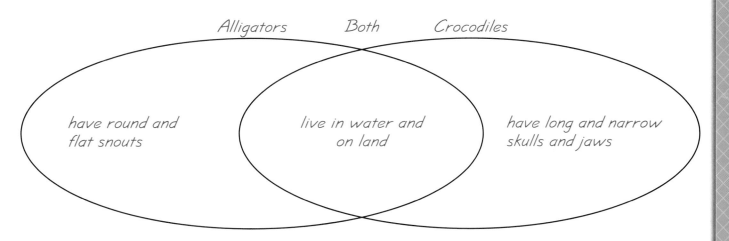

Alligators   *Both*   *Crocodiles*

have round and flat snouts   *live in water and on land*   *have long and narrow skulls and jaws*

Process Diagrams

When you are learning about a **step-by-step process**—like in science or health—use a **process diagram** that shows steps or stages.

Have you ever wondered how you get cavities? The part of the tooth that you can see is called a crown. The crown of each tooth is covered with enamel, a very hard surface. Enamel protects the tooth. You have millions of bacteria, or very tiny germs, in your mouth. When you eat foods with sugar, like candy bars, the bacteria produce acids that eat through the enamel. The bacteria then get inside the tooth and cause it to decay. The decay can spread down into the tooth and cause it to die.

We have bacteria in our mouths. When we eat foods with sugar, the bacteria makes acids.

↓

Acids eat through the enamel (hard covering) of the tooth.

↓

Bacteria get inside the tooth and cause the tooth to decay.

Now practice making your own diagram. Read about why and how snow falls.

A cloud is a mixture of air and very tiny droplets of water. When the droplets of water get very cold, they turn to ice. Ice particles start very small. As they travel through the air, more water freezes on them, and they become larger, forming ice crystals. When the ice crystals are big enough, they join together and make snow flakes. If the snow flakes are heavy enough, they fall to the ground.

Timelines

When you are reading about an important **event in history**, make a **timeline**. Read the passage and complete the timeline below.

> It is difficult to climb Mt. Everest. Many mountain climbers have died trying to reach the summit. In 1921, the first British team tried to reach the top. They couldn't make it, but they did discover a route to the summit. Many attempts followed. In 1924, British climbers George Mallory and Andrew Irvine attempted to climb Everest and were last seen just below the summit. No one knows if they reached the top before they disappeared. The first people we know reached the top were Edmund Hillary and his Sherpa guide, Tenzing Norgay, who succeeded in 1953. Both men became heroes. In 1980, the Austrian climber Rheinhold Messner climbed Mt. Everest alone—without bottled oxygen! He is considered by many to be the greatest mountain climber of all time.

1921	The first British team tried to climb Mt. Everest. They discovered a route, but didn't reach the top.
1924	George Mallory and Andrew Irvine tried to climb Mt. Everest. No one knows what happened to them.
1953	
1980	

3. Practice It Read these two passages. Decide which type of graphic organizer to use for each. Then take notes on a separate piece of paper. Compare your notes with a partner's.

Reading 1.

The Changing Look of America's Population

The United States is becoming more racially diverse than ever before. The most diverse group is people who are 18 years old and younger. Almost 40 percent of these people are members of a minority group, which in this case is a racial group smaller than the larger group that it belongs to.

Many Americans thought that America was becoming more diverse, but we weren't sure about it until the 2000 census was complete. A census is a count of the population of an area. Before 2000, people had to choose one race from a list of races to describe themselves in a census. But in Census 2000, people were allowed for the first time ever to choose more than one race. About 7 million people identified themselves as multiracial. Almost half of these people were 18 or younger than 18.

According to people who study population information and numbers, we are seeing increased racial diversity in the U.S. because of growing numbers of immigrants and interracial marriages here in the past several years.

Reading 2.

That volcano is about to erupt!

Do you know how and why a volcano erupts? To find out, we have to look inside the volcano. Under the ground, we find magma. Magma is hot, melted rock. Liquid magma moves around under the ground and can flow toward the surface inside a volcano. When this happens, the gas in the magma starts to bubble up, forcing the magma upward. If earthquakes happen near a volcano, you can be sure that the volcano is active because the upward movement of magma can cause earthquakes.

If you see the rocky top surface of a volcano bulging outward, run fast, because it means that gas and magma are collecting and the volcano might erupt. But before the eruption occurs, steam and gas will shoot out of cracks and holes in the volcano to release some of the pressure that's building up inside. When there is too much magma and gas to be released through these small cracks and holes, or if the top of the volcano breaks open because of an earthquake, the volcano will erupt, shooting out steam, ash, and sometimes lava, which is what magma is called when it reaches the surface.

When you summarize, you find the most important ideas in something you've read, then *restate* them in your own words. Writing a summary shows how well you understand something.

1. Talk It Over Talk with a partner. Write down one reason that summarizing might help you in school. Be ready to share.

2. Learn How to Do It Read the passage. Then read the summary.

Reading Passage

> ### The Changing Look of America's Population
>
> The United States is becoming more racially diverse than ever before. The most diverse group is people who are 18 years old and younger. Almost 40 percent of these people are members of a minority group, which in this case is a racial group smaller than the larger group that it belongs to.
>
> Many Americans thought that America was becoming more diverse, but we weren't sure about it until the 2000 census was complete. A census is a count of the population of an area. Before 2000, people had to choose one race from a list of races to describe themselves in a census. But in Census 2000, people were allowed for the first time ever to choose more than one race. About 7 million people identified themselves as multiracial. Almost half of these people were 18 or younger than 18.
>
> According to people who study population information and numbers, we are seeing increased racial diversity in the U.S. because of growing numbers of immigrants and interracial marriages here in the past several years.

Summary

More and more kids in the U.S. belong to more than one race. For the first time, in the 2000 census, people were allowed to identify themselves as members of more than one racial group. About seven million people did this. This change is the result of an increase in immigration and interracial marriages.

How to summarize:

1. Read the passage, taking notes.
2. Review your notes, underlining the important ideas. Next, circle absolutely essential information.
3. Write a paragraph that includes the important ideas and details.

3. Practice It Summaries are short, and they are in your own words. You will need two pieces of paper for this activity. Number each one in the upper right hand corner. As you do the activity, be sure that your handwriting is the same size on each sheet.

1. Fold sheet #1 in half so you have a short, wide piece of paper. Read the passage below. Write down the most important ideas and details from the passage.
2. Fold sheet #2 in three parts so you have a very short, wide piece of paper. Study the notes on sheet #1, crossing off less important ideas or details. Then fill up sheet #2 with the notes that you think are the most important.
3. Use the notes from sheet #2 to write a short paragraph about the reading. Remember to write complete sentences and use your own words.

Why Egyptians Learned to Make Mummies

Ancient Egyptians believed that a person's soul lived on after a person died, but didn't stay near the body after death. Instead, it left its body after death and returned to find it later. The body needed its soul to go to the mythical Next World. But the *soul* couldn't return if it couldn't find or didn't recognize its body.

When Egyptians buried their dead in the sand, the hot, dry weather dried up the bodies and stopped them from rotting. But sand burials weren't good enough for wealthy Egyptians. They started to bury their family members in beautiful stone tombs. However, they soon realized that this was a horrible mistake because the bodies didn't dry up in the tombs like they did in the sand. They became skeletons. What would the Egyptians do? The souls wouldn't be able to recognize their bodies if the bodies turned into skeletons! These people would never be able to go to the Next World!

The wealthy Egyptians didn't want to go back to burying their loved ones in sand, but they had to solve this problem of bodies rotting away and becoming unrecognizable to their souls. They learned from the sand burials that bodies could be preserved if they were kept dry. They tried different things for many years until they finally discovered the perfect way to preserve bodies without burying them in the sand. They found a way to make mummies. Their techniques were so good that some of the mummified bodies still exist.

Appendix A: Common Prefixes

Prefix	Meaning	Example
anti-	against	**Anti**freeze keeps water from freezing.
auto-	self, same	Helen Keller wrote a famous **auto**biography.
bi-	two	Tran rides his **bi**cycle to school every day.
circum-	around, about	A very large ship can **circum**navigate the earth.
de-	opposite	The veternarian **de**clawed the cat. Now she won't scratch.
dis-	not, opposite of	Maria often **dis**agrees with her parents.
ex-	out	We painted the **ex**terior walls of our house.
in-, im-	in	The murderer is in prison. He is **im**prisoned.
in-, im-, il-, ir-	not	I don't believe your story. It is **in**credible.
inter-	between	Most people enjoy **inter**acting with others.
micro-	tiny	An amoeba is a **micro**scopic animal.
mid-	middle	Lori stopped talking. She stopped **mid**sentence.
mis-	wrongly	She realized that she had **mis**spoken.
mono-	one, single	We rode the **mono**rail at Disneyland.
non-	not	What you are saying is absolute **non**sense!
post-	after	My dad **post**dated the check.
pre-	before	You should **pre**view the chapter before you read.
pro-	favoring	Is Senator Smith **pro**war or antiwar? No one is sure.
re-	again	Stefan **re**wrote his essay. Now it is perfect.
semi-	half	Mr. Smith is **semi**retired. He works just two days a week.
sub-	under	A **sub**marine is an underwater vessel.
super-	over	Jennifer Lopez isn't just a star. She's a **super**star.
trans-	across	The QE2 is a **trans**atlantic ocean liner.
un-	not	Juan told us an **un**believable story.
under-	under	An octopus is an **under**water creature.

Appendix B: Common Suffixes

1. Suffixes that make nouns:

Suffix	Meaning	Example
-ance, -ence	state, condition	Maria is always concerned about her appear**ance**.
-ee	one who receives	Senator Lee is the presidential nomin**ee**.
-er, -or	one who does	Ms. Vasquez is an excellent teach**er**.
-ion, -tion	action, process	The lions are the main attrac**tion** in the circus.
-ity	state, quality	Lake Tahoe is known for the clar**ity** of its water.
-ment	state of	Most people watch TV for the enjoy**ment** of it.
-ness	state, quality	In spite of her blind**ness**, Helen Keller wrote books.
-ure	act, process	Playing with my dog Chipper gives me pleas**ure**.

2. Suffixes that make verbs:

Suffix	Meaning	Example
-ate	to act upon	You must compens**ate** me for my work.
-ify	to cause to become	We can ampl**ify** the sound by getting better speakers.
-ize	to cause to be or become	Our teacher will critic**ize** us if we don't do the assignment.

3. Suffixes that make adjectives:

Suffix	Meaning	Example
-able, -ible	capable of being	Chipper is a lov**able** dog. He is ador**able**.
-al, -ial	of, relating to	The bat is a nocturn**al** animal.
-en	made of	We live in a wood**en** house.
-ese	of, from	Tran is Vietnam**ese**.
-ful	full of	Everyone loved the movie. It was wonder**ful**.
-ic	of, relating to	Math is an academ**ic** subject.
-ish	somewhat	The sky has a redd**ish** glow in the evening.
-ive	tending toward	Snakes are repuls**ive**.
-less	without	Her advice was foolish. It was worth**less**.
-ous, -ious	having the characteristics of	Stanford is a prestig**ious** university.
-y	tending toward, characterized by	Juan saves his money. He is a thrift**y** young man.

Appendix C: Common Irregular Verbs

Simple Form	Past Form	Past Participle	Simple Form	Past Form	Past Participle
be	was/were	been	lay (= put)	laid	laid
beat	beat	beaten	lead	led	led
become	became	become	leave	left	left
begin	began	begun	let	let	let
bend	bent	bent	lie (= lie down)	lay	lain
bite	bit	bitten	lose	lost	lost
break	broke	broken	make	made	made
bring	brought	brought	mean	meant	meant
build	built	built	meet	met	met
buy	bought	bought	pay	paid	paid
catch	caught	caught	put	put	put
choose	chose	chosen	quit	quit	quit
come	came	come	read	read	read
cost	cost	cost	ride	rode	ridden
cut	cut	cut	ring	rang	rung
do	did	done	rise	rose	risen
draw	drew	drawn	run	ran	run
drink	drank	drunk	say	said	said
eat	ate	eaten	see	saw	seen
fall	fell	fallen	sell	sold	sold
feed	fed	fed	send	sent	sent
feel	felt	felt	set	set	set
fight	fought	fought	show	showed	shown
find	found	found	shut	shut	shut
fly	flew	flown	sing	sang	sung
forget	forgot	forgotten	sit	sat	sat
forgive	forgave	forgiven	sleep	slept	slept
get	got	gotten	speak	spoke	spoken
give	gave	given	spend	spent	spent
go	went	gone	stand	stood	stood
grow	grew	grown	swim	swam	swum
have	had	had	take	took	taken
hear	heard	heard	teach	taught	taught
hide	hid	hidden	tear	tore	torn
hit	hit	hit	tell	told	told
hold	held	held	think	thought	thought
hurt	hurt	hurt	throw	threw	thrown
keep	kept	kept	understand	understood	understood
know	knew	known	wake	woke	woken

Spelling Activities

Spelling Listen to the following words. What do you notice about the spelling?

fragrance   difference   avoidance   patience

Supply the missing letters for each incomplete word. Use your dictionary for help.

a. Our teacher took attend_____.

b. Juan plans to attend the confer _____ on Friday.

c. My doctor has over 20 years of experi_____.

d. The store is having a clear_____ sale.

e. The audi_____ loved the play.

f. Stefan is an acquaint_____ of mine.

UNIT 2

Spelling The sound /sh/ can be spelled in many ways. Listen to the following words.

show   attention   species   machine   issue

Supply the missing letters for each incomplete word. Use your dictionary to check your work.

a. _sh_ ell

b. fa____ion

c. reddi____

d. vaca____on

e. ti____ue

f. informa____on

g. court____ip

h. sec____on

i. se____ion

j. musta____e

k. pa____ion

l. spe____al

Spelling The sound /ē/ can be spelled many ways. Listen to the following sentence.

Many teens believe that studying with a friend can be a good way to make homework fun and easy.

-y	e	ee	ie	ea
scary	scene	teen	belief	leave
hairy	me	queen	grief	heat

Find the eleven words in the list below that have the /ē/ sound. Underline them. Then circle the letters that are pronounced /ē/.

thirteen	key	peace	piece	easy
reed	Hey!	read	thief	geography
seed	Peter	break	friend	fly

Spelling Listen to the following words. What do you notice about the spelling?

pharoah   fairy   laugh   off

Supply the missing letters for the incomplete words. Use your dictionary for help.

a. Juan has had enou_____ to eat.

b. The boy's name is Je_____.

c. The rock singer autogra_____ed my CD cover.

d. Turn le_____t at the next street.

e. I have a bad cou_____.

f. That animal with the long neck is a gira_____e.

g. This is a _____oto of my sister.

h. Carlos dove off the cli_____.

i. Do you know how to write a paragra_____?

Spelling The sound of the letter *g* can be hard (*dragon*) or soft (*angel*). Listen to the following words. Put the words with the same *g* sound in the correct column.

huge	ugly	danger	strangely	give	cargo
forget	gold	getting	tiger	guard	gift
geology	dog	ages	generous	diagnose	agitated

hard *g* (dragon)	soft *g* (angel)

UNIT 6

Spelling Listen to the following words. Pay attention to which syllable you hear stressed. Then look at the final consonant when an ending is added. What do you notice?

travel   traveled   expel   expelled

Listen carefully as your teacher reads each word. Write the word, adding the letters *–ed*. Decide whether you need to double the final consonant. Use your dictionary to check your work.

a. edit   _____edited_____   f. focus   _____

b. commit   _____   g. offer   _____

c. worship   _____   h. prefer   _____

d. open   _____   i. occur   _____

e. vomit   _____

UNIT 7

Spelling Words with the letters *ie* and *ei* are often misspelled. Listen to the words containing the letters *ei*. What do you notice?

weigh   eight   vein

Supply the missing letters for the incomplete words. Use your dictionary for help.

a. A fr_____ghter is a ship.

b. Tran is a fr_____nd of mine.

c. May I have a p_____ce of cake?

d. I bel_____ve you!

e. Maria is Juan's n_____ghbor.

f. Sau-Lim is from Taip_____.

g. The police caught the th_____f.

h. Santa rides a sl_____gh.

i. Rudolph is a r_____ndeer.

UNIT 8

Spelling Listen to the following words. What do you notice about the spelling?

independent   observant   resident   assistant

Supply the missing letters for the incomplete words. Use your dictionary for help.

a. Jorge is a flight attend_____.

b. My mother is very observ_____.

c. Christiane is wearing a differ_____ hairstyle today.

d. My perman_____ address is 1234 Main Street.

e. I have a persist_____ cough.

f. Your argum_____ is not relev_____ to the issue.

UNIT 9

Spelling Listen to the following words. What do you notice about the spelling?

impossible   available   flexible   capable

Supply the missing letters for the incomplete words. Use your dictionary for help.

a. Harry Potter is a remark_____ boy.

b. I have a terr_____ headache.

c. Juan is a respons_____ young man.

d. The movie is unforgett_____.

e. Your excuse is not believ_____.

f. Our cafeteria food is ined_____!

UNIT 10

Spelling Listen to the following words. What do you notice?

condense   existence   vase   face   recluse   reduce

Supply the missing letters for the incomplete words. Use your dictionary for help.

a. You don't have any sen_____e!

b. The fen_____e is painted white.

c. I need to tie my shoela_____es.

d. Where is your briefca_____e?

e. I am taking a math cour_____e.

f. We need to enfor_____e the law.

ChecBrics*

ChecBric for Autobiographical Reflection

Focus	Overall rating
Organization ____ I focus on one important event, incident, or experience. ____ My reflection has a beginning that sets the scene. ____ The middle describes the incident. ____ My conclusion tells what happened and why I remember the incident.	____ 4 = Wow! ____ 3 = Strong ____ 2 = Some strengths ____ 1 = Needs work
Content ____ I tell who, what, where, and when. ____ I describe what happened in time order. ____ I use descriptive words and dialog. ____ I make it clear why this incident or experience was important to me. ____ I let the reader know how I felt about the experience.	____ 4 = Wow! ____ 3 = Strong ____ 2 = Some strengths ____ 1 = Needs work
Style ____ My beginning grabs the attention of the reader. ____ I talk to the reader, showing that I am part of the story. ____ I "show, not tell."	____ 4 = Wow! ____ 3 = Strong ____ 2 = Some strengths ____ 1 = Needs work
Grammar and mechanics ____ Each sentences is complete. ____ I use the past perfect tense correctly. ____ Each verb agrees with the subject. ____ I use a comma in compound sentences with "and" or "but."	____ 4 = Wow! ____ 3 = Strong ____ 2 = Some strengths ____ 1 = Needs work

*ChecBric name and concept created by Larry Lewin

ChecBric for Field Guide

Focus	Overall rating
Organization ____ My introduction identifies the animal and what makes it interesting to read about. ____ Each body paragraph develops a different detail, or idea about the animal. ____ My conclusion summarizes the information.	____ 4 = Wow! ____ 3 = Strong ____ 2 = Some strengths ____ 1 = Needs work
Content ____ I provide important information about the animal. ____ I include at least one unusual fact others probably don't know. ____ The information I provide is accurate.	____ 4 = Wow! ____ 3 = Strong ____ 2 = Some strengths ____ 1 = Needs work
Style ____ My introduction "hooks" the reader. ____ I use figurative language, including similes. ____ I use adjectives that relate to the five senses. ____ My conclusion leaves the reader wanting to tell others or learn more.	____ 4 = Wow! ____ 3 = Strong ____ 2 = Some strengths ____ 1 = Needs work
Grammar and mechanics ____ Each sentence is complete. ____ Every verb agrees with its subject. ____ I use the correct forms of adverbs and place each at the correct place in the sentence.	____ 4 = Wow! ____ 3 = Strong ____ 2 = Some strengths ____ 1 = Needs work

ChecBric for Essay of Advice

Focus	Overall rating
Organization ____ My introduction catches the attention of the reader. ____ Tips are presented clearly. ____ Details support each point. ____ Quotes provide good ideas.	____ 4 = Wow! ____ 3 = Strong ____ 2 = Some strengths ____ 1 = Needs work
Content ____ I state the complaint clearly. ____ I provide tips that are useful. ____ My reader will learn good ideas.	____ 4 = Wow! ____ 3 = Strong ____ 2 = Some strengths ____ 1 = Needs work
Style ____ I use quotes from other students. ____ Tips are short and snappy. ____ My essay is fun to read.	____ 4 = Wow! ____ 3 = Strong ____ 2 = Some strengths ____ 1 = Needs work
Grammar and mechanics ____ My sentences are complete. ____ My grammar is correct. ____ My quotation marks and punctuation are correct. ____ I use countable and uncountable nouns correctly.	____ 4 = Wow! ____ 3 = Strong ____ 2 = Some strengths ____ 1 = Needs work

ChecBric for Research Report

Focus	Overall rating
Organization ____ My introduction has a thesis statement and identifies my research question(s). ____ Each body paragraph focuses on a different subtopic—and includes facts, examples, quotes, and/or statistics. ____ The ideas are presented in logical sequence. ____ My conclusion makes a final statement about why the topic is important, making my reader want to learn more.	____ 4 = Wow! ____ 3 = Strong ____ 2 = Some strengths ____ 1 = Needs work
Content ____ My report is about an interesting topic. ____ My report develops the topic completely, providing facts, details, and examples. ____ The information in my report is accurate and relevant. ____ I use my own words to restate information. ____ I cite, or name, sources of information.	____ 4 = Wow! ____ 3 = Strong ____ 2 = Some strengths ____ 1 = Needs work
Style ____ I use straightforward sentences. ____ I combine sentences to help make my writing flow.	____ 4 = Wow! ____ 3 = Strong ____ 2 = Some strengths ____ 1 = Needs work
Grammar and mechanics ____ I use complex sentences. ____ I use passive sentences appropriately. ____ The verbs agree with their subjects.	____ 4 = Wow! ____ 3 = Strong ____ 2 = Some strengths ____ 1 = Needs work

ChecBric for Comparison and Contrast Essay

Focus	Overall rating
Organization ____ I introduce the subjects being compared. ____ I describe one thing and then the other. ____ I summarizes the comparison in my conclusion.	____ 4 = Wow! ____ 3 = Strong ____ 2 = Some strengths ____ 1 = Needs work
Content ____ I describe how two things are the same and/or how they are different. ____ I compare the same features of both things. ____ I provide concrete details.	____ 4 = Wow! ____ 3 = Strong ____ 2 = Some strengths ____ 1 = Needs work
Style ____ I use words that signal things are being compared. ____ I use similes and descriptive language.	____ 4 = Wow! ____ 3 = Strong ____ 2 = Some strengths ____ 1 = Needs work
Grammar and mechanics ____ My sentences are complete. ____ I use tenses correctly. ____ My punctuation is correct. ____ All words are spelled correctly. ____ I use plural nouns correctly. ____ I use contractions correctly.	____ 4 = Wow! ____ 3 = Strong ____ 2 = Some strengths ____ 1 = Needs work

ChecBric for How-to Instructions

Focus	Overall rating
Organization ____ My introduction tells the reader what I am going to explain. ____ I list the materials that are needed. ____ I put the steps in time order. ____ I use formatting (subheads, bold face, etc.) to make my instructions easy to follow. ____ I use transition words to help the reader move to the next step.	____ 4 = Wow! ____ 3 = Strong ____ 2 = Some strengths ____ 1 = Needs work
Content ____ My instructions are easy to follow and "reader friendly." ____ I use graphics to help the reader understand. ____ I provide important details. ____ I use specific terminology.	____ 4 = Wow! ____ 3 = Strong ____ 2 = Some strengths ____ 1 = Needs work
Style ____ My sentences are short and simple. ____ I write in the second person ("you"). ____ My "writer's voice" is appropriate for my audience.	____ 4 = Wow! ____ 3 = Strong ____ 2 = Some strengths ____ 1 = Needs work
Grammar and mechanics ____ Each sentence is complete. ____ I use the correct articles. ____ Each verb agrees with its subject. ____ I put a comma after time adverbs that begin sentences.	____ 4 = Wow! ____ 3 = Strong ____ 2 = Some strengths ____ 1 = Needs work

ChecBric for Oral History

Focus	Overall rating
Organization ____ My interview begins with personal questions. ____ I organize my interview questions by categories, or topics. ____ My questions follow a logical order and build on each other.	____ 4 = Wow! ____ 3 = Strong ____ 2 = Some strengths ____ 1 = Needs work
Content ____ My interview focuses on a specific time or topic. ____ My interview questions are open-ended to draw the person out. ____ I ask follow-up questions that get my interviewee to provide interesting facts and details.	____ 4 = Wow! ____ 3 = Strong ____ 2 = Some strengths ____ 1 = Needs work
Style ____ I record the person's words the way they said them. ____ I use either an interview or narrative format.	____ 4 = Wow! ____ 3 = Strong ____ 2 = Some strengths ____ 1 = Needs work
Grammar and mechanics ____ I ask well-formed questions. ____ I use *would*, *could*, and *used to* correctly to express repeated actions in the past. ____ I use apostrophes to show possession.	____ 4 = Wow! ____ 3 = Strong ____ 2 = Some strengths ____ 1 = Needs work

ChecBric for Persuasive Essay

Focus	Overall rating
Organization ____ My introduction identifies the book I am reviewing and states my reaction. ____ The body of my review explains why I liked (or didn't like) the book. ____ My conclusion summarizes my reaction and makes a recommendation to the reader.	____ 4 = Wow! ____ 3 = Strong ____ 2 = Some strengths ____ 1 = Needs work
Content ____ I summarize the book I am reviewing. ____ I provide reasons for my reaction and give examples to support each reason. ____ I tell others why they might like (or not like) the book.	____ 4 = Wow! ____ 3 = Strong ____ 2 = Some strengths ____ 1 = Needs work
Style ____ My introduction makes others want to read my review. ____ I use varied types of sentences.	____ 4 = Wow! ____ 3 = Strong ____ 2 = Some strengths ____ 1 = Needs work
Grammar and mechanics ____ I use well-formed complex sentences. ____ I use complex tenses correctly. ____ The verbs agree with their subjects. ____ I use conditionals correctly. ____ I use commas with adverbs correctly.	____ 4 = Wow! ____ 3 = Strong ____ 2 = Some strengths ____ 1 = Needs work

ChecBric for Response to Literature: Book Review

Focus	Overall rating
Organization _____ My title communicates the issue. _____ My introduction identifies the issue and states my position. _____ My body paragraphs support my position.	_____ 4 = Wow! _____ 3 = Strong _____ 2 = Some strengths _____ 1 = Needs work
Content _____ I provide at least three reasons to support my position. _____ I provide facts and examples to support each reason. _____ I state my arguments logically and clearly. _____ I cite opinions, using quotes.	_____ 4 = Wow! _____ 3 = Strong _____ 2 = Some strengths _____ 1 = Needs work
Style _____ My introduction grabs my reader's attention. _____ As much as possible, I show, not tell.	_____ 4 = Wow! _____ 3 = Strong _____ 2 = Some strengths _____ 1 = Needs work
Grammar and mechanics _____ I use complete sentences. _____ I use adverbs correctly. _____ I use commas correctly. _____ I use the present perfect tense correctly. _____ I format titles correctly.	_____ 4 = Wow! _____ 3 = Strong _____ 2 = Some strengths _____ 1 = Needs work

ChecBric for Feature Article: Explaining a Process

Focus	Overall rating
Organization ____ My introduction identifies the process I will explain. ____ Each paragraph describes a stage in the process I am explaining. ____ I organize the stages in logical sequence, or time order. ____ My conclusion summarizes the process or brings my explanation to a natural end.	____ 4 = Wow! ____ 3 = Strong ____ 2 = Some strengths ____ 1 = Needs work
Content ____ I provide details that make my explanation clear and understandable. ____ I use correct terminology. ____ I use visuals, as needed, to help explain the information.	____ 4 = Wow! ____ 3 = Strong ____ 2 = Some strengths ____ 1 = Needs work
Style ____ My introduction grabs the attention of the reader. ____ I use formal, serious language. ____ I use complex sentences with adverbial clauses to help my writing flow.	____ 4 = Wow! ____ 3 = Strong ____ 2 = Some strengths ____ 1 = Needs work
Grammar and mechanics ____ Each sentence is complete and well-formed. ____ I use correct clause connectors. ____ I set off adverbial clauses with a comma.	____ 4 = Wow! ____ 3 = Strong ____ 2 = Some strengths ____ 1 = Needs work

Glossary

UNIT 1

abusive—hurtful to another person

Achilles tendon—the band of tissue attaching the heel bone to the calf muscle in the leg

balance—when your weight is evenly spread so that you are steady and don't fall

be diagnosed with—to find out from a doctor that you have a particular illness

cure—a treatment or medicine that stops a disease and makes you healthy again

currency—money

devastated—very badly damaged

devastating—making someone feel extremely sad or shocked

dignity—the ability to remain calm in difficult situations

engaging—extremely interesting

exacerbate—to make a bad situation worse

excruciating—extremely painful

expanding—growing larger; more distant

expression of regret—a type of apology

fault—to blame someone

flat-soled—used for describing shoes with flat-bottoms

flex—to bend part of your body so your muscles become tight

focus—when you are paying close attention

growth-spurt—a sudden increase in the growth of your body

hardship—something that makes your life difficult

imposed—forced on you

incredible—unbelievable

judgment—an opinion about someone else

lavish—luxurious, often expensive

ligament—one of the bands that joins your bones together

literally—according to the most basic meaning of a word or expression

outrun—to run faster than other people

overcome—to succeed in dealing with a problem

perspective—the way you see and think about the world around you

physics—the study of natural forces

predominantly—mostly

preposterous—completely unreasonable or silly

pressure—the force or weight that is put on something

prevail—to win or triumph

racial profiling—a racist practice by which police stop people of some groups just because of their race

recapture—to experience or feel something again

recitation—something you say that you remember well, like a poem or story

regret—to feel sorry that you have done something

resent—to feel angry about something someone has done to you, often unfairly

sense of identity—a feeling that you are special and belong to a group that is different from other groups

strip someone of—to take away something from someone

syndrome—a set of symptoms that show you have a certain medical condition

taut—stretched tightly

Tour de France—the popular bicycle race held in July, mostly in France

traditional values—beliefs about the importance of education, hard work, family etc. that have been around for a long time

upbringing—the way someone was raised

verisimilitude—the appearance of being true

UNIT 2

ball—a dance

bark—the sound a dog makes

bellow—to make a very loud, low noise

brandish—to wave something around in a dangerous way, like a weapon

bray—the sound a donkey makes

buoy—an object that floats in the water as a marker

canine—a long sharp tooth

carcass—the body of a dead animal

carnivore—a meat-eating animal

carrion—the flesh of dead animals

courtship—when two people or animals are trying to gain each other's affection

croak—the sound a frog makes

defend—to protect someone or something from being attacked

den—a cave where an animal lives

display—to show something

echo—to make a sound you can hear again and again

endangered—used to describe a type of animal that may soon die out, or not exist anymore

environment—the land, water, and air in which people, animals, and plants live

feast—to eat a lot of something with enjoyment

grunt—the sound a pig makes

habit—something you do all the time, without thinking

hatch—to come out of an egg

high-pitched grunt—a short sound like a pig makes

hoot—the sound an owl makes

howl—the sound a wolf makes

in check—under control

inhabitant—one of the people or animals that lives in a particular place

intimidate—to make someone afraid, often by using a threat

loner—someone who often prefers to be alone

mating—related to animals' having sex to produce babies

mournful—very sad

muzzle—the nose and mouth of an animal

nestled—located comfortably

opponent—a person or animal that tries to defeat another in a contest of some sort

piercing—sounding very sharp and unpleasant

presence—the state of being in a particular place

prey—an animal that is hunted for food by another animal

protrude—to stick out

rid—to remove something bad

ritual—a detailed procedure or set of actions that is regularly followed

roar—the sound a lion makes

savanna—the flat grasslands in tropical regions

scavenger—an animal that eats food that other animals don't want

shoot—the new part of a plant

snout—the long nose of certain animals

species—a group of animals that can breed with each other

steal away—sneak away

swamp—land that is always very wet and covered with water

tropical—existing in the hottest, wettest parts of the world

trumpet—the sound an elephant makes

tusk—the very long tooth of an animal, like an elephant's

unfortunate—unlucky

vocal cords—the thin bands of muscle in the throat that produce sound

ward off—to fight off

UNIT 3

absorb—to learn and understand something

adjustment—a small change

ace—(informal) to get the best grade possible on a test or asignemnt

assignment—something that someone like a teacher has told you to do

assume—to believe something is true without knowing

attain—to achieve or reach

be in the mood—to want to do something or feel you might enjoy something

bomb out—(slang) to do very poorly

brainiac—(slang) an intelligent person

break for—to take time for

burn out—(slang) to become exhausted

calculation—a step in doing math

catch some z's—(slang) to take a nap

caw—to make a crowing sound

chip away at—to reduce something slowly

circulate—to flow

concentrate—to think about one thing with all your energy

cram—(slang) to study a lot of information quickly

distraction—something that takes your attention away from what you are doing

ease the pain—make easier and more fun

fine-tuning—the process of making something perfect

flatterer—someone who gives a compliment that is not sincere

fresh—not tired and able to think clearly

fridge—a refrigerator

goal—something that you want to accomplish

go bonkers—(slang) to feel crazy

have the urge—to suddenly want to do something

hit the books—(slang) to study hard

improve—to make better

interior designer—a person who gives ideas about color, style, furniture, and art in a home or building

Inuksuks—human-like stone figures found in Nova Scotia

manage—to succeed in doing something difficult

marathon—used to describe an event that lasts a long time

Master—a title for the male head of a household used in the past

Mistress—a title for the female heads of a household used in the past

motivated—very eager to do something

move it—(slang) to get out of the way

panic—to sudenly feel frightened

pile on—(slang) to give someone a lot of something

priority—something that is most important and needs attention before anything else

procrastinate—to delay doing something you ought to do

project—a carefully planned piece of work

progress—the process of getting better

reinforce—to practice what you learn so that you remember or understand it

reward—something good that you get for doing something

schedule—a plan of what someone will do and when he or she will do it

segement—a section or piece

stare—to look at steadily

surpass—to be better than something else

tackle—to start dealing with a difficult problem

time frame—a period of time

topic—a subject that people talk, read, or write about

upcoming—happening soon

abandon—to leave someone or something

acro- —high, top

advanced—having the most modern ideas and ways of doing things

burial—the ceremony of putting a dead body into a grave

calculate—to use numbers to find out something or measure something

civil war—a war between groups of people from the same country

computer imaging—creating pictures on a computer

crane—a large machine used to move heavy things

curse—a magical power that does something bad

drought—a long period without any rain

dwell—to live in a place

eerily—in a strange and frightening way

eliminate—to get rid of something completely

embalming—using chemicals to prevent a body from decaying or rotting

equipped—provided with things that have a specific purpose

erupt—to happen suddenly

essential—extremely important and necessary

ex- —out of

fiber—the woody part of a plant

flint—a type of very hard stone

formula—a method you use to do something over and over

geo- —Earth

-graph—something drawn

heave—to throw, with effort

hieroglyphic—used to describe writing that uses pictures for words

high-tech—the most technologically modern

influence—to have an effect on the way someone thinks or behaves

intact—not damaged

internal organ—a body part inside your body, such as the heart, stomach, and lungs

linen—a type of light cloth

-lith—rock or stone

malnourished—poorly fed

mega- —giant, a million

mystery—something that is difficult to explain or understand

papyrus scroll—a long piece of ancient Egyptian "paper" that is rolled up and has official writing on it

picto- —like a picture

pre- —before

priest—someone who performs religious duties

quarry—a place where rock is dug out of the ground

raft—a flat floating structure used as a boat

represent—to mean something

restore—to make something as good as it was before

-ridden—filled with large numbers or quantities of something unpleasant

ritual—a set of actions or a ceremony that is always done in the same way

scattered—thrown around in many directions

spirit—a living being without a body, like an angel or ghost

steamy—hot and humid, or wet

symbolize—to represent or be a sign for something or someone else

UNIT 5

accompany—to go somewhere with someone

agitated—very upset

associate—to make a connection in your mind between one thing and another

body language—body positions and movements that show what you are thinking or feeling

cargo vessel—a ship that carries goods or products

chemical—involving reactions between different substances

compare—to describe how two or more things are similar to or different from each other

conclusion— something you decide after thinking about all the information you have

copycat—someone who copies other people's clothes, actions, etc.

disorder—a medical condition that keeps a part of your body from working like it's supposed to

exasperated—very annoyed

flail—to wave your arms and legs in a wild manner

frenzy—the state of being very excited or anxious

in favor of— supporting one thing over another

keeshond—a type of dog from the Netherlands

motivated—very eager to do or achieve something

on cue—at just the right moment

peep—a small sound

pinpoint—to find the exact location of something

pneumonia—a disease of the lungs in which people have a lot of trouble breathing

predict—to guess what will happen before it happens

reportedly—according to what people say

retrieve—to bring back something

rotate—to turn something around a fixed point

seizure—a short time when someone passes out and cannot control their shaking bodies

species—a group of animals of the same kind that can breed together

static electricity—electricity in the air

talent—a natural ability to do something well

tightrope—a rope or wire above the ground that someone walks on in the circus

unconscious—unable to see, feel, or think often because you are very sick or have had an accident

urinate—to get rid of liquid waste from your body

vibration—a continuous slight shaking movement

yowl—to make a long, sad cry

UNIT 6

assemble—to build something by putting all its parts together

asthma—an illness that causes difficulty in breathing

awl—a pointed tool for making holes in something soft

bacteria—very small, one-celled living things, sometimes causing disease

bi- —two or double

cell—the smallest part of a plant or animal that can exist on its own

component—one of several parts of a machine

construct—to build a building

credit with—to recognize someone as the person who did something important

daunting—making you feel a lack of confidence

duct tape—a type of cloth tape used for heating ducts or pipes

excess—a larger amount of something than is needed

instrument—a tool used in work such as science or medicine

inter- —among or between

lathe—a tool for shaping wood

leverage—lifting power

lice—(*plural of* louse) very tiny insects that live in the hair of people and animals

magnify—to make something appear larger than it is

manufacture—to produce a product in a factory

mend—to fix something that is cracked or torn

metal file—a tool used to file down, or reduce, a metal object

microscope—an instrument that makes very small things appear large enough to be seen

mite—a very tiny insect

modesty—being shy about showing your body

mono- —one or single

mounting hardware—a metal device used to attach one object to another

multi- —many

no-brainer—(*slang*) something that is so easy you don't need to think about it

non-binding—allowing free movement

nutdriver—a tool used to screw a nut to a bolt or screw

optional—not required to do if you don't want to

patch—to try to seal something that is leaking water or air

petroleum jelly—a mixture used in lubricants like Vaseline

-phone, -phono- —sound

plaster—to stick things like decals all over the surface of something

power drill—an electrical tool used to make holes

prepared slide—a small glass plate with a specimen to be examined under a microscope

professional—someone who does a job, sport, or activity for money

puppy—(*slang*) a way of referring to an object you like

refurbish—to fix up an old room or building by cleaning, making repairs, painting etc.

safety knife—short, very sharp knife that retracts, or goes back, into its handle

semi- —half

set up—to make a piece of equipment ready to be used

sit in—(*dialect*) to stay after

specs—(*short for* specifications) the details of how something should be made

stethoscope—an instrument used by doctors to listen to sounds within a person's body, like the heart or breathing

tadpole—a small creature that matures into a frog

trade secret—a tip known only by experts

tri- —three or triple

troubleshoot—to figure out what is wrong with a piece of equipment

uni- —one or single

urban—found in a city

wheeze—to breathe with difficulty, making a whistling kind of sound

UNIT 7

air raid warden—someone with the job of warning the community when an air attack in coming

animule— (*dialect*) an animal

-aqua- —water

artifact—an object made or used a long time ago

-biblio- —book

-bio- —life

blackout—an occasion when all lights are turned off in a city during an air attack

bond—a promise the government makes to pay back money it has borrowed

cemetery catalog—a list of people buried in a graveyard

critter—(*dialect*) creature

-dent- —tooth

-derm- —skin

disintegrate—to become weaker and be destroyed

downfall—the cause of a sudden loss of money, happiness, or health

draft—to officially order someone to join the military

Fenway Park—a baseball park in Boston

-geo- —earth

-graph- —writing

Great Depression, the—a long period throughout the 1930s when businesses had trouble selling their products and many people had very little money

gritty—rough, like stone

holler—(*dialect*) a small valley between mountains (a word used only in the Appalachians)

income—the money you earn from working

keen—very good at something

ker-plunk!—the sound something very heavy makes when it falls

-log- —word

-man- —hand

-mater- —mother

New Deal, the—new government programs that President Franklin D. Roosevelt introduced during the 1930s to help people without jobs and to help the U.S. economy improve

-nym- —name

-onym- —name

Pearl Harbor—an attack by the Japanese on an American naval base in 1941 that made the U.S. decide to join World War II

-phone, -phono- —sound

professional—someone who does a job, sport, or activity for money

raised—brought up

ring-tailed roarer—(19th-century dialect) a wild and uncontrollable boy

scholarship—money that is given to someone to pay for his or her education

-scrib- —write

-script- —write

-simil- —same

sit in—(*dialect*) to stay after

snappin' turtle—(*dialect*) a type of turtle with very powerful jaws

-spect- —see

stock market crash of 1929, the—the day that many stocks, or shares in companies, lost all or most of their value, or worth

tater—(*dialect*) a potato

-therm- —heat

wee—little or young

whippin'—(*dialect*) a punishment of being hit with a switch, or thin branch from a tree

World War I—a war fought from 1914 to 1918, in which Great Britain, France, Russia, Belgium, Italy, Japan, the United States, and other allies, or partners, defeated Germany and its European allies

World War II—a war fought from 1939 to 1945, in which Great Britain, France, the Soviet Union, the United States, China, and other allies defeated Germany, Italy, and Japan

UNIT 8

administrator—a person who is in charge of the school

adrift—not having any plan or purpose

argument—a reason you give to explain why something is right or wrong

asteroid—one of a group of small planets between Jupiter and Mars

automated—done or controlled by machines

blare—to make a loud, unpleasant noise

channel of communication—a way of communicating

come from the heart—to be sincere

commitment—a promise to do something

compensate—to make up for a lack in another area

confiscate—to take away someone's property, usually as punishment

considerable—large and noticeable

constitutional amendment—an addition to the U.S. Constitution

courageous—brave

desecration—the action of damaging something that is highly respected

dinky ping—a little "pinging" sound

distraction—something that takes your attention from what you are doing

distracting—making you lose your concentration

drift—a movement somewhere without a plan or purpose

economically—carefully, without wasting money

efficiently—without wasting time, money, or effort

ensue—to happen as a result of something

expedition—a carefully planned trip, especially to a dangerous place

explorer—someone who travels to places no one has ever visited

extinction—the state of no longer existing, like dinosaurs

facility—a place used for a particular purpose

financial—related to money

fragile—very delicate

golden age—the time when something was at its best

illicit—against the law or what most people approve of

imposed—caused by a situation

impulse—a sudden desire to do something

independent—able to do things on your own

invasion of privacy—a situation where people try to find out about your personal life when it is none of their business

issue—a subject or problem people discuss

launch vehicle—something that takes people into space

life-support—what is needed to keep a person alive

Louisville Slugger—a type of baseball bat

manufacturing—making things in factories

massacre—the killing of many people at one time, in one place

mistrust—a feeling among people that they do not trust each other

obstacle—something that gets in the way

overcome—to succeed in dealing with a problem

peace of mind—when you are not worried

peers—other students your age

penalty—a disadvantage or drawback

phased series—actions that are planned and happen one after the other

pine tar—a substance used to help the batter hold the bat

pop up—to appear suddenly

position—an opinion about a subject

presence—the fact that something or someone is in a particular place

primary mission—the most important purpose

prohibit—to make something illegal or against the rules

remain wedded to—to be unwilling to change something

reliable—dependable

research—the study of a subject to learn new facts

revolution—a complete change in how we do things

risk—the chance something bad might happen

robot—a machine that moves and does the work of humans

sophisticated—well made and complicated

surveillance—the activity of watching a person or place that could be related to a crime

susceptible—likely to be affected by a problem or illness

suspicion—a lack of trust

universe—all of space, including the planets and stars

unknown, the—a place no one has ever been

valid—based on strong reasons or facts

venture—to risk going somewhere or doing something new

vision—an idea or dream of what could happen

whereabouts—the area where someone is

worthy—good enough to deserve attention or support

UNIT 9

account—a description of things that have happened

adventure—a type of story that involves survival in a strange, often harsh or exotic, land

adversary—an enemy

aura—a feeling other people get about someone

autobiography—a story about someone's life written by that person

bully—a person who picks on people who are weaker

character—a person in a book, play, or movie

civil—polite, but not quite friendly

clarity—the quality of being clear and easy to understand

comparable to—similar to

concoction—an unusual mixture

craze—a popular new fad or fashion

crude—offensive or rude

definitive—considered the best and unable to be improved

delver—someone who is searching for information

emanate from—to come from or out of something

exuberance—a feeling of being very happy and full of energy

fantasy—a type of story often set in imaginary lands where the natural and the supernatural meet. The hero often has magical powers.

fiction—books and stories that are not about real events

forge—to form a strong relationship

giddy expectation—a happy, excited sense that something good will happen

gloom—darkness

hanker—to have a strong desire for something

horror—a type of story that involves the unknown, the forbidden, or the supernatural. A horror story can frighten the reader and often involves ghosts, werewolves, and vampires.

identity—a sense of who you are and how you are different from other people

insight—an ability to notice and understand something

installment—one of several parts of a story that are published at different times

medium—a method by which something, especially communicating, is done

mesmerized—totally interested in or absorbed by something

mind-blowing—(informal) making you feel very surprised

mystery—a story about a crime, often a murder. A detective usually solves the crime.

mystical—having magical powers people cannot understand

novel—a long written story with characters and events

orphan—a child whose parents have both died

Pokemon—a popular Nintendo Gameboy game that both young and old enjoy

protagonist—the main person in a book, play, or movie

puberty—the time when you change from a child to an adult

quirky—unusual or strange

raggedy—in poor condition

rake in the profits—to make a lot of money

realm—a place ruled by a king or queen

reel in—to pull in or interest someone

science fiction—a type of story that takes place on another planet or in the future

sensory detail—an explanation of how things look, smell, sound, taste, and feel

sequel—a book that continues the story of a previous book

series—a set of books with the same characters or on the same subject

shatter—to break something completely

sibling—a brother or sister

sober up—to recover from the effects of drinking alcohol

sober—to make someone feel serious

spirit—someone's strong, enthusiastic attitude

take revenge—to do something to punish or harm someone who has harmed you

talk down to—to talk to someone as if you are smarter or more important than they are

thriller—a story with an exciting plot and lots of action and suspense. The hero usually defeats an evil villain.

tone—the general feeling of a piece of writing

transformed—changed into something different

unconquerable—not able to be defeated

underfed—not having enough to eat

universal appeal—the quality of being liked by everyone

venture—to risk going somewhere

warlock—a boy or man with magical powers

western—a story about life on America's frontier, usually involving conflict between cowboys and outlaws

wherewithal—the money and ability to do something

wholeheartedly—completely

wisecracking—always making funny, slightly unkind remarks

young adult—a type of story with a main character in the 12 to 16 age range

zest—a feeling of enjoyment

altitude—the height of something above sea level or the earth's surface

boast—to brag

circulate—to move around in a circle

clockwise—in a circular motion to the right, the same direction the hands of a clock move

cluster—a group of things of the same kind that are very close together

column—something with a long, narrow shape

con- —together, with

concurrent—happening at the same time

counter- —opposite, against

counterattack—to go after an enemy that has struck the first blow

dangle—to hang

degree—a measurement equal to 1/360 of the distance around a circle

detector—a piece of equipment that finds or measures something

e- —out (of)

elevation—the height of something above sea level

encounter—to meet

energy—the physical force that something gives off

environment—the land, water, and air in which people, animals, and plants live

ex- —out (of)

exhale—to breathe out

forecaster—someone who says what is likely to happen, especially with the weather

gauge—an instrument used to measure the amount or size of something

gravity—the force that makes objects fall to the ground when dropped

hala—a type of tree in Hawaii with nice-smelling flowers

hemisphere—one half of the globe

inter- —between, among

intercom—a communication system to different parts of a building

kahuna—a Hawaiian priest or priestess

latitude—the distance of a point on the earth from the equator measured along an imaginary line that runs north and south

mass—a large amount of something

molecule—a group of atoms that form the smallest possible unit of a particular substance

mph—(*abbreviation*) miles per hour

ocean liner—a ship that carries passengers

post- —after, later

postsecondary—after high school

pre- —before

pressure—force or weight that is put on something

preview—to see a movie or play before the general public sees it

principle—a rule that explains the way something works

Puna—the district on the Big Island of Hawaii from north of Hilo to the Hawaii Volcanoes National Park and all the land south of that

slosh—to move the liquid in a container from side to side

spiraling—moving up or down, winding around a central point

sub- —under

submarine—a ship that can travel under water

sup- —under

super- —over

superhuman—having powers that are much greater than usual

tame—to change something from violent to gentle

trigger—to cause an event to happen

tropics—the hot, wet areas north and south of the equator

uproot—to pull a plant and its roots out of the ground

vapor—very tiny droplets of water that float in the air

wham into/onto—(*informal*) to hit something very hard

zone—a part of an area that has something special about it

Listening Script

A. 1. Tuning In. (page 4)

Patty (now): I'm an adult now, but when I think back to when I was a kid, I can remember many funny stories. Here's one of my favorite memories.

Sometime during the seventh grade two things happened to me. The first was that I got hooked on salami—Salami sandwiches, salami and cheese, salami on crackers—I couldn't get enough of the salty, spicy sausage! The other thing was that my mom and I weren't getting along really well. We weren't fighting really badly or anything, but it just seemed as if all she wanted to do was argue with me and tell me what to do. We also didn't laugh together much anymore. Things were changing, and my mom and I were the first to feel it.

As far as the salami went, my mom wouldn't buy any because she said it was too expensive and not that good for me. So one day I used my allowance to buy a full sausage of dry salami. I didn't want my mom to see it. So I hid it in the only place that I knew was totally safe—under my bed.

A couple of weeks later, I peered beneath the bed and saw—not the salami I had hidden, but some green and hairy object. The salami had grown about an inch of hair! I was not interested in consuming any of *this* object! The best thing I could think of to do was... *absolutely nothing.* Sometime later, my mom became obsessed with spring cleaning, which in her case meant cleaning places that had never seen the light of day. Of course, that meant under my bed. ... She washed, she scrubbed, she dusted ... she *screamed!*

Mother (then): *Ahhhh! Ahhhh! Ahhhh!*

Patty (then): *What is it, Mom?*

Mother (then): *There is something under your bed!*

Patty (then): *What's under my bed?*

Mother (then): *Something ...something...I don't know what it is. Maybe it's alive! Watch out! I don't know what it is!*

Patty (now): I was amazed at what I saw. The salami's hair had grown another three inches. I looked at my mom. Abruptly, she got up and left the room, only to return with the broom. Using the handle of the broom, she poked the salami. It didn't move. Finally, my mom got up her nerve and pushed the salami really hard. At that same exact moment, the laughter I had been trying to hold back exploded. She dropped the broom and looked at me.

Mother (then): *What's so funny? ...WHAT IS SO FUNNY?*

Patty (then): *Salami...It's a salami!*

Patty (now): My mother gazed at me in disbelief. I gasped for breath.

Mother (then): *What is the salami doing under your bed?*

Patty (then): *I bought it with my allowance.*

Patty (now): My laughter was subsiding, and fear was beginning to take its place. I looked at her. She had the strangest expression on her face: a combination of disgust, confusion, exhaustion, fear—and anger! I couldn't help it. I started to laugh. And then the miracle of miracles happened. My mom started to laugh, too. When we finally were able to stop laughing, my mom shoved the broom into my hands.

Mother (then): *OK, Patty Jean Shaw, clean it up, no matter what it is!*

Patty (now): My mom never got mad at me for buying the salami. I guess she thought I had already paid a price. The salami provided a memory of shared, unrestrained laughter. For years to come, all I had to do was threaten to buy a salami to make my mom laugh.

Before You Begin. (Page 25)

Brady Barr: I've been chomped on by crocodiles and tickled by tarantulas. I've wrestled a 14-foot python. I've swum among the great white sharks. But do you know what really scares me? Bats.

My name is Brady Barr. (That's me, reluctantly getting acquainted with some new "friends" called big brown bats.)...I'm a herpetologist, a biologist who studies reptiles and *amphibians*—animals that live both on land and in the water. While I'm doing that, I often run into other critters...like bats.

My fear of bats started when I was a kid in Bloomington, Indiana. One day when I was bringing firewood in from the garage, I heard a strange squeaking sound. At first I couldn't figure out where it was coming from. Then I looked down and realized that a little brown bat was crawling up my neck—it must have been sleeping in the woodpile. I started screaming and ran into the house.

Another time, I was cleaning leaves out of the gutters on our house. As I reached behind one, I put my hand into the middle of a whole family of bats! I almost fell off the ladder. I've objected to bringing in firewood or cleaning gutters ever since, and my family *still* thinks I was just trying to get out of doing my chores.

Narrator: Now listen to Brady tell about his scariest time with bats ever!

Brady: My scariest experience with bats was last year, in Myanmar, a country in Southeast Asia. I was deep in a cave as a team member on an expedition to find a new species of cobra. I looked up and saw thousands of bats hanging from the cave ceiling. I was wading through five inches of guano, or bat poop, supplemented by a constant rain of more guano and urine from the bats above. Can you imagine the smell?

This particular cave happened to be a sacred shrine, or holy place, so we had all taken off our shoes before entering to show respect. With every barefoot step, I felt the crunch and ooze between my toes of the decomposing bats that had died and fallen to the cave floor. When I aimed my flashlight down into the muck, I saw that the dead bats bobbing in the muck were swarming with maggots. Soon maggots were crawling up my legs.

I've been to a lot of horrible places in my life, but that cave was the worst. I was convinced I was going to die of some killer germ I'd picked up in there. But in the end, I never even got sick.

Narrator: Of course, Brady doesn't really *hate* bats! Listen why.

Brady: I really do love all animals. As much as they bother me, bats actually come in handy to help me find my favorite animals in the wild. Underneath bat roosts—places where bats rest and sleep—is always a good place to find crocodiles. And snakes often hang out at the cave entrances, too. Not only are they a help in my work, bats are crucial to ecosystems—or other plants and animals—around the world. They eat pesky insects, they pollinate flowers, and they spread seeds so new trees grow. These flying mammals fascinate me. But if a bat gets into *my* house, somebody else is going to have to chase it outside, because they still give me the creeps!

A. 1. Tuning In. (page 26)

1. I've never seen an animal quite like this ugly creature. It looks like it's a pig—except that it has huge, curved tusks coming out of its head! It uses its tusks like swords—for fighting off its enemies. It has a thick hide, or hairy skin, and is often covered with mud.

2. This beautiful animal lives in trees, in the forest. It's a cousin of the plain, brown pheasant. When its enemies come near, it screeches so loudly you can hear it a mile away! When the male wants to find a lady friend, he screams in a high-pitched voice, spreads his blue-green tail to make a fan, then walks around displaying that beautiful tail!

3. What is that I hear laughing? It must be time for dinner! These animals live in Africa, and they always seem to be laughing! When they laugh, these animals show their sharp teeth and powerful jaws. Their screams scare away their enemies—they can even frighten lions!

4. Most people don't like this ugly, *repulsive* animal. That's partly because of the way it looks—with a naked head, long, hooked beak, and needle-sharp claws. And it's also partly because its favorite food is dead bodies! These animals circle in the sky, waiting for their victim to die. Then, when their prey is dead, they gather around the body, ripping the flesh right off its bones.

5. This animal is all head and arms. Its eight tentacles are covered with rows of suction cups that can hold onto most anything! It hides between underwater rocks, waiting to grab its victims—usually crabs and lobsters. Even though it's kind of creepy-looking, this creature is really very shy and won't attack humans.

6. This is the noisiest, most loud-mouthed reptile on Earth. It sounds like a lion! This animal lives both in the water and on land. When you hear a cry come from its huge snout, that means it is trying to pick a fight with other males.

UNIT 3

A. 1. Tuning In. (page 48)

Stefan: This a disaster! My parents will be so mad at me!

Lori: What do you mean, a disaster? What do you mean, they'll be mad at you?

Stefan: I got an A in PE … but the rest of my grades are C's and D's!

Lori: What's happening? Usually you get A's and B's in everything.

Stefan: I don't know. I work really hard. I'm always busy. I play on the soccer team … and the softball team … and the basketball team …

Lori: … and you're on the Student Council …

Stefan: Right … and I'm in the drama club …

Lori: … and you take music lessons …

Stefan: And I … and I … I do my homework … sort of …

Lori: How do you get your homework done? You don't have time …

Stefan: But I like after school activities … and I don't really like homework …

Lori: If you want A's and B's, you've got to do your homework!

Stefan: I guess you're right. What do you think I should do?

A. 1. Tuning In. (page 70)

Narrator: Hiram Bingham had spent the summer of 1911 hacking through the thick forest of Peru, sticking to "a trail which not even a dog could follow." He dodged poisonous snakes and sometimes crawled on his hands and knees "six inches at a time."

Bingham, a Yale University archaeologist, was joined by two friends, several mules, and a Peruvian guide on his journey through the Andes Mountains. They were looking for the fabled "lost city" of Vilcabamba [Veelka-bamba] and searching for clues that would explain why the once-mighty Inca empire had vanished.

As their journey progressed, Bingham and his party had to navigate the steep and slippery cliffs on the eastern edge of the mountains. One wrong step could have caused Bingham and his group to tumble hundreds of feet to their deaths.

On July 24, Bingham's determination paid off. After struggling up the side of a treacherous mountain, he peered through thick bushes. He could hardly believe his eyes!

Hiram: Suddenly, I found myself confronted with the walls of ruined houses built of the finest quality of Inca stone work. It fairly took my breath away. What could this place be?

Narrator: Bingham thought he had discovered Vilcabamba. After studying the site, however, he determined the ruins were actually that of the lost city of Machu Picchu [Ma-chew Pitt-chew].

Bingham returned to Machu Picchu several times over years. He was sure the Incas had used the site for centuries as a holy city, a place where priests prayed to the sun god.

Modern archaeologists now say that Machu Picchu was not a spiritual center but a vacation home built for the Inca ruler Pachacuti [Pah-cha-KOO-tee] and his royal court.

Pachacuti hunted and entertained foreign visitors at Machu Picchu and used the resort to escape the city of Cuzco [Kooz-koh].

As Richard Burger, an archaeologist who studies the Incas today, says, "It was just a country palace where they would go to get away from the capital."

C. 3. Unlocking Meaning: Before You Move On. (page 75)

Narrator: For 3,000 years, mummies were Egypt's hidden treasures. Writing found inside the tombs told us a lot…but it never told us how the Egyptians made mummies! Several years ago, Dr. Bob Brier, a college professor of Egyptology, decided to find out how…

Dr. Brier: In Egypt, mummy-making was a trade secret, passed on from father to son. I wanted to find out how the Egyptians did it. I decided to make my own mummy!

Narrator: People who know him weren't surprised. His license plate reads M-U-M-M-Y. His living room is decorated with small statues from Egyptian tombs. One time, his wife gave him a wrapped mummy's arm for a gift!

Dr. Brier: It was the best Valentine's Day present I ever got! We call the mummy's arm "Lefty."

Narrator: The first problem was finding a body. Ronn Wade, the director of the Maryland State Anatomy Board helped with that. Mr. Wade decided to help Dr. Brier with the project. He gave him the body of an elderly man who had died of a heart attack. Before the man died, he donated his body to science.

Dr. Brier: Our first job was to remove the brain. We were in for a big surprise! The brain didn't come out the way we thought it would!

Narrator: The Egyptians removed the brain through the nose. They didn't want to cut open the skull because they wanted to keep the body as perfect as possible.

Dr. Brier: At first, we thought we could insert a long hook into the nose and pull out the brain. But that didn't work!

Narrator: So what did Dr. Brier and his partner do? Let's find out!

Dr. Brier: We decided that the Egyptians probably used an instrument like a whisk—you know, the kitchen utensil you use to whip cream or beat eggs. We decided that the Egyptians probably stuck the tool up the person's nose and rotated it around and around until the brains turned to liquid.

Narrator: So…were you right?

Dr. Brier: We sure were! The brains ran out of the nose! What a discovery!

UNIT 5

A. 1. Tuning In. (page 92)

Lori: Oh, no! I got a C in science!

Juan: And I got a D in math. That's because math is harder, I guess.

Lori: What do you mean harder? Science is a lot harder!

Juan: It is? How so?

Lori: Well, we have a lot more reading to do in science.

Juan: But we have reading to do in math, too—word problems. Plus, our teacher is much harder! She gives a lot more tests!

Lori: But in science the vocabulary is a lot harder. I don't know what a lot of the words in our book mean, and the teacher won't let us use a dictionary!

Juan: At least science is *interesting*. We get to do experiments … Math is so *boring* … All the teacher does is write on the board and talk. Plus, she doesn't explain things … I always feel lost!

Lori: We have more homework in science …

Juan: But the homework in math is so … *repetitious*. Every night, we have a bunch of problems to solve …

Lori: Well, all I know is that I'm getting an A in math and a C in science. That proves it's harder!

Juan: Hmmmmm.

UNIT 6

A. 1. Tuning In. (page 114)

Carlos: That's really cool, Juan. Can you show me how to make one?

Juan: Sure. You start with a sheet of paper. Binder paper is good. Then you lay the paper on a table with one of the long edges closer to you.

Carlos: Uh, huh.

Juan: Next, fold the paper in half, lengthwise. When the two edges match up, make a sharp crease along the fold.

Carlos: OK.

Juan: Now take the upper left corner and fold it down diagonally …

Carlos: Diagonally?

Juan: You know, that's when a line goes in a slanted direction…Anyway, you take the upper left corner and fold it down diagonally, toward you, until the edge lines up with the first crease you made. When the edges match up, make a sharp crease along the new fold. That makes a small triangular flap.

Carlos: Then you turn the paper over and do the same thing!

Juan: Right. On the other side, you take the upper left corner and fold it down diagonally, toward you, making another triangular flap.

Carlos: What's next?

Juan: OK. Pay attention. Take the newly formed diagonal edge on the right side of the paper and fold it straight down toward the first crease you made. When the edges match, make another sharp crease.

Carlos: Then you turn it over and do the same thing to the other side.

Juan: Just one more step. About 4 or 5 inches from the nose, make a small rip in the bottom, then another rip about one-half-inch behind it. Fold this tab up.

Carlos: Cool! Can we try it?

Juan: Wait, class is about to start. We can try it outside at lunchtime.

E. 1. Listen Up. (page 121)

1. Boy: Is there the shoe store in this mall?
   Girl: Yes. There's a shoe store on the second floor!
2. Girl: Do you have a pencil? Mine broke!
   Boy: Here. Take the red one. It's sharper than the others.
3. Boy: Can you tell me where a principal's office is?
   Girl: Go all the way to the end of the hall.
4. Girl: You're the best friend I've ever had.
   Boy: So are you! You're the nicest person I've ever known.
5. Boy: I'd like to be an astronaut some day.
   Girl: Me, too. I'd like to go to a moon.
6. Girl: A vicious dog chased me home!
   Boy: Who ran faster—you or the dog?

UNIT 7

A. 1. Tuning In. (page 136)

Girl: This is an interview with my grandmother, Sally Mae Smith. When were you born?

Grandmother: I was born on April the ninth, 1921.

Girl: Who were your mother and father?

Grandmother: My mother was Minnie Viola Johnson. My father was William Smith.

Girl: What did they do for a living?

Grandmother: They ran a farm and sold produce, butter, and eggs in West Virginia.

Girl: What did you do for fun when you were small?

Grandmother: Well, I can remember my parents went to bed early. We didn't have electricity. They didn't even light a lamp. They worked hard and they went to bed by dark.

We children would play in the yard. We would run and play tag and I remember my brother would put me in a big tire and roll me around the yard.

Girl: What were your chores around the house?

Grandmother: There are almost too many to mention. I helped milk the cows. I churned the milk to make butter. And I worked in the field. I cleaned house, and I always baked a cake on Saturday. I didn't learn much about cooking because I was always out in the field somewhere—working all summer long.

Girl: What was your favorite meal?

Grandmother: Corn bread and beans. My mother could cook the best corn bread, and we had corn bread twice a day. She baked it in an iron skillet, and it was always crusty on top and bottom, good and brown. I really enjoyed mother's corn bread. I still like corn bread and milk with a little sugar in it to this day.

Girl: Where did you go to school?

Grandmother: Went to a one room school house in Silver Creek, through the eighth grade.

Girl: What was the school like?

Grandmother: That little one room school? Well, the building was heated with a pot-bellied stove. We didn't have any water in the building. We didn't even have bathrooms. We had to go to the Jonny-House.

Girl: The Jonny-House?

Grandmother: An outhouse. We had outside toilets!

Girl: What did you study?

Grandmother: Very little. I think I had four subjects. Let's see...I had math and English and literature together. We worked our spelling in with our English. And history.

Girl: Did you ever get into trouble?

Grandmother: Sure!

Girl: What did you get into trouble for?

Grandmother: My mouth! Always! I was always talking when I was supposed to be listening! You have one mouth and two ears. You're supposed to listen twice as much as you talk!

UNIT 8

A. 1. Tuning In. (page 158)

Son: Hey, Mom, did you hear the story on TV about parents getting report cards?

Mother: Report cards? *Parents*?

Son: It's true! They said that the Chicago public schools are giving parents report cards. Every five weeks, parents get a grade on whether their children are doing their homework, on whether the kids are absent too often, and on whether the kids are suitably dressed for school!

Mother: Hmmm...Sounds like a strange idea! I'm not sure I like the idea of giving parents report cards!

Son: I think it's a good idea!

Mother: Why? Why do you think it's a good idea?

Son: Well, for one thing, a report card would get parents involved in their children's education. That means kids would do better in school.

Mother: OK...

Son: And a report card might also let parents know what they are doing well—*and* what they are not doing very well. It would help them be better parents.

Mother: Hmmmm. Good point!

Son: Finally, when parents get good grades, then they will feel rewarded—just like their kids!

Mother: You've made some good points, but I'm still not sure I like the idea.

Son: Why not?

Mother: Well...to begin with, parents should be able to raise their children the way they want to. Teachers shouldn't be telling parents how to raise their children because they don't know the whole story.

Son: Oh...I hadn't thought of that...

Mother: Besides, if a child isn't doing well in school, it might *not* be the parent's fault! Maybe it's the *school's fault*. Maybe the classrooms are too crowded, or maybe there aren't enough books, or maybe the teachers are overworked.

Son: Yeah, that does happen I guess...

Mother: Plus, some parents would be insulted. I mean, if I got a failing grade, I would feel rather...*irritated*!

Son: Don't worry, Mom. I'm sure you'd only get straight A's!

UNIT 9

A. 1. Tuning In. (page 180)

Juan: So, Lori. You like to read, too! What are you reading?

Lori: This book is one of my favorites. It's about the deadliest season in the history of Mount Everest. The author climbed with 13 others to the top of the mountain. They ran into a terrible storm. When the storm passed, five were dead and the sixth was so frostbitten that his hand had to be amputated!

Juan: They had to cut off his hand? Wow! I'm reading a book by a former president. The book tells the stories of brave people who made the United States what it is today—people like John Quincy Adams, Daniel Webster, and Sam Houston. Each of them did what they thought was right. The book won many important prizes.

Lori: I just read a book about a Jewish girl whose family hid from the Nazis during World War Two. She kept a diary. The diary tells what it was like for Jewish families in Europe and how they always lived in fear, never knowing when the German soldiers might come and take them away. This book really helps you understand how much the Jewish people suffered!

Juan: That sounds like an interesting book! Have you read this one? It's about evil space aliens who arrive on Earth in yellow spaceships and totally destroy the planet in order to build a freeway throughout the universe. The book is about two survivors and their funny adventures. It's really a hilarious book! I couldn't stop laughing!

Lori: Have you read this one? It's great! It's a novel about a team of people who go into the jungle of Africa to try to solve the mystery of who killed another team. When the group finds what they're looking for, it's a lot more than they expected! This is a book for people who like a lot of action and who also like to learn about the world as they read.

Juan: Cool. This is one of my favorites, too. After I read this book, I knew why it was a best seller for almost a year! The story goes back and forth between the lives that four Chinese women lived back in China and the lives of their American-born daughters in California. The author really knows how to write just the way people really talk. But I don't want to ruin it by telling you what happens. You'll have to read it yourself! I just couldn't put it down!

Lori: I will! I love to read! And that story will have a lot of meaning for me and my mom as well!

UNIT 10

A. 1. Tuning In. (page 202)

Mieko: That morning I got dressed as usual. I was just leaving for school when I noticed that my shoes were filthy. I went back inside to polish them. Staying home those five extra minutes probably saved my life.

When I came outside again, my mother was on the lawn picking flowers. Somebody yelled "tsunami!" We thought it was an April Fools' joke. Then I looked up and saw a huge wall of dirty water. Palm trees 35 feet tall were covered by water. My mother pushed me inside and slammed the door, just as the wave struck our house. It felt like we'd been hit by a train.

The wave picked up the house, and we floated away. Seawater came up to my knees. I decided to change clothes, in case we had to swim. When I opened the closet, the back wall was gone! All I could see past my hanging clothes were waves and dead fish. It looked like a strange painting.

Through the windows we could see people floating by, holding onto whatever they could. A boy was clinging to a piece of lumber. The waves carried us far out into Hilo Bay and back again three times.

Finally, our house slammed into a factory wall. Somehow, my parents and I climbed into the factory, where we found some neighbors on the upper floor. We all got busy tearing burlap sugar bags into strips to make a rope. Whenever someone floated by, we threw them the rope.

Our family was fortunate. And I'm not nervous about tsunamis anymore. But when I got married, I told my husband, "We're not living at the beach. We're going to live in the mountains!"

MINI-UNIT

A. Listening and Taking Notes: Practice It. (page 223)

Let's talk about the grizzly bear.

A large grizzly bear is one of the strongest animals in the world. A full-grown male is over eight feet long from nose to tail and can weigh over 700 pounds. Grizzlies are omnivores. They eat everything from squirrels to deer, and from berries to birds. Almost any animal in grizzly country may wind up as a meal for this mighty hunter.

There is no doubt that a grizzly bear is a dangerous animal and should be left alone. If you see a bear that is far away or doesn't see you, turn around and go back. If the bear is close or does see you, remain calm. Do not run. Instead, stand tall or back away slowly and wave your hands and speak loudly. The chances are that the bear will not bother you and will disappear.

Index

Predicting, 28
Prereading, 6, 12, 28, 34, 50, 56, 72, 78, 94, 100, 116, 122, 138, 144, 160, 166, 182, 188, 204, 210
Previewing,
    using pictures, 72, 100
    using titles, 4, 48, 92, 114, 136, 158, 180, 202
    using topic sentences, 182
Process diagram, 204
Questioning the author, 6, 12, 138, 145, 167
Quick writing, 79
Reading like the writer, 160
Rereading, 122
Summarizing, 211, 230
Text features (subheadings, visuals, labels), 116
Venn diagram, 94, 225

Real World Applications
Animal idioms, 110
Animal terms, 44
Book review (tongue-in-cheek), 198
Class debate, 176
Class dictionary (animal idioms), 110
Diagrams, 132, 220
Eye dialect, 154
Journals, 22
Review (book), 198
Time capsule, 88–89
Tongue-in-cheek book review, 198

Spelling
-able/ -ible, 186
-ance/-ence, 10
-ant/-ent, 164
Doubling consonants with suffixes, 120
/ē/ sound as in *see* and *tea*, 54
-ei-/-ie-, 142
/f/, 76
g, 98
s/c, 208
/sh/, 32

Style
Audience, 127
Conclusions, 171
Figurative language, 39
Formatting, 86, 126–127
    titles, 196
Fragments, 149
Introductions, 215
Punctuation,
    apostrophe to show possession, 152
    commas with adverbial clauses, 218
Quotes, 61
Run-on sentences, 149

Sentences,
    beginnings of, 193
    combining, 83
    run-ons, 149
Showing not telling, 17
Similes, 105
Visuals, 129
Writer's voice, 127

Visual Literacy
Book covers, 180
Charts, 5, 15, 19, 26, 27, 34, 41, 59, 71, 81, 84, 93, 94, 104, 106, 107, 125, 129, 141, 147, 159, 164, 169, 171, 173, 181, 185, 186, 191, 195, 214
    T chart, 94
Comic strips, 154
Diagrams, 132, 173, 203, 220
Illustrations, 37, 41, 44, 81, 85, 88, 114, 115, 116, 117, 118, 119, 122, 123, 124, 128, 132, 150, 151, 198, 204, 205, 206, 213, 216
Maps, 28, 29, 30, 35, 36, 41
Memory web, 18, 62, 173, 194
Photographs, 9, 14, 26, 40, 70, 136, 202, 210, 212
Pictures, 72–74, 100–102, 202
Posters, 144
Timelines, 18, 129
Schedule, 66

Vocabulary, 5, 6, 7, 12, 13, 14, 27, 28, 29, 30, 34, 35, 36, 37, 49, 50, 51, 52, 56, 57, 58, 59, 71, 72, 73, 74, 78, 79, 80, 94, 95, 96, 100, 101, 102, 103, 105, 115, 116, 117, 118, 122, 123, 124, 137, 138, 139, 140, 144, 145, 146, 154, 159, 160, 161, 166, 167, 168, 169, 172, 177, 181, 182, 183, 184, 188, 189, 190, 191, 203, 204, 205, 206, 210, 211, 212, 213
Academic, 49, 50, 51, 52, 56, 57, 58, 100
Ancient worlds, 71, 72, 73, 74, 78, 79, 80
Animals, 27, 28, 29, 30, 34, 35, 36, 37, 94, 95, 96, 100, 105
Dialect differences, 139, 154
Earth science, 203, 204, 205, 206, 210, 211, 212, 213
Fiction, 181, 182, 183, 184, 188, 189, 190
    types of, 191
History, 137, 138, 139, 140, 144, 145, 146
Interviewing, 147
Issues, 159, 160, 161, 166, 167, 168, 172, 177
Making things (technical material), 115, 116, 117, 118, 122, 123, 124
Medical conditions or problems, 100, 101, 102
Narrative, 5, 6, 7, 12, 13, 14
Qualities, 103, 105, 169
Slang, 59
Technical material, 115, 116, 117, 118, 122, 123, 124

Word Analysis Skills

Writing

Text and Audio Credits

p. 4 Adaptation of "Green Salami" by Patty Hansen, *Chicken Soup for the Kid's Soul: 101 Stories of Courage, Hope, and Laughter.* © 1996 Patricia J. Hansen. Used by permission of the author; *p. 4* From "The Night the Bed Fell" by James Thurber. Copyright © 1933, 1961 by James Thurber. Copyright renewed 1987 by Rosemary Thurber. Used by permission of the Barbara Hogenson Literary Agency; *p. 6* "Facing 'Growing Pains' and Overcoming Them," by Henry Magram from *New York Times Upfront*, April 5th 2004. Copyright © 2004 by New York Times & Scholastic Inc. Reprinted and reproduced by permission of Scholastic Inc.; *p. 13* "What Racial Profiling Feels Like," by Jemelleh Nurse from *New York Times Upfront*, February 7th 2003. Copyright © 2003 by New York Times & Scholastic Inc. Reprinted and reproduced by permission of Scholastic Inc.; *p. 14* "Visiting Vietnam and Finding a New Identity," by Son Tran from *New York Times Upfront*, February 2nd 2004. Copyright © 2004 by New York Times & Scholastic Inc. Reprinted and reproduced by permission of Scholastic Inc.; *p. 20* From "Turning a Wreck of a Chevy into a Dream Car," by Dan Rudolph from *New York Times Upfront*, November 17th 2003. Copyright © 2003 by New York Times & Scholastic Inc. Reprinted and reproduced by permission of Scholastic Inc.; *p. 23* "Oranges" from *New and Selected Poems* by Gary Soto, © 1995 by Gary Soto. Used with permission of Chronicle Books LLC, San Francisco. Visit ChronicleBooks.com; *p. 25* Adaptation of "The Icky Adventures of Brady Barr: Going Batty," by Brady Barr as told to Margaret Zackowitz, *National Geographic World*, October 2001. Copyright © 2001 the National Geographic Society. Used by permission of the National Geographic Society; *p. 28* "The Indian Peafowl" from *The Loudest: Amazing Facts about Loud Animals* written by Mymi Doinet. © by Editions Playbac. Reprinted and reproduced by permission; *p. 29* Adaptation of "The Spotted Hyena," *The Loudest: Amazing Facts about Loud Animals* by Mymi Doinet. © Editions Playbac. Reprinted and reproduced by permission; *p. 30* "The American Alligator," *The Loudest: Amazing Facts about Loud Animals* by Mymi Doinet. © Editions Playbac. Reprinted and reproduced by permission; *p. 35* "The Nubian Vulture," *The Ugliest: Amazing Facts about Ugly Animals* by Mymi Doinet. © Editions Playbac. Reprinted and reproduced by permission; *p. 35* "The Babirusa," *The Ugliest: Amazing Facts about Ugly Animals* by Mymi Doinet. © Editions Playbac. Reprinted and reproduced by permission; *p. 36* "The Octopus," *The Ugliest: Amazing Facts about Ugly Animals* by Mymi Doinet. © Editions Playbac. Reprinted and reproduced by permission; *p. 45* "How Owl Got His Feathers" from *How and Why Stories: World Tales Kids Can Read and Tell* by Martha Hamilton and Rich Weiss. Copyright © 1999 by Martha Hamilton and Rich Weiss. Published by August House Publishers, Inc. Reprinted and reproduced on their behalf by permission of Marian Reiner; *p. 50* From "Too Much Homework!: American kids spend more time than ever on homework. Will their hard work payoff?" *Time for Kids*, January 29, 1999. Used with permission from Time for Kids Magazine; *pp. 51, 52, 57, 58* Excerpts from "Get Motivated" and "Slow Motion" and "Concentration" and "Cramming 101" by Cathy Spalding. © 2001 by Cathy Spalding (http://homeworktips.about.com). Used with permission of About, Inc. which can be found on the Web at www.about.com. All rights reserved; *p. 66* Homework poem from *Love Me When I'm Most Unlovable: Guide to the Middle School Years* by Robert Ricken. Copyright © 1984 National Associaton of Secondary School Principals. www.principals.org. Reprinted and reproduced with permission; *p.67* "The Fox and the Crow," from *Aesop's Fables*; *p. 70* Adaptation of "Machu Picchu: Uncovered," *Weekly Reader, Senior Edition*, April 4, 2003; *p. 72* "Mummies: The Inside Story," by Albert Dumatt, *National Geographic World*, June 1999. Copyright © 1999 the National Geographic Society. Used by permission of the National Geographic Society; *p. 75* Adaptation of "I Made a Mummy!" by Alison Delsite, *Boys' Life*, January 2002. Reprinted and reproduced by permission of the author, Alison Delsite Everett and Boys' Life Magazine published by the Boy Scouts of America; *p. 79* "Heads May Roll: Giant Stone Sculptures Help Reveal the Secrets of an Ancient People," by Vicki Leon, *National Geographic World*, November 2001. Copyright © 2001 the National Geographic Society. Used by permission of the National Geographic Society; *p. 80* From "The Secrets of Easter Island," by M. Barbara Brownell, *National Geographic World*, January 1995. Copyright © 1995 the National Geographic Society. Used by permission of the National Geographic Society; *p. 86* Adaptation of "The Secrets in the Stones," by Michael Burgan, *National Geographic World*, May 1999. Copyright © 1999 the National Geographic Society. Used by permission of the National Geographic Society; *p. 89* Adapted from *Appleseeds'*, December 2003 issue: "Children of Ancient Mexico," © 2003, Carus Publishing Company, published by Cobblestone Publishing, 30 Grove Street, Suite C, Peterborough, NH 03458. All Rights Reserved. Used by permission of the publisher. Revision of English and Spanish by Suanna Gilman Ponce; *pp. 94, 101* "Who's smarter...cats or dogs?" *National Geographic Kids*, March 2004; *p. 111* From "Fifth Chinese Daughter," by Jade Snow Wong, © 1989 by Jade Snow Wong, published by University of Washington Press; *p. 116* "Making a Microscope" by Anthony Joseph as appeared in *Boys' Life*, September 2003. Reprinted and reproduced by permission of the author, Anthony Joseph and Boys' Life Magazine published by the Boy Scouts of America; *p. 117* From "Make Your Own Stethoscope," *Boys'*

Photo Credits

Cover Images: From the Getty Images Royalty-Free Collection: peacock; Easter Island statues; Great Wall of China; girl on cover; **From the Corbis Royalty-Free Collection:** Chichén Itzá; **Other Images:** proboscis monkey: Gavriel Jecan/CORBIS; teenagers: Creatas/PictureQuest; mummy painting: Archivo Iconografico, S. A./CORBIS; depression-era migrant woman and child: Library of Congress, Prints and Photographs Division [LC-USF34-9093-C]; riveters: Harold M. Lambert/Getty Images; space shuttle Columbia launch: NASA; Anne Frank: Getty Images; tornado: Aaron Horowitz/CORBIS; boy on cover and spine: Ryan McVay/Getty Images; Globe spread: William Westheimer/CORBIS.

Interior Images: From the Getty Images Royalty-Free Collection: *p. 3*; *p. 28*; *p. 30*; *p. 40*, elephant; *p. 70*, Easter Island; *p. 70*, pyramids; *p. 70*, Machu Piccu; *p. 70*, Great Wall; *p. 80*; *p. 84*; **From the Corbis Royalty-Free Collection:** *p. 3*; *p. 26*, top left; *p. 26*, top right; *p. 26*, bottom right; *p. 70*, Chichén Itzá; *p. 70*, Stonehenge; *p. 136*, 1960s; *p. 199*, stack of books; *p. 202*, photo 4; **Other Images:** *p. 3*: Royalty-Free/CORBIS/PictureQuest; *p. 3*: Tim Pannell/CORBIS; *p. 3*: Photodisc/PictureQuest; *p. 5*: Bettmann/CORBIS; *p. 9*, photo a: Bettmann/CORBIS; *p. 9*, photo b: John Springer Collection/CORBIS; *p. 9*, photo c: Rufus F. Folkks/CORBIS; *p. 14*: Owen Franken/CORBIS; *p. 23*, oranges: Photodisc/PictureQuest; *p. 24*: Robin Chittenden; Frank Lane Picture Agency/CORBIS; *p. 26*, top center: Robin Chittenden; Frank Lane Picture Agency/CORBIS; *p. 26*, bottom left: Marvin E. Newman/Getty Images; *p. 26*, bottom center: Art Wolfe/Getty Images; *p. 29*: Tom Brakefield/CORBIS; *p. 35*, top: Gallo Images/CORBIS; *p. 35*, bottom: Art Wolfe/Getty Images; *p. 36*: Jeffrey L. Rotman/CORBIS; *p. 40*, donkey: Rosemary Calvert/Getty Images; *p. 40*, lion: Daniel Cox/Getty Images; *p. 40*, howler monkey: Theo Allofs/CORBIS; *p. 40*, proboscis monkey: Gavriel Jecan/CORBIS; *p. 40*, frogfish: Stuart Westmorland/CORBIS; *p. 40*, uakari: Brand X Pictures/PictureQuest; *p. 40*, mole rat: Scott Camazine/Photo Researchers, Inc. ; *p. 45*: Dede Hatch; *p. 46*: Image Source/PictureQuest; *p. 47*: Dex Images/CORBIS; *p. 49*: Creatas/PictureQuest; *p. 50*: Image Source/PictureQuest; *p. 67*: Diego Rodriguez de Silvay Velasquez/Getty Images; *p. 67*, crow: Photodisc/PictureQUest; *p. 68*: Danny Lehman/CORBIS; *p. 72*: Charles Walker/Topfoto/The Image Works; *p. 72*, pyramids: Photodisc/PictureQuest; *p. 73*: Archivo Iconografico, S.A./CORBIS; *p. 73*, pyramids: Photodisc/PictureQuest; *p. 74*, pyramids: Photodisc/PictureQuest; *p. 79*: Danny Lehman/CORBIS; *p. 89*: Randy Faris/CORBIS; *p. 111*: Creatas/PictureQuest; *p. 133*, shark: Brand X Pictures/PictureQuest; *p. 134*: Courtesy Wilma H. Briggs; *p. 135*: Library of Congress, Prints and Photographs Division [LC-USF34-9093-C]; *p. 136*, 1950s: ABC/The Kobal Collection; *p. 136*, 1940s: Lucien Aigner/CORBIS; *p. 136*, 1930s: Library of Congress, Prints & Photographs Division, FSA-OWI Collection, [LC-USF33- 001163-M1]; *p. 138*: Courtesy Bland County History Archives, Rocky Gap High School, Rocky Gap, VA; *p. 144*, top: CORBIS; *p. 144*, bottom: Harold M. Lambert /Getty Images; *p. 145*: Courtesy Brown University and South Kingston High School, South Kingston, RI); *p. 145*: Courtesy Wilma H. Briggs; *p. 145*: Courtesy Wilma H. Briggs; *p. 155*: Burstein Collection/CORBIS; *p. 156*: NASA; *p. 167*: NASA; *p. 168*: NASA; *p. 177*: Rafiqur Rahman/Reuters/CORBIS; *p. 177*, baseball bat: Brand X Pictures/PictureQuest; *p. 179*: Tom & Dee Ann McCarthy/CORBIS; *p. 179*: Jose Luis Pelaez, Inc./CORBIS; *p. 180*, photo a: From *Congo*-Jacket Cover by Michael Crichton, copyright Reprinted by permission of Ballantine Books, a Division of Random House Inc. Used by permission of Ballantine, a divsion of Random House, Inc.; *p. 180*, photo b: "Jacket Cover," from *Anne Frank: The Diary of a Young Girl* by Anne Frank. Used by permission of Doubleday, a division of Random House, Inc.; *p. 180*, photo c: "Jacket Cover," from *Into Thin Air* by Jon Krakauer. Used by permission of Doubleday, a division of Random House, Inc.; *p. 180*, photo d: From *The Joy Luck Club*-Book Cover by Amy Tan, copyright Reprinted by permission of Ivy Books, a Division of Random House Inc. Used by permission of Ballantine, a division of Random House, Inc.; *p. 180*, photo e: "Jacket Cover," from *The Hitchhiker's Guide to the Galaxy* by Douglas Adams copyright © 1979 by Douglas Adams. Used by permission of Harmony Books, a division of Random House, Inc.; *p. 180*, photo f: Entire Book Cover (Harper paperback 2004 edition) from *Profiles in Courage* by John F. Kennedy. Copyright © 1955, 1956, 1961 by John F. Kennedy. Copyright renewed © 1983, 1984, 1989 by Jacqueline Kennedy Onassis. Foreword copyright © 1964 by Robert F. Kennedy. Reprinted by permission of HarperCollins Publishers Inc.; *p. 199*: Courtesy of the Harvard University Portrait Collection, Gift of councilors and class agents of the Harvard Fund Council, 1961; *p. 200*: Warren Bolster/Getty Images; *p. 201*: Aaron Horowitz/CORBIS; *p. 202*, photo 1: Lloyd Cluff/CORBIS; *p. 202*, photo 2: Galen Rowell/CORBIS; *p. 202*, photo 3: Najlah Feanny/CORBIS SABA; *p. 202*, photo 5: Warren Bolster/Getty Images; *p. 202*, photo 6: G Brad Lewis/Getty Images; *p. 210*: CORBIS ; *p. 212*: Bettmann/CORBIS; *p. 212*: Beawiharta/Reuters/CORBIS; *p. 212*: Punit Paranjpe/Reuters/Corbis; *p. 221*: © 2004 Herb Kawainui Kane, Artist.